Dead Reckoning:
The Six Phases of a Funeral

Michael K. Jones

Vogelstein Press
Calgary, Alberta

Dead Reckoning: The Six Phases of a Funeral
Copyright © 2015 by Michael K. Jones

ISBN: 978-0-9949088-1-0 (epub)
ISBN: 978-0-9949088-0-3 (paperback)

Published by Vogelstein Press
Calgary, Alberta, Canada

Website: www.vogelsteinpress.com
Email: vogelsteinpress@shaw.ca

The views expressed in works published by Vogelstein Press are those of
the author and do not necessarily represent the official position of
Vogelstein Press.

Cover design: Danah Cox

To Wib MacLennan, Bob Kotow, and James Lundblad.

Each of you left us far too soon.

Contents

Preface

One would be hard–pressed to find someone more competent than Mike Jones to write a book on funerals. He is the expert. He did not necessarily plan to be Canada's foremost thinker on death and the rituals that surround it. The opportunity fell into his lap. After helping a church to die well, Mike found himself wanting to take a little time off before jumping back onto the ministerial treadmill. When a funeral home tapped him to conduct a service, he did so, and he did it well. And they approached him again, and again. Roughly a thousand funerals later, Mike has emerged as someone who understands the ending of life, death, and funerals — better than anyone. He speaks from a deep experience that is rare.

Mike has a pastoral nature. Yes, he understands the ins and outs of funerals, he knows what scholars have said about the topic, and he has done his homework. But what distinguishes Mike is the fact that he is an everyman. Having grown up in blue–collar, Eastern Canada, he never lost his street sense. During his university and seminary years he held onto that ability to relate to ordinary people. Breakfast at the Tim Horton's, cracking jokes at the mall, a conversation in the front yard — these are comfortable places for Mike. He relates to people. He understands them. He's one of them. He doesn't think of himself as "The Reverend" or "The Father", rather, he's the pastor who walks alongside his sheep, encouraging them, and listening to them.

Funerals are crucial events. We all want to be remembered well. And we want to remember our friends well. We want to get it right. Yet sometimes funerals go so wrong. There is tension in the room, there is anger, there is confusion and sadness. This is not the place for a public speaker or religious leader to fall flat, or worse. Most of us can recall a funeral that just wasn't quite right. But the funeral isn't the place for a religious leader to figure things out on the fly. We need thoughtful people who can show us the ropes and explain the bigger picture … *before* we find ourselves addressing a tense room full of people grieving.

What's the funeral all about? What should it be about? How should each funeral be approached with sensitivity? These are questions Mike has thought about deeply. And taking his words seriously will help those of us who lead funerals to do it better. Mike's task is a noble one: to equip us to conduct a more graceful funeral, and to offer more dignity to the departed.

Dead Reckoning is Mike's gift to all those who will either lead a funeral or help to arrange a funeral. This is truly his life's work and he has a treasure trove of ideas to offer. Religious leaders and funeral directors will appreciate having this book as a handy resource. Professors in the seminaries, bible colleges, or theological institutions need this book. For schools that offer a practical ministry program, this book will serve as the ideal text for helping students to navigate the complexity of a modern funeral.

Mike's wit shines through in these pages, as does his ceaseless ability to see humor in all areas of life. His humility is evident on every page, but so is his competence. Perhaps it is not the most cheerful activity in the world — to read a book about funerals — but for those who need to read a book such as this, Mike's relatability will make for enjoyable reading … and even a few smiles.

After all, it shouldn't kill us to have to read a book about death. Hopefully it will breathe new life into how we approach this most sacred transition.

Dyron Daughrity, PhD
Associate Professor of Religion
Pepperdine University
Malibu, California

Acknowledgements

When learning that I was writing a book about the six phases of a funeral a friend asked if I was going to "keep it light". While I'm not certain the final product is something we could describe as being "light" I do hope readers find it helpful and accessible. For helping me to do just that I'd like to thank a number of people. These friends, family, clients and colleagues have helped keep me on track with their stories, encouragement, questions, insights, experiences, and just about everything else a project like this demands.

First of all, I would like to thank The Rev. Dr. Dyron Daughrity for writing the preface to this book. Dyron and I have known each other for years and I'm really glad he responded positively to my invitation to contribute to this project. I'd also like to thank The Rev. Danah Cox for the design and artwork appearing on this book's cover. Stan Litke has been really helpful with his technical advice.

The Rev. Peter Smith read through an early draft and offered some extremely helpful feedback, and most of his insights have been incorporated into this final text. Peter also provided a sentence for the back cover. I'd also like to thank Pastors Fred Massey and Michael Hathaway for their thoughts and stories. I am thankful for the many clergy who have taken the time to share their thoughts, experiences, and questions with me.

I can't complete this book without a nod to the people in my Friday afternoon coffee group. Dr. Irving Hexham, The Rev. Dr. Tim Callaway, Dr. Ron Galloway, The Rev. Dr. Chang Han Kim, The Rev. Doug Barrie and Jeremy Hexham (a PhD candidate at the time of this writing) have been extremely helpful. They've helped with the proofreading of this text, listening to my somewhat coherent ideas and helping solve problems. That last item, alone, is perhaps the biggest gift of all. Along with Peter Smith, Tim and Doug also helped out by providing a sentence for the back cover.

Much of this book wouldn't have been possible without the funeral directors and clients with whom I work on a daily basis. Their observations, assistance, questions, comments, and concerns have been extremely helpful in our work over the past several years. I'd try and list everyone but I know I would miss somebody and that's something I don't want to do. You all know who you are and hopefully you also know how grateful I am.

Another group that has my profound gratitude is the management and staff of Vogelstein Press. Irving Hexham, PhD and Karla Poewe, PhD, have given me a tremendous opportunity and I hope I don't disappoint them with this current offering. Without their help and resources this project would never have been completed.

Finally, a special thank you has to go to my wife, Trish. Without her support *Dead Reckoning* would not be in your hands right now.

Introduction

I'm at that age when I find myself reading a lot of retirement planning books. I guess it's never too early to start getting things in order for that day when I no longer "work". One thing I've noticed about these books is that they've organized life into chapters. Gail Vaz–Oxlade, for example, talks about "kid", "teenager", and "parenting" chapters. Her book *Never Too Late* focuses on the retirement chapter.[1] If I were to follow this practice and organize life into a series of chapters I'd suggest that *Dead Reckoning* deals with the final chapter of our time here on earth. It would focus on the end of this final chapter, in particular. It would address those final words we would offer as we gather and say goodbye.

I've learned a lot about endings and the power of words and silence in recent years. Roughly ten years ago the congregation I was serving closed and that process taught me about final chapters and saying goodbye. It was a harsh and frightening conclusion for me because I didn't have any idea what I was going to do once the congregation's doors had been closed for the final time. Fortunately, this conclusion wasn't the end. This conclusion led to the opening chapter of a new story. In the days and weeks following the final service an interesting thing happened. I began receiving phone calls from funeral directors asking if I could officiate funerals for families without a church connection. As the years have progressed I've averaged about 100 services per year. When it comes to funerals I've been through a lot and *Dead Reckoning* is the result of this experience.

In each and every one of the services I've led I've learned a lot about the funeral ritual. For one thing, I've learned how important funerals are in people's lives. Ninian Smart once wrote, "The power of religion does not rest in simple beliefs or theologies; it rests in the deep words and rites which enable us to face death and make a good end to living."[2] As I have made my way through so many funerals I've come to agree with his statement. Funerals are powerful and that's why we have to invest so much time and energy into them. It's also why we need to work harder at understanding how they work.

To understand how they work we first have to learn more about their structure. Once we understand the structure of the funeral we can learn more about how to lead them with some effectiveness. For me the Christian funeral can be divided into two main components. Christian funerals have a worship component and a celebration component. There are many who believe that these two components cannot be combined into one ritual act. I disagree and will explain how and why in the pages that follow. When we worship we bring heaven and earth together acknowledging God's place among us as we grieve the loss of a loved one. We also celebrate the life of the deceased whenever we gather for a Christian funeral.

For me, each and every individual is a creation of God and has been created in God's image. Christian ethicist Richard McCormick once said that we are all "of incalculable worth."[3] When a person dies we need to learn more about their "worth". We need to hear about their experiences and encounters; we need to hear about what they held to be important and we can also learn about those ideas and things that inspired them. So these two main components can be divided further still. In *Dead Reckoning* I've outlined the six phases to help ensure that worship and celebration come together to help create a meaningful and effective funeral. These six phases are: planning and preparation; warm up; inspiration; education; transition; and closing. Each phase will have a dedicated chapter introducing us to a different piece of the funeral ritual. Each phase and chapter will help us ensure that we create, lead and offer a service that honours and respects both God and the deceased.

Regardless of how important funerals are, however, each and every funeral is a challenge for the person asked to lead it. It can be difficult to find words to tell the story of the deceased and address the intensity of grief and loss experienced by those left behind. It can be difficult to shape the words we can find into something that brings people together to mark the beginning of a long and often painful road. Edwidge Danticat once wrote, "Through recent experiences with both birth and death, I have discovered that we enter and leave life as, among other things, words."[4] These words can be memories and stories. These words can help create pictures in our minds that can help us remember the one's whom we've lost. So, as difficult as the funeral task can be *Dead Reckoning* will help us find the words we need to address the loss and grief in people's lives. These words can be offered as statements and prayers. They can be offered as memory and story. They can also be shared as questions.

Dead Reckoning will also help us find the questions we need to ask. We humans are a curious, questioning people. From the very beginning we have experienced strange and confusing things and tried to figure out what has happened by asking a series of questions. What? When? Why? Where? Who? How? Even in the present day there always seems to be something around the next corner we want to know more about. When confronting the death of a loved one and dealing with the arrangements surrounding this loss people generate lists of questions to ask the individuals to whom they have turned for help and guidance. Perhaps the most frequent question I'm asked by friends and family of the deceased is, "What do we do now?"

What do we do now? This question has a number of possible responses. In *Dead Reckoning* we sift through these possibilities. Perhaps the first response is for friends or family members to go ahead and do the service themselves. It would be difficult yet possible. We do not need a license or credential in order to lead a funeral. For those of us who are asked to do so there are resources available to help those who accept the challenge. There are books, websites and other resources on the "bits and pieces" that comprise religious funerals. What seems to be lacking are books that walk us through the process from beginning to graveside and beyond. Longfellow once wrote, "Great is the art of beginning, but greater is the art of ending."[5]

Being asked to deal with beginnings and endings and officiate at a funeral and tell a person's story is a tremendous honour but, as I have already mentioned, it's also a tremendous challenge. It is also one of the toughest pieces of public speaking we will ever do. Most human beings fear two things: death and public speaking. Of these two death is probably the front runner. Officiating funerals incorporates both and with a much higher degree of intensity and difficulty. This is why it's an extremely frightening possibility. There are different ways in which we can navigate this intensity and difficulty. The first thing we can do is confront the reality of death. Poet W.B. Yeats challenges us to "Cast a cold eye / On life, on death."[6] In *Dead Reckoning* I intend to focus a "cold eye" on the funeral service itself. I will be addressing issues such as preparation, presentation and content. I will even consider some of the mixed messages offered to grieving people throughout the years. On one hand, we have Jesus advising listeners to "let the dead bury their own dead"[7] while on the other we have churches and other religious organizations placing funerals at the centre of what they do to serve their followers. We'll find a way between both sides.

There is more than enough material available to help us with our task. The funeral service has been studied for centuries. Much of this work has been done under the general titles such as ritual studies. A number of scholars within these disciplines have published a lot of thought provoking material. Arnold Van Gennep, for one, uses the term "Rites of Passage" to describe rituals like funerals. Perhaps a better translation is "Rites of Transition"[8] as that label more accurately describes what is happening in the ritual and how it is affecting the people sharing in this ceremony. Van Gennep writes, "The life of an individual in any society is a series of passages from one age to another and from one occupation to another."[9] Funerals are one, if not the most important transition times for individuals, families, workplaces, and communities. An anthropologist by the name of John Beattie labeled rituals such as funerals "transition rituals".[10] Angela Sumegi argues that for humans funerals mark this transition from a person's physical reality to their bodily place among the ancestors.[11] Funerals are a time of "counting the cost" of this transition and being

4

reminded that, to borrow a phrase from the late Gonzo journalist Hunter S. Thompson, "the tribe is smaller by one."[12]

These transition times have been described in many ways throughout human history. What I set out to accomplish in *Dead Reckoning* is built on this scholarly tradition and outline a way we can take this theory and translate theory into practice. This practice will be simple yet challenging. For this reason we will begin *Dead Reckoning* with a review of the literature dealing with the funeral ritual. This gives us a foundation from which to proceed through the six phases of the funeral. Some cultures have compared the death journey to crossing a one–way bridge[13] and we'll be learning more about this passage. It's a passage that goes by many names and we will explore some of these. For example, Bronislaw Malinowski describes death as being a "gateway to the other world in more than the literal sense".[14]

Building on this and other material we can build on this term "gateway experience" and apply it throughout *Dead Reckoning*. These gateways continue to mark the transition between life and death.[15] Gateways can also give us a slight glimpse of what may lie beyond. Madeleine L'Engle suggests that we are being sent through this gateway and "into the unknown".[16] Some, including the ancients, would even hint that we are entering upon a new journey of sorts[17] and this notion of gateway helps us visualize and understanding the beginning or starting point. Historically, this journey's destination depended on the religious tradition to which the person belonged. In many aboriginal traditions of North America, for example, the deceased proceeded to the underworld from which they emerged.[18]

Even if we narrow and limit our work here to Christian funerals it's important to consider various beliefs of the afterlife and we'll be doing this in a couple of places.[19] Plato, for example, argued that when we die our new journey would include the separation of spirit and body. He suggested that the spirit was indestructible and eternal and that it continued on its way while the body was left behind.[20] In medieval art this is shown as a person's spirit leaving the body through their mouth.[21] The spirit is believed to leave the body and take flight. Perhaps this is why some visions and descriptions of heaven include people wearing wings. Some pagan traditions use terms like "crossing over" to describe this transition and movement.[22] In these traditions it was hoped that the trip was one way and their funeral services reflected that hope and prayer.[23]

The oldest of human literature speaks of this search for knowledge about the afterlife.[24] The Ancient Greeks, for example, spoke of journeys into the land of the dead. Homer, himself, referred to human beings as being "searchers".[25] These works offered descriptions of what happened when we crossed over to this land. The Ancient Roman Lucretius once wrote, "Death is therefore nothing to us and does not concern us at all, since it appears that the substance of the soul is perishable. When the separation of the body and soul, whose union is the essence of our being, is consummated, it is clear that absolutely nothing will be able to reach us and awaken our sensibility, not even if earth mixes with sea and seas with heaven."[26] Victor J. Stenger is more precise when he writes, "… when our brains die, we die."[27]

All of this underlines the appropriateness of using a term such as "gateway transition" when describing a funeral. It also supports our work of finding out more about these transitions and how we can create rituals that help us understand this journey more deeply. A critical part of this gateway transition is the naming of the reality of death and the beginning of the grief process for people left behind. This is an important point because death can affect families in deep and profound ways. And it's something we cannot avoid as we all face death at some future time. As *Star Wars* character, Yoda, said in the movie *Return of the Jedi*, "That is the way of things."

Religious leaders throughout the centuries have helped individuals, families, and communities confront the movement of our loved ones through the gateway. Perhaps the shaman is the best example of this. Curtis Hoffman writes, "The shaman is a communicator between the worlds …"[28] Being this "communicator" is not a job that can be taken lightly. It was and still is a powerful responsibility. Jay Dolan describes the

Shaman as being "religious specialists, both male and female, who cured sickness, cast spells, controlled the weather, and predicted the future."[29] Regardless of whether or not we want to admit it much of the Shaman's work finds its way into the expectations of contemporary service leaders, especially when it comes to working with people experiencing the natural reality of death. In a way whenever we confront the worlds of life and death we become shamans of a sort. As shamans we help bridge these two worlds for those around us.

Death and funerals may build bridges and be the way of things but we still struggle with them. Wade Davis writes, "Every culture honours its dead, even as it struggles with the meaning of the inexorable separation that death implies."[30] This is true for both religious and nonreligious people. In fact, atheists find themselves extremely "helpless"[31] when faced with the loss of a loved one. French philosopher Andre Comte–Sponville writes, "For you, there can be neither consolation nor compensation — only sometimes, a faint sense of relief at the thought that at least that person is no longer suffering."[32] Silverstone and Hyman write, "Some widows and widowers, after a short time, reflect this quality in the midst of sadness."[33] The six phases of a funeral help us deal with the emotions death generates within us.

They can also help us offer a thought or a word to the people around us. Those who join us for funerals may represent a number of beliefs beyond our own but we still gather for one timeless purpose. This represents a bit of a historical shift. There was a time when people turned to the church when they experienced a death in their family.[34] It was conventional thinking that the clergy in particular would preside over the rituals of life and perhaps many other details as well. Joyce Youings summarizes this conventional thinking well when she writes, "To all Christian people only the clergy can give a child a name and admit it to full church membership, join men and women in holy matrimony, and preside over the burial of the dead."[35] In most cases this continues to be the case today and this may be surprising.

The world around us is changing, however. Nicholas Wade uses the term "waning" when describing the decline in religious belief across western society.[36] To describe the shrinking number of Christians, in particular Philip Jenkins has coined the term "ever shrinking remnant" and it certainly seems to fit here,[37] especially in our North American context. In terms of the Canadian experience Northcott and Wilson write, "… Canada is a secularized society; that is, the importance of religion as a central social institution has declined. Church and state are separated, and weekly attendance at church has declined substantially, especially since the mid–twentieth century. Increasingly, death is defined by secular rather than religious elements of society and culture."[38] Retired Episcopalian Bishop John Shelby Spong has noticed these changes happening throughout his career as both a priest and bishop. He agrees that not everybody who attends a funeral is religious. Many attend a funeral because they want to remember and celebrate a life. They're not there to worship any particular deity. Still others are members of religious communities beyond the Christian community.[39] Spong later writes, "A century ago Christian funerals asserted the ability of God to overcome the power of death. Today Christian funerals are more likely to be memorial services intended to remember and extol the virtues and the example of the deceased."[40] The six phases offered throughout this book help us respect the variety of thoughts and beliefs of those joining us.

As frightening and difficult as these situations may be, on those occasions when people turn to church leaders for funerals we are presented with a unique opportunity. We are also presented with a tremendous responsibility. We need to approach this opportunity and responsibility with both prayer and caution. I'm constantly hearing complaints about clergy being too religious and eulogists trying to force their views onto others. I've also experienced situations in which clergy did not "mind their manners", so to speak. It all goes back to a service I attended a couple of years ago. It was in a large, evangelical church here in Calgary. A colleague had passed away and I wanted to attend the funeral. As I listened to the pastor and members speak about my friend's life a word kept running through my mind. That word was "insider" and it described the service perfectly. It was a Christian funeral for a Christian person and this is where the problem began. The speakers seemed to make it clear that if you did not buy into their particular take on the Christian message then you were somehow lacking something. Even though I am both a Christian and a pastor, I still felt like an outsider. I felt as if I was living beyond some invisible circle that was almost impossible to enter. The exact phrase I wrote on my service bulletin was this: "Insider services create outsiders". As pastors and service leaders we need to be told and reminded that funerals are for both insiders and outsiders. Christian funerals should be more than simply having the pastor at the front "kicking the tires and lighting the fires"

In saying this we need to acknowledge that it's difficult to maintain the balance between the needs and desires of both religious and nonreligious people. It is important to try, however. Both religious and nonreligious people confront the reality of their loss and grief. Grief and the need for mourning cannot be ignored, resisted, or buried. Canadian poet Erin Moure expresses this notion wonderfully when she writes, "To leave this world is not only to vanish ... (it) is to leave a terrible and beautiful bond."[41] Pagan witch and theorist Starhawk defines grief by claiming that "grief is our healing response to loss, and if we let ourselves fully feel it and go through all of its stages, it will bring us through rage and despair, back to acceptance and restoration."[42]

Grief and mourning are closely related but still very different. When it comes to mourning Paul Irion writes, "Mourning, painful though it is, has to be faced if comfort is to follow."[43] Irion also writes, "... the funeral must provide a sense of finality. We have to have an opportunity to say farewell in whichever way we feel is appropriate. Mourning is a process which entails the breaking of ties with the deceased."[44] We have to learn to "live with the memory of the deceased."[45] Funerals help start the work of rebuilding, regrouping, and reconnecting in people's lives, regardless of where the grieving survivors are on their spiritual journeys. Again, it's not something we can escape or run away from. Moving through the six phases of a funeral helps keep us from running away. It's in working through these six stages that we move forward. Put another way, Alla Bozarth–Campbell writes, "Ultimately, the only way to get through something is to get *through* it — not over, under, or around it, but all the way through it."[46] I experienced this in a personal way not too long ago. A brain–injured friend went in for his seventh brain surgery and didn't come out of the anaesthetic. Because of geography and financial realities his friends and I were uncertain whether or not there was going to be a funeral. His family lived across the country and they planned a service in his hometown. Luckily, parishioners in the church he attended made arrangements for a memorial service here in town. Before we knew about the service things seemed to be on hold since he died. I felt as if I was in a sort of limbo. It wasn't until I actually experienced the local funeral that I felt I had actually passed through the gateway and moved on in my personal grief journey.

Scholars will tell us that naming the reality of loss is an important part of the funeral ritual.[47] I recently had a dream about one of the people to whom this book is dedicated. Wib died all too suddenly and I was unable to attend either of the services held in his honour and memory. In this dream Wib was going about his life as if nothing had happened. He was teaching his adult students and consulting for different provincial government departments. He was meeting people in restaurants for coffee and debating the issues of the day. As the dream progressed its message seemed to be that Wib hadn't really died. The rest of us were wrong about his death. Whatever news I had received of his death was either a miscommunication or a complete lie. The funeral was an empty and meaningless gesture. When I awoke from the dream I was once again faced with the harsh reality that he had, indeed, died. I had to remind myself that his death was real. Funerals help us face this reality. They help us break out of that dream state we may find ourselves experiencing following a loss. They help us realize that life has indeed changed and in a bigger way than we may think. Those of us left behind are beginning the long process of rebuilding their lives. We're trying to move towards that point where we can carry on with life as best as we can.

In confronting death we face an unknown future that can be both confusing and frightening. Gateways may offer a hint of where we go when we die but there is often not enough information to be helpful. Regardless of how religious we are we want to know what's going to happen after we or someone close to us dies. We want to know what happens next. Aristotle once said, "All humans, by their nature, desire to know."[48] But we cannot really know what happens next for the dead loved one so we need a place where we reflect on our questions and uncertainties. We also need a place where we try to come to some understanding of our own belief concerning death and afterlife. We need a place where we can think about what one writer named as "a great perhaps".[49] What will happen to us when we die? Where will we go? Who will we meet? The six phases I present here will help us bring order to the chaos we encounter and messiness we experience.

We, as leaders and listeners, approach a funeral with all of these questions, dilemmas and more. We gather hoping for a glimpse of not only where the deceased has gone but where we will go as well. The response to these issues and needs have changed as human history has developed and evolved. Ronald Grimes writes, "Whatever the reason, the past two decades have witnessed a resurgence of interest in the construction of rites of passage." Grimes goes on to add, "Without rites that engage our imaginations, communities, and bodies, we lose touch with the rhythms of the human life course, just as we become temporarily disoriented without seasonal and commemorative rites that recreate our connections to the natural world and the course of human history."[50] People today want something above and beyond the traditional. They want something that speaks to their particular situation. The families that I have worked with constantly identify the need for a service that combines both personal and spiritual dimensions. They want a celebration of life with spiritual components. The six phases of the funeral can incorporate all of these needs.

Perhaps one of the more practical reasons for the increase in attention on funerals is simple demographics. As the so–called "Baby Boomers"[51] move into their older years the frequency of funerals will only increase. More and more people, both religious and nonreligious will be called upon to lead services marking these earth–shattering transitions. Gerald Hodge states that as the population grows older there will be more of a demand for certain "support services".[52] While he doesn't state this explicitly one can only hunch that one of these support services will be the funeral home. I'll spare you an extensive statistical analysis but at the beginning of the 21st century, for example, the number of seniors living in Canada was 3.9 million. By 2006 this number had grown to 4.3 million.[53] Those numbers, alone, speak volumes.

Both religious and secular organizations are going to have to keep up if each person is going to have a meaningful "send–off". Clergy and celebrants will be faced with the challenge of leading more than one type of service. We'll be called upon to provide an incredible variety of ritual possibilities throughout our working lives. Ron Grimes writes, "To live, rite and the traditions they moderate need constant revision."[54] We will not be able to lead the same funeral twice. This will be difficult for those of us having files and books from which we pick and choose services and fill in the blanks with the name of the deceased.

Perhaps Grimes captures this best when he states, "A good funeral is one that celebrates a life, comforts the bereaved, and facilitates working through grief."[55] Paul Irion would perhaps add that a "good funeral" also has to include the participation of as many people as possible.[56] *Dead Reckoning* will help us build services that celebrate a life, comfort and call on people to begin their grieving, and include as many people as possible in the ritual itself. This is not as easy as it sounds, however. There are so many ways we can twist things around and make a situation more difficult than it has to be. One of the ways things can get twisted is when different beliefs are in conflict.

Van Gennep writes, "Funeral rites are ... complicated when within a single people there are several contradictory or different conceptions of the after world which may become intermingled with one another, so that their confusion is reflected in the rites."[57] He goes on suggest that the deceased and survivors are in a kind of neutral space "situated between the world of the living and the world of the dead."[58] One of the ways a funeral situation can become more difficult and complicated is when some clergy see the funeral as an opportunity to spread the Gospel and offer an evangelical message to the so–called "unchurched". Some would call it a "God–sized opportunity".[59] While it may seem like a good idea at the time this is not always appropriate, requested, or desired. One pastor has told me that this approach "does not bring glory to God". He also said that we "cannot pray people into heaven". Christian clergy can do effective work in a funeral situation without having to resort to what I would call a hard sell approach. I would suggest that this is one of the reasons why so many individuals and families are increasingly turning to so called "secular funerals"[60] to honour and remember the lives of their loved ones. This does not have to be our reality. As service leaders we can untie whatever gets twisted and offer something that helps bring clarity and comfort. Paul Irion reminds us that the word "comfort" means "to make strong"[61] so our efforts can also bring strength to those who both grieve and gather to offer support.

Individual Christians and congregations have done a lot of good work without attaching strings or conditions to what they do. Habitat for Humanity, for example, is an organization that lives out a strong Christian vision without trying to convert the people they serve. Habitat volunteers build houses for people who need it and it doesn't matter whether clients are Christian or not.[62] The foundational belief at work is that God loves everyone. I've heard clergy say the same thing when it comes to leading funerals for people beyond their congregations.

There are other reasons why funerals often have a bad name, however. Some voices have described them as being "stiff" and "unemotional".[63] Other people have used stronger language to describe what they think of funerals. French writer Gustave Flaubert once talked about the "Grotesquerie (sic) of the whole ceremony".[64] Elizabeth Cady Stanton once described them as being "the sad pageantry of death".[65]

Margaret Laurence uses stronger language by referring to them as having a "bizarre cruelty".[66] Each of these examples may contain extreme language but they capture the thoughts and feelings of many throughout human history. In fact, the negativity would grow to a point where people wondered if we should be having them at all. An ancient Chinese reformer by the name of Mo Ti, for example, claimed that funerals were "useless" and that they should be "abolished".[67] The six phases of a funeral help us move away from this negativity in order to help us focus on the more realistic and hopeful things we can say. The six phases can help us find that place where we can celebrate and offer thanks.

When we focus on the hopeful and creative dimension of our work we can help people realize that there are some real and meaningful advantages to having funerals. Funerals, for one, offer a sense of community and inclusion. There are people around us who share our journeys. Edward Myers writes that funerals "can reassure you of your sense of belonging."[68] There can be something therapeutic about knowing that your family and friends are there to support you throughout this difficult time.

As we will be discussing in the next chapter, funerals can have a certain symbolic power and effect that helps people in ways they may not even know. Symbols help us deal with realities that cannot be described or understood by simply using words. I.M. Lewis states that symbols are "something that connects the known with the unknown."[69] Symbols also take the big indescribable things in life and put them into words and things. It's difficult to describe and define love, for example so we come up with visuals like hearts in order to help us show or say what we mean. When it comes to things like love and respect gestures can be just as powerful as anything we say. One of the Buddha's most powerful sermons is believed to be that one occasion where he simply held up a yellow flower for his disciples to see.[70] Symbolic gestures can help us acknowledge the change that has come into our lives. They can help us reflect on the new realities we face when someone dies. People may not always remember what is said at the ceremony itself but they may remember a gesture, sound, or even smell.

It is for these reasons that depriving people of this funeral ritual is extremely risky. People sometimes request that there be no funeral service when they die. While this may seem to be a compassionate and thoughtful gesture it often does little to meet the needs of survivors. People want and perhaps need to do something in response to word that someone they know and have been close to has died. They want to do something tangible and say something helpful. They want some active and communal way to say "Goodbye".[71] This only makes sense. As Betty Jane Wylie wrote in her book *Beginnings*, "… a little howling at the moon might save a little tension later on."[72] James Turner writes, "deprive individuals of their rituals and you may unglue the whole structure of their beliefs."[73] Even though Reformation scholars looked down on the funeral ritual, itself, they called for the deceased "to be accompanied prayerfully by their friends and family to the cemetery." They would also be prayed for during Sunday service.[74]

Dead Reckoning helps with the planning and design of contemporary funeral services. I'll walk you through these six phases of the funeral and we'll see how each of these phases fit together and work as a unified entity. Assistance is offered in the creation, revising, and writing of everything from prayers to meditations to closing dismissals. My hope is that this will be a resource every service leader can use.

Because this book deals with people from a variety of spiritual "places", perhaps a brief comment about terminology is important here. Throughout this book I will be using terms such as "client" and "clients" to deal with people we encounter when planning and leading a funeral. I will also refer to "family" and whenever I do so I rely on a broad definition of the word. We're either born into families or we choose the people who will share the journey with us. Professionals use terms like "fellow travelers"[75] but I find these awkward and slightly "new agey".

Regardless of the words we choose the end product should be our focus. Celebrating a person's life is key. I've already mentioned the importance of telling the story of the deceased. This is something I'll be repeating often throughout this book. Stories are often underrated as forms of communication. Too often we dismiss them as being untrue and without power. This assessment has not always been valid. In fact, stories have been a critical part of human life from almost the very beginning. According to John Shaw entire cultures have been based on the art of storytelling. This is especially true of the Scottish Gaels who eventually found their way to Nova Scotia's Cape Breton Island. Shaw writes, "There's been a culture whose most important monuments are not in the form of buildings, paintings, or statues but rather in the less tangible but equally real form of stories ... that have been enthusiastically transmitted over centuries by the common people."[76] Gunter Grass once said in a Nobel Prize acceptance speech that humans have always told stories. He said, "Long before humanity learned to write and gradually became literate, everybody told tales to everybody else and everybody listened to everybody else's tales."[77] "Everybody" is one of the key words in this quotation. We all tell stories. Novelist and critic V.S. Pritchett once described the act of storytelling, itself, as being a "universal habit".[78] This book will help you bring stories and other resources together so that we can perpetuate this "universal habit" and perhaps give it a more personal touch. What these writers may also tell us is that stories are told in steps and stages. One thing has to happen before another in a particular sequence if the plot is to move forward and tell us something. The six stages of a funeral will help us move in a similar way.

There is a tremendous amount of pressure on the service leader to do an excellent job each and every time they are requested to officiate at a service. Family and friends remember even the smallest mistakes. As one baseball umpire once said, "We're supposed to be perfect our first day on the job and then show constant improvement ..."[79] While it's impossible to achieve perfection from day one, there are ways we can "show constant improvement" and grow in how we officiate at funerals. Peter Urs Bender writes, "When you acquire a new skill or perform a task for the first time, there is an initial start–up period during which the amount of work we put in far exceeds the results gained."[80] We can find poems and readings appropriate to the many different kinds of funerals we will be asked to lead. We can develop a filing system from where this information can be easily retrieved. We can find courses that help us deal with grief and people's response to the loss of a friend or family member. This book will offer advice on how to do these things and more through a chapter helping us evaluate our work.

If you find me going off topic please bear with me. Some of my theory is grounded in different disciplines so you may encounter some strange and distant examples and connections. I rely on everything from books on grief counseling to material from the latest business gurus. Don't worry and bear with me — I'm usually going somewhere with everything I include. Or, to quote a friend of mine, "Trust me — I'm a professional".

Perhaps these phases are necessary because the ground on which funerals are positioned is constantly changing and people are turning to a variety of sources for help and answers. One pastor told me that he has seen a serious shift in funerals. Funerals used to stress order and tradition and that no longer works for many people today. People don't want funerals that have been described as being "stifling", "stuffy" and "stagnant". They certainly don't want something that's read out of a book. According to this pastor funerals have developed into something that is more centred on the deceased. Some may disagree with our use of the word "shift" but regardless of our word selection something is happening and not everybody likes it. Thomas Long, for example, suggests that "funeral practices have drifted off course."[81] Long is correct but probably not for the reasons he would expect. But I will explain all of this as we proceed through the six phases. *Dead Reckoning* is intended to help us recognize the "drift", where we've gone and find our way back on course.

There may be many reasons for this "drift" but for me one stands out from the crowd. This may come across as being rather harsh but many of us simply don't know what we're doing when it comes to funerals. This isn't necessarily our fault either. For many service leaders funerals have not been a part of their formal training. Few clergy have had an extensive introduction to funerals in either seminary or in Bible college. Given the number of funerals we'll be asked to lead in our working and retired lives this is quite simply stunning. But maybe we should be careful in what we wish for. From what clergy have told me when training is available it is not always helpful. Perhaps the situation is best summarized in a phrase Harvard medical students were once offered: "Half of what we have taught you is wrong. Unfortunately, we do not know which half."[82] *Dead Reckoning* addresses this deficit by helping us navigate many of the shifts happening in the world and work of funeral ritual.

So as we make our way through the six phases of a funeral let us keep our boat between the navigational beacons and the best way to do this is to start at square one and try to answer a simple question.

Funeral Ritual

Many of us need to picture something in order to understand it. It's how we learn. When we read or hear about an idea or concept we may picture a shape or diagram of some sort. When I think of the six phases of a funeral I picture a six story building where each floor represents an element of a funeral service. When we picture this building we also have to visualize what's beneath ground level. One of the things a contractor will tell us is that buildings need strong foundations and we have to establish a similar foundation prior to launching into a detailed examination of the six phases of a funeral. This foundation is important because we don't always know what a funeral is or what it is for. We need a body of information that helps inform what we say and do. This became apparent in a very public way a couple of years ago.

On January 8th, 2011 nineteen people were shot in a supermarket parking lot near Tucson, Arizona. Six people died as a result of their wounds. One of the wounded was U.S. Representative Gabrielle Giffords and among the dead was Judge John Roll of the U.S. District Court for the District of Arizona. On January 12th a memorial service was held to remember those killed in the shooting. The following evening *The Daily Show* host, Jon Stewart, made some observations about media pundits' response to this service. He talked about how these pundits seemed to think that it was somehow similar to the broadcasting of an awards show like the Emmy's. After listening to a number of inane statements Stewart blurted out, "It's not a show!" While he did have a point he wasn't completely correct either. We can say that he was half–right. A funeral is not a "show" as we may see on television or the internet but it is something similar. Television shows and funerals share the same roots. They both find their roots in drama. To be more specific it's similar to a drama as we would see on a live stage. A variation of this type of drama is ritual and, as we'll be discussing in this chapter, funeral services are rituals and funeral rituals are a part of each and every culture.[1]

We can begin our discussion of the funeral ritual with one general, simple question: What is ritual? My immediate answer is "it depends". Rituals come in many different shapes and sizes and often go by different names. As we've already mentioned one such name is "drama". Perhaps the simplest way of defining ritual is by saying that it is a belief converted into an action.[2] Historically, as Kingsley Davis indicated in his study of human societies decades ago, rituals have been "activities" tied to religion. This goes back to a time when humans began developing the belief that we, as individuals are made up of two main components: body and soul. These early humans wondered what happened to the soul when the body physically stopped working. What happened when the body and soul "part ways"? Many concluded that the soul must go somewhere and they devised ways to help the soul on its way. They felt that this would be the best outcome. Perhaps the worst thing that could happen to a person's soul or spirit was for it to somehow remain with the family and friends who survive the deceased. This is why Kingsley Davis suggested that the first human ritual was a funeral ritual.[3] He also suggested that "the first altars were tombs".[4] John Casey believes that these early funeral rituals eventually "morphed" into other forms of worship such as Christianity's various Sunday morning liturgies.[5]

Today, while rituals can express spiritual realities surrounding such things as death and the afterlife, they don't have to be tied to particular religious traditions. Weddings no longer require clergy leadership. Baptism services have been replaced by secular "Welcomings". The changes that affect our current rituals began a long time ago. Jean Meslier once described rituals as being "superstitious practices of religion" and dismissed them as being "human inventions".[6] While he may not have thought much of these "human inventions" they were an important part of how people organized their spiritual and community lives. This human inventiveness continues in the present day. Rituals such as funerals may be "human inventions" they still have importance, relevance, and value. They still have a place in our lives regardless of how religious or nonreligious we are.

Ritual names spiritual reality and can also be a way of ordering the chaos we experience in our everyday lives, especially when we experience loss. In the case of funerals perhaps we can use the word "taming" instead of "ordering". "Ordering" implies that we organise people or items in a way that make sense. It suggests that we should tell people what to do. We order toy blocks, for example, when we place them in a line or some other shape. Taming, however, suggests that we change behavior or outlook. It also suggests that we have begun the process of bringing order out of chaos. It doesn't seem as organized but it is still important. French historian Robert Fossier writes, "Since no one could avoid death's sentence, death had to be "tamed", rendered accessible, admitted as a beginning and as something desirable, thus limiting the force of our vulgar ties to things of this world."[7]

Regardless, funeral rituals tame and order for a particular reason and that is because of how we're wired as human beings. Clifford Geertz writes, "The drive to make sense out of experience, to give it form and order, is evidently as real and as pressing as the more familiar biological needs."[8] In taming chaos we may find ourselves doing things like venting emotional energy in a unique and profound way. Even ancient writings such as the Gospel of Thomas acknowledge the need to vent in a time of loss. It is stated in this writing, "If you bring forth what is inside you, what is inside you will save you. If you do not bring forth what is inside you, what is inside you will destroy you."[9] An example of this wisdom can be found in ancient Egypt where women used to plaster mud on their faces and parade half–naked through the streets beating themselves as they went.[10] This told witnesses that someone had died. It also provided the grieving women a way of channeling their emotional energy. Each and every culture needs a way to accomplish this. Ancient cultures knew that venting was important because they also knew the cost of burying emotions. Phyllis Kosminsky writes, "Feelings are signals, and if we ignore them, they continue to break through any way they can."[11]

Ritual is a way we show people, in both a physical and symbolic way, that we care about them as they process the emotional energy of loss and make their way through important transition times in their lives. Geertz writes, "But a ritual is not just a pattern of meaning; it is also a form of social interaction."[12] Tom Jokinen writes, "All sacred customs were ways to signal to one another that we're not alone, that there's some continuity even in death, a consensus that we could beat back the senseless, arbitrary fact of it by holding hands and chanting."[13] In some communities this commitment to caring means we set aside our class and economic distinctions for the good of the group. The Kabylia people of Algeria, for example, once expected individuals to attend each and every funeral held in their respective villages. The main reason for doing this was to establish a level playing field between rich and poor. Each funeral was important and each deceased person should be shown the same respect.[14] It was a way of telling each and every member of the community that they were loved and cared for, regardless of how much money or power they had.

In addition to emotional and other pastoral considerations perhaps the most pragmatic reason for having ritual in our lives is the communication of information from one person or group to another. When it comes to funerals in particular this information will be in the form of memories, stories, insights, and shared experiences. This "information" helps us mark crucial transitions as death. Emile Durkheim has suggested that it's one way for an individual to connect with a wider group such as family or community.[15] This is especially important in times of crisis. We'll be talking about the content of a person's life and the effect this life had on the people around him or her in a later chapter.

Paul Radin and Thomas Long compare rituals such as funerals to dramas and this is a connection made at the beginning of this chapter. Drama entertains and it also teaches. Radin, for example, writes, "In the broadest sense of the term ... (rituals) are dramas, for they contain elements that are, at least in part, re–enactments of deeds ascribed to some mythical character or characters."[16] Long supports his argument by writing, "It has a script, a plot, actors, and a stage on which it is performed."[17] According to John Stubbs drama "sent people out full of possibilities, voices raised re–running half–remembered dialogues with their companions, simply enlivened by a funny show, or aware of things they had not known about themselves before ..."[18]

Ancient rituals were, indeed, extremely dramatic and tried to touch as many of the human senses as possible. Funerals were important as they, of all the available rituals, affected most people.[19] Royal funerals, especially, helped reassure subjects that there will be a smooth transition of power and that everything will be under control.[20]

The same is true today. In a funeral the drama is built around the history and legacy of the life of the deceased. It's built around a gap that's been opened in our lives and now we're trying to bridge that gap. This is why storytelling is so important. Storytelling is akin to drama so it also entertains and educates. We can say that storytelling feeds drama. On New Brunswick's Grand Manan Island, for example, people gather around their kitchen tables telling stories about the deceased and reviewing their life and family history. According to Joan Marshall, "a conversation might recount a whole series of events that place the person ... and finally conclude with: 'Oh, that's who she is!'"[21] That's one statement we want people proclaiming as they leave the funeral. We want them to hear what is said and respond by saying something like, "Oh, that's who he or she is!"

Stories help build memories of the deceased and they can also offer examples and inspiration for the survivors. Stories also show us how a person's life has changed, evolved, and moved through the years and decades. It's as if we say something like "Jane Doe, this is your life". Or perhaps in this context it's best to say, "This is Jane Doe's life." This retelling of Jane Doe's story can be done in several different ways and we will be touching on many of these throughout this book. Each of the six phases we'll be addressing in the chapters that follow can address a piece or section of the life in question but we cannot get ahead of ourselves. First we have to talk about food and other aspects of the funeral ritual.

In the ancient world this ritual drama and storytelling were usually combined with a meal. Perhaps these were the earliest dinner theatres. Meals were an important part of these funeral rituals because they brought people together and helped them maintain their relationship with the deceased. They also nourished people so that they had to energy to endure their loss and fulfill their ritual commitments. People gathered in homes for these ritual meals and would sing hymns, share in emotional laments, tell stories, and drink toasts.[22] There would also be dramatic expressions of these grieving survivors.

The Romans called this ritual the "meal of the dead"[23] and similar rituals were played out across the Mediterranean. These different rituals came to comprise what has come to be called the "cult of the dead".[24] They thought about the future and the immediate challenges of rebuilding and regrouping. It has been argued that these meals inspired Biblical accounts such as the miraculous feeding of the 5000.[25] Kathleen Corley argues that these meals were so important they helped develop the Eucharist itself.[26] They also helped establish the place of women in the early church. Women have shared in these funeral meals since around 200 B.C.E.[27] These rituals were seen as being mandatory. People believed that failure to offer a funeral meal could lead to some very bad things, including frequent visits from the ghost of the deceased. People were terrified by the possibility that ghosts would find their way back to the world of the living. Rituals helped keep a strong wall or barrier in place preventing this from happening but these things only worked if the ritual was properly carried out.[28] Threatened haunting aside, funeral meals were often positive, upbeat affairs where the life and accomplishments of the deceased were celebrated and honoured.[29]

One of the reasons why these meals were often considered mandatory was because of their importance to both individuals and communities. Yes, they celebrated the life of the deceased but they were so much more. Community meals can help build connections between people. This is why team meals are so important in the sports world. They bring players and coaches together with the goal of improving overall performance. These meals also strengthen relationships and a commitment to work as a group. A similar thing happens during a funeral. When a person dies a meal can help bring a community together and mend the tear in the fabric that holds people in relationship. We have to address these tears in each and every ritual.

Addressing these tears cannot easily be accomplished in one move. Arnold Van Gennep argues that rites of passage incorporate three main stages: separation, transition, and incorporation.[30] These stages help us acknowledge that a person has moved from life to death or from life to afterlife. We've already discussed the notion of a funeral as being a "gateway experience". In this part of our discussion this "gateway" can take the form of a bridge. This bridge takes us through and across what we can call a "liminal" or "in between" time.[31] That's the gap between realities and it's usually the space in which funerals happen.

It's for this reason Paul Radin was wise to move one step beyond Van Gennep and cut ritual down to two stages. He writes, "... the rites for the dead, in spite of all other constituents, remained basically a ritual of separation to which there was soon added the ritual of the soul's entry into a new non–human and altogether desirable world."[32] While the word "separation" may be accurate it seems rather tame given the sheer intensity of shock we experience. Mircea Eliade uses the word "rupture" when describing the first stage of an initiation ritual and this word can also apply to the funeral ritual as well. "Rupture" is appropriate because the tear between the deceased and survivors can be, to borrow another term Eliade uses, "brutal".[33] Regardless of how intense our work is, however, we can still work with the two–step system Radin introduces and discusses.

These two steps help keep us on track when it comes to our present work. When we're planning and leading a funeral service we're trying to accomplish several things at once. One thing funeral rituals help us do is confront the reality of death.[34] Northcott and Wilson write, "Funeral and memorial services do much to assist those who grieve by providing an opportunity to reflect upon the life of the person who has died and to publicly and collectively acknowledge the person's death."[35] This may sound harsh but it's important when it comes to the early steps in the grief and bereavement experience. When we first experience death we may experience a fog of sorts. Fog obscures our surroundings and makes it difficult to make our way from point A to point B. When we try to drive through fog we can only see a short distance in front of us and it's almost impossible to see what's ahead of us. We can only see what's immediately surrounding us. When someone dies our world shrinks so that we only have the energy and resources to deal with what's immediately surrounding us in our lives.

Ritual helps us begin the process of clearing this fog or perhaps some would use the term "dream". Beverley Raphael says that when we confront the reality of death, we "come out of the dream."[36] When we come out of this dream we may begin a frantic and ultimately fruitless search for the deceased and this is also a reality of bereavement. Adam Gollner writes, "Bereavement brings with it a sense of having embarked upon a lengthy search for something that can't be found."[37]

Funerals also help us offer clarity and they also give people a chance to say goodbye, express their emotions, acknowledge changes in families and relationships, and share their grief and condolences with friends, colleagues, and family. bell hooks has coined the term "rituals of regard and recollection" and these words certainly apply to the funeral.[38] Sharing this experience with one another can help survivors make the transition mentioned earlier. Transition and transformation are important terms when it comes to funerals. Mary of Guise is believed to have said "In our end is our beginning"[39] and when it comes to death and what comes after she was correct. When it comes to death and funerals endings become beginnings. Our lives turn and spin in a radical way. That may be a big switch for a lot of people. It's often tough to see the new beginnings when we're still assessing our losses. We can still recognize and name this shift, however.

Transition and transformation are not always neat and tidy and ritual helps us restore some order and balance. Elaine Ramshaw writes, "The taken–for–granted everyday world is disrupted, one's place in the social structure is shifted, a relationship one has depended upon for continuity has ended,"[40] When we experience endings we may be tempted to completely turn away from the situation completely. We don't like messy things and loose ends. We want our lives to run smoothly and that cannot happen in times of loss. Ritual is one way that can help us set our individual and collective journeys back on track.

Some would argue that ritual acts like funerals are a waste of time. As I have previously stated, many request that there be no funeral held when they die. This request may be based on personal experience. Let's be blunt here — many ritual acts can come across as being extremely cold and insensitive. We've reviewed many of the ugly and negative things that have been said about funerals in this book's introduction. We can also address this negative outlook here. Indeed, why should we bother? Why should we go through the tears and emotional stress of a funeral?

It turns out there are many good reasons why we should bother. In dealing with the significant transitions in our lives, ritual presents us with the opportunity, and perhaps the responsibility to address human needs.[41] This is true whether or not the ritual is religious or nonreligious. Ritual is like a cord that farmers in the early west would run between the house and the barn before a blizzard arrived.[42] When the storm hit and visibility went to nil that cord helped them make their way between buildings so that they could survive and get things done in extremely difficult and threatening circumstances. It was real and it helped people move when they had to, even in the most difficult conditions. The animals still needed to be fed and the family still needed water. Life had to continue regardless of the weather and the same is true today.

So to present a counter argument to those who think that there's no need for a funeral we can ask the question: How is it supposed to help us? To some extent we've already begun to answer this but perhaps we need to pursue this question farther. Ramshaw is realistic when she suggests, "For many people, the most a funeral can do is to get them out of the initial state of shock, numbness, and denial, and into grief, that is, to help them *into* rather than through or out of grief. This is why the crucial moments for the family and close friends are usually the signs of finality: the closing of the casket, the lowering of the casket into the ground, the first shovelful of dirt."[43] Another crucial moment is when we're reminded of the gaps left behind by the departure of the deceased.

These are gaps that need to be bridged and resolved. Bronislaw Malinowski writes, "A small community bereft of a member, especially if he be important, is severely mutilated. The whole event breaks the normal course of life and shakes the moral foundations of society."[44] He goes on to add, "Death in a primitive society is, therefore, much more than the removal of a member. By setting in motion one part of the deep forces of self–preservation, it threatens the very cohesion and solidarity of the group, and upon this depends the organization of that society, its tradition, and finally the whole culture."[45] This is like a house of cards — remove one card and the entire structure may fall. We find ourselves with a house that requires some effort to rebuild. We, as service leaders are in a unique position to help with this rebuilding. At the very least we're in a position to help hold the house of cards together. In the Christian context especially the presence and work of ritual can be critical for both pastors and other church leaders. How does ritual work when it comes to Christian funerals in particular? What are we trying to do? One pastor told me that there are two goals to a Christian funeral: "Bring glory to God" and reconciliation to family and friends left behind. Reconciliation can be the healing of rifts between God and survivors of the deceased. Rifts can also be healed between groups and individuals struggling with their loss. Paul Johnson writes, "This is a time for the Christian community to rally around the bereaved in sympathetic understanding and loving concern."[46] The death of a loved one can awaken memories and experiences that may have been buried for a long time. These divisions may need to be addressed if people are to move on.

Reconciliation can bring healing at a time when conflict seems natural, especially when it comes to our emotional state. There are several contradictory emotions at work when we deal with the death and funeral of someone we love. Malinowski writes, "The emotions are extremely complex and even contradictory; the dominant elements, love of the dead and loathing of the corpse, passionate attachment to the personality still lingering about the body and a shattering fear of the gruesome thing that has been left over, these two elements seem to mingle and play into each other."[47] Malinowski identifies two of the main emotions in play at a time like this as being "fear" and "hope". He writes, "Man's conviction of continued life is one of the supreme gifts of religion, which judges and selects the better of the two alternatives suggested by self–preservation — the hope of continued life and the fear of annihilation."[48]

Hope is an important and timeless word here. What is hope and how can we find hope in Christian funerals? For me the first part of the definition of hope is simply the expectation that something is going to happen. We hope we're going to have a good day for the picnic this weekend. We hope we're not going to sprain an ankle when we run that marathon next month. We hope that we're going to live a long and relatively pain free existence. Hope is expectation and hope is so much more. The great preacher G. Campbell Morgan once wrote that hope is also active. He defines hope as being "confidence in something yet to be, with an accompanying endeavor to reach it."[49] In other words it's not good enough to sit around and wait for good things to happen. We have to plan and prepare. If we're running a marathon we have to prepare ourselves physically and psychologically. We actually have to hit the pavement, start running and try to break a sweat. If we want to remember someone who has died we can do things like serve the causes they valued or complete the community projects they helped initiate.

Christian hope in particular offers that sense that death is not the end and that there is new life with God. We can both expect that and pursue it. Yes, we are sad but we can also be relieved knowing that a loved one is transformed, at peace and with God. Robert Millet captures this notion when he writes, "when we pass through the veil of death, all those impediments and challenges and crosses that were beyond our power to control — abuse, neglect, immoral environment, weighty traditions, private temptations and inclinations ... will be torn away like a film and perfect peace will prevail in our hearts." In other words, whatever is not working in our lives here and now will be somehow sorted out when we die. Millet goes on to say, "We as mortals simply do not have the power to fix everything that is broken."[50]

This is a hope we can hold on to and hold onto it we must. Losing hope, especially in a situation of loss and grief can be crippling. Viktor Frankl observed this in an up close and personal way during his detention in a concentration camp during the Second World War. People who survived the experience, for the most part, did so because they looked forward to a new and better reality. He wrote, "The prisoner who lost faith in the future — his future – was doomed."[51]

Regardless of what we believe about what happens at that moment of our death hope helps us when it comes to dealing with and releasing our emotions. Catholic theologian Richard Neuhaus writes, "Life feeds on hope, and hope is by definition hope for something better ..."[52] Hope is considered a virtue and virtue, according to Neuhaus, is one of many human "strengths".[53] Sometimes we don't know how strong we experience loss and make our way through the ritual expression of this loss. Perhaps one of the strengths we will discover is that of dealing with feelings and emotions, especially when it comes to something like crying.

As we've previously discussed, when it comes to funerals, emotional processing and release is an important component. Bozarth–Campbell writes, "These rituals provide release and an opportunity to express what needs to be expressed among persons involved."[54] We've been created with the ability to cry and yet, for some reason, many of us have been discouraged from doing so. We've joined the western effort to numb whatever pain is in our lives and spirits. In a way, crying is often seen as being almost completely contrary to human nature. But regardless of how hard we try we cannot hold back the tears. There are times when we have to cry. Joan Chittister writes, "Tears fall despite the fact that we resist them so strongly."[55] Chittister goes on to add: "Of all the expressions of human emotion in the lexicon of life, weeping may be the most functional, the most deeply versatile."[56]

Crying and the shedding of tears presents a problem for many, if not most mourners. Whether we're in prison[57] or church or almost anywhere else, for that matter, crying has been discouraged. This is why, in many parts of Africa "professional wailers" facilitate this release.[58] Conversely, the Chinese help release their emotions by the use of fireworks.[59] This makes sense as the emotional release experienced at a funeral can be quite explosive. People have often said to me, for example, that they become so occupied with planning a funeral they don't cry or release their emotions until the funeral itself. I'm not certain how this restraint is helpful. Crying seems to have a natural place in the funeral ritual. Perhaps it will take time for this change to take place.

Hooyman and Kramer write, "Cultural norms and variations help determine how grief is expressed, especially in the rituals that surround grieving."[60] In military culture, for example, the expression of this grief can be equally strong and intense. In his memoir of life in the United States Marine Corps, Anthony Swofford describes one of his experience with death and funerals and writes, "We continued cussing during the viewing, profanity being as clear a trumpet of grief as any. Profanity and then silence."[61] Profanity is an emotional release and can be helpful. Like many clergy I've had to inform people of the death of a loved one and on many occasions they've responded by saying things like "Shit". While I would not recommend using profanity in a funeral service we can be aware of its power and uses beyond the ritual.

Considering the sheer amount of emotional release that can happen at a funeral it seems strange to use terms like "celebrations of life". I've heard many people refer to funerals in this way. The roots of this terminology may extend back into church history and perhaps even prior to that. Bonnie Effros writes, "Saints' funerals theoretically represented occasions of great joy for their followers, even if the most devout

Christians sometimes had difficulty expressing their elation at the loss of one of their own."[62] The ancient druids lead rituals that could be called "celebrations". These celebrations included meals and games. People found ways to show their excitement at the thought of someone achieving rebirth in the afterlife.[63]

The word "celebration" can be easily misunderstood in this and many other contexts. I've often been asked to keep a service "upbeat" and "positive" and that's extremely difficult to do. Not everyone attending a funeral is in a space where they can be "upbeat". Contemporary celebrations are not always about laughter and being upbeat. In many cases they're about acknowledging and saluting good work and a life well lived. What I do suggest is that we respect the need to balance laughter and tears and focus on the many gifts the person has offered in life. We may not always accept that laughter and tears can be experienced together but they can. In fact, Joan Chittister suggests that "both laughter and tears come from the same place."[64] Funerals are one of those moments when this happens. When it comes to the grief experience tears and laughter can both be gifts. These gifts can be shared in many different ways.

Recent advances in technology are changing how we remember and celebrate people's lives. This is one of the ways in which ritual has evolved. Susan White writes, "To be a contemporary human being is to be caught up in the web technology has set for us."[65] She later adds, "(Men) and women in every age have had to integrate technology into their personal and communal perspectives, and to manage the social, moral, and intellectual anxieties that the relationship with technology occasions."[66] Marshall McLuhan once wrote, "Each new medium alters permanently our psychic environment, imposing on us a particular pattern of perceiving and thinking that controls us to an extent we scarcely suspect."[67] Even the invention and introduction of the common microphone has had its affect. Each and every new technological innovation changes the way we experience a funeral.

A couple of years ago I was helping a family plan a service when they asked if we could "Skype the service" to a distant community so that elderly relatives there could see and hear the service. This was the first time I've ever heard this request so I thought about it and told the family that we could give it a try. I couldn't see any reason why it would be a problem. So on the day of the funeral the younger relatives showed up early with all of their equipment and set everything up. Everything seemed to work well and when I checked in with the family a few days after the funeral they told me that it was really meaningful for distant relatives to watch the service on their monitors. A few months later a funeral director told me that Skyping was becoming more common in services and this makes sense given the experience I've just mentioned. A few weeks later this same director showed me where cameras had been installed in the funeral home's chapel so that Skyping would be a lot easier for their clients.

Even the locations of churches and cemeteries have changed how we do funerals. Susan White writes, "By the time of the Reformation, the ritual included a procession from the house of the deceased to the church, the office of the dead, the funeral mass, the procession to the grave, and the burial."[68] This separation became important when cemeteries were located a great distance from the communities they served. Service books from this time contain service materials that reflect this division.[69]

Regardless of how technology and other considerations change some of the funeral's content it's important that we ensure that the essential structure of the ritual remain intact. Change has to be managed so that ritual development moves in a positive direction. Julian Huxley once wrote, "Change must come; it can, on balance be good; it is our business to try and guide it and ensure that it shall be not merely change but progress."[70] When we manage change we have to sort out what we need to keep and what we need to remove. We need to figure out what works and what doesn't work.

Regardless of where the winds of change take us there are some elements of the funeral ritual that endure and need to continue. Naming realities such as separation continue to be critical as is the reflection on what happens when we die. A.C. Grayling describes the funeral as being an "absolute parting".[71] This "parting" has to be experienced in order for the loss to be understood and accepted. This experience has to include most of our senses. We can smell the flowers and see the burning candles. We can feel the touch of a friend or family member when we hug or shake hands. We can also feel the dirt as we throw handfuls of it into the grave following the graveside service. Tom Jokinen underlines this reality when he writes, "We need to see it to know it, touch its hair or hands, feel how cold it is."[72]

In speaking of the need for reality and innovation in ritual Ronald Grimes writes, "Ritual, like art, is a child of imagination, but the ritual imagination requires an invention, a constantly renewed structure, on the basis of which a bodily and communal enactment is possible."[73] Invention and imagination are both important when comes to funerals because each situation is unique and developing sense of separation is sometimes difficult. This is why the word "negotiation" has to be a part of our work when it comes to funerals. Each service will have its own twists and turns and surprises. Grimes goes on to add, "But neither imagination, nor invention is a creation out of nothing."[74] The funeral has to be built on the real experience of separation and the need to rebuild and renew our lives. This is why we need to move the deceased to a new place in our continuing journeys. It's also why we need to embrace one another as we struggle with new realities. Andre Comte–Sponville writes, "What religion affords us, when we lose a loved one, is not only the possibility of consolation but also a sorely needed ritual — a ceremony, with or without pomp, a sort of ultimate courtesy, which helps us confront and integrate death ... perhaps accept it as well, since we shall eventually have to do so, or at least acknowledge it."[75] Comte–Sponville also writes, "Wakes, funeral orations, chants, prayers, symbols, postures, rites, sacraments, ... All these things help us grow accustomed to the horror, humanize it, civilize it — and this is no doubt necessary."[76] He then adds, "Nothing prevents atheists from seeking an equivalent — and indeed, they often do so."[77]

Why have I introduced and dwelt on all of this? For me the answer is simple: effective ritual requires skilled, informed and innovative leadership. This leadership can be provided by many thoughtful and capable people. Historically, high priests have led rituals. Although the titles may have changed this remains true today. There was a time when people turned to the priests and clergy for, to borrow Irvin Yalom's terminology, "magic, mystery, and authority".[78] For the most part, this has become a thing of the past but some thread of this thinking may still remain to some extent. This is why clergy continue to be asked to lead funerals and celebrations of life.

If given the choice between formal worship and a celebration of life I'd rather focus on the deceased and the legacy they leave behind. This can be done in a warm and respectful way. I agree with something Confucius wrote long ago: "… in mourning, it is better to err on the side of grief than on the side of formality."[79] In saying this, however, it's important that we maintain order and dignity when combining formal worship and celebrations of life. When we design less formal services we potentially lose something important. We could lose a sense of order and solemnity. We may also lose that sense of movement that presses the reality that our loved one has died and life will be forever altered. *The Globe and Mail* columnist Margaret Wente once wrote, "I hate the modern loss of ritual and solemnity surrounding death. Something is lost when people get together and have a party and pretend the loved one has done nothing more dramatic than move to Cleveland."[80]

Regardless of whether we focus on worship or celebration we cannot lose sight of the need for effective ritual. Rituals have power and can move us emotionally, spiritually and intellectually. Burial rites, for example, are so important many throughout history have believed that there is a tremendous amount of power in denying these rites. Plato, for one, recommended denial of burial rites for those who have been executed for a crime. He felt that this would have some punitive effect on the person's journey through the afterlife.[81] The ancient Greeks, among others, seemed to agree and left the bodies of execution victims to be eaten and consumed by scavengers.[82] While this seems harsh it was thought to be effective. In our present day, however, that view seems to have softened. Even mass murderers have a few words said over their graves when they die. Perhaps this is one way we try and set things right, offer some dignity in traumatic circumstances and get back to whatever our "new normal" is going to look like.

When led effectively funerals can also have the ability to restore order in chaotic times. They can help us process and release intense emotional energy. They can also inspire, educate, and rebuild individual lives, families, and communities. Ritual leaders are similar to actors in that they do so many jobs at once. Pine and Gilmore write, "Acting is the taking of deliberate steps to connect with an audience."[83] This connection is critical in so many different ways. When American President John F. Kennedy was assassinated it was argued that the funeral helped restore a sense of stability to a badly shaken nation.[84] People had experienced a tremendous loss but they knew that they could find strength, hope, and new beginnings by sticking together as a community.

So now the stage is set so let us begin our travels through the six phases of the funeral.

Phase One: Planning and Preparation

Arctic explorer Vilhjalmur Stefansson once began a lecture by boldly stating, "An adventure is a sign of incompetence."[1] This may come across as a rather harsh thing to say but it does contain both a surprising and critical truth: a strong leader plans well and anticipates any and all potential challenges, surprises and accidents so that the given project or journey can run without a problem. Without the proper planning and training problems arise and an adventure begins. Some of us may find adventure fun but the flip side is that there is always a serious risk of something tragic happening. This "something tragic" can derail and disrupt a journey before it even begins. One of the most important parts of any journey is gathering the necessary maps, charts, and tables so that we can figure out which course will get us to our destination with the minimum of risk. While it may sound like quite a stretch between arctic exploration and a funeral service they both have their risks, require appropriate amounts of preparation and have no room for adventure.

This is nothing new either. The importance of funeral planning is something to which even the ancients were committed. Confucius, for example, once wrote, "Conduct the funeral of your parents with meticulous care ..."[2] "(M)eticulous care" are two words to hold before us as we plan and prepare a funeral service. In our present day service leaders have to focus a fair amount of time and attention on the "meticulous" work of creating and officiating a funeral. We also have to invest a lot of energy in caring for the people with whom we work. Detailed planning and preparation help prevent adventures and ensure a job well done. This is why I name it as being the first phase of a funeral.

Sprinters will tell us that one of the keys to winning any race is that first explosive instant out of the starting block. Professionals in many different disciplines will agree with this. Engineers, for example, need accurate drawings if their projects are going to stand a chance of succeeding. They need to have a crystal clear idea of what their clients want and need before any trades people can proceed. When discussing improved productivity on the industrial production line W. Edwards Deming once wrote, "quality must be built in at the design stage."[3] Preparation and design take many different forms and we will be focusing on many of these in this chapter.

The first thing we need to do once we've agreed to lead a service is connect with the family. This marks the beginning of a brief but intense relationship. Calgary Funeral Director Kimberly Stevenson describes the nature of the relationships we develop when we plan and officiate a funeral as being "hyper–intimacies".[4] I've found this term to be extremely accurate. We meet a group of people under extremely difficult circumstances and have to establish some sort of rapport with them in an extremely brief period of time. This working relationship will cover a lot of ground in a real hurry and we'll have to work hard in order to keep up.

Once contact has been initiated and introductions have been made we'll have to make arrangements for a planning meeting held with friends and family. This is that place where the hyper–intimacy begins. These meetings are a critical part of the process because we have to find out how the deceased contributed to the lives of the people who shared his or her world. We also have to find out what the mourners need in terms of the service itself. This body of knowledge is what we feed off of throughout the entire funeral process. Building this body of knowledge doesn't have to be complicated. We can begin with some rather simple questions such as "Where was the deceased born?" and "How did they contribute?" What is their legacy? The meeting will be built around these and many other questions.

Planning meetings come in many different shapes and sizes. There are many ways we can touch base with friends and family of the deceased and gather the information we need. One of these ways is to simply use the telephone. Sometimes family live a fair distance from where the funeral is going to be held. They may not arrive in time to have a separate planning meeting. Telephone conversations are not always ideal but they sometimes have to suffice. For me, an actual meeting with the family is the most effective option and I say this for a number of reasons. Perhaps the best reason is simply matching faces with names. Surviving friends and family will also want to get to know us as well. One of the things that make the funeral more meaningful is the mutual nature of the working relationship between the service leader and the survivors.

When it comes to the planning meeting the first challenge is trying to figure out when and where to meet. I try to focus on the convenience of the family, as they are the ones who have to juggle a number of commitments over a fairly brief time line. Studies have shown that the death of someone close to us is one of the most stressful times we can experience in life.[5] Finding a place where people feel safe and comfortable may help reduce the amount of stress people are experiencing. When people are comfortable they find it easier to talk and this helps with our information gathering. This is why the lobbies of many funeral homes are beginning to resemble coffee shops. Coffee shops are often places where we meet people and have some of our deepest conversations.

There is some discussion as to whether or not we meet families at their homes or at the funeral home. Some pastors claim that it is important to consider the family's comfort zone and meet in a place they are familiar with. The home that is best for this is the deceased's or so–called "Primary Person's" home. People will be there from time to time anyway as they will have to get the deceased person's earthly affairs sorted out. But home visits, regardless of where they're held, may not work for everyone. Not everyone wants visitors in their homes at a time like this. With all of the sudden activity they may not have time to clean up, organize and prepare. This is an added chore for which they do not have the time or energy.

This is one of the reasons why I've heard other clergy make the case that it is best to meet in a funeral home, as it can be a central location where people may need to drop by for visitations, decorating, etc.. This reduces the need for clients to find extra meeting time in their already constrained schedules. Some clergy will try to make the appointment for roughly the same time as a visitation or viewing as this ensures that the maximum number of people is available for the meeting. Funeral homes also offer neutral territory in case there is conflict between individuals or within a group. We've already mentioned the conflicting emotions that emerge in times of loss. Walter Whitaker III suggests that emotions will sometimes be expressed as aggression.[6] This aggression can be aimed at fellow family members, the deity we worship and/or ourselves. When we have a sense that people are being aggressive with the people around them we can arrange for this safe place so that we can move on with our work.

I try and schedule an hour–long meeting with mourners either before or after their appointment with the funeral home staff. Most, if not all funeral homes will allow family, friends, and clergy to meet and plan the service there. Just make sure you contact the director and let them know you'll be needing a place to meet on a certain day and time. Funeral homes can be extremely busy places and some time slots may be off limits because of services, meetings or seminars.

One other place I've met families is at a decent and quiet restaurant just around the corner from where I live. It's a little rough around the edges but it's quiet, accessible, and has enough parking for everybody. We can plan the service while people enjoy a coffee or quick meal. Some of my clients have enjoyed the food so much they've returned to the restaurant on numerous occasions and a few have even become regulars. It's best to offer clients a choice and let them decide where they would like to meet.

While I try and schedule one hour for these meetings I am open to the possibility that the time we need to cover all of the bases will vary depending on the identified needs of the family. For whatever reason, some clients simply don't have much to say about the deceased. There's really not much we can do about that. Forcing information from people is less than helpful. A friend of mine used to respond to a lack of information in a rather creative way. If he felt he was not getting enough information from a group or family he would simply say something like: "So you want me to tell folks that the deceased was ugly and that nobody liked them." While this was somewhat effective, it's not something I would recommend to every reader, however.

Some meetings will require a time commitment of more than an hour or so. There are situations that will call for more time and energy on our part. There are many reasons for this. Perhaps the main reason concerns the type of death. There may be issues within the family that need addressing. Families may even want to talk about issues they're having with the funeral home itself. On a couple of occasions I've had to listen to complaints about a funeral home or staff person before anything can be accomplished. We couldn't begin to prepare for the service before the air was cleared. Regardless of how long the meeting takes the important thing is that everything that needs to be discussed is taken care of. There should also be time set aside for a brief question and answer session. I'll talk more about this later.

When making arrangements for the meeting, one question we are often asked by families is "What can we do to prepare for our meeting?" There are a couple of simple responses to this question. As I've already mentioned, families can bring information about what I call the details of the service. This would be things like the music we'll be listening to and the names of people who will be speaking about the deceased. If we've never met the deceased then the family will have to bring stories and memories to help build a history. Families can also bring photographs to the meeting. This helps give us a mental picture of what the deceased looked like and it also helps with the story telling process. We can ask about the time and place in which the photo was taken. We can ask about the people in the photo and whether or not there are any important memories of the occasion.

Perhaps the most helpful thing they could do is bring written notes so that the service leader can take them when they leave so that they don't have to rely on memory. As we will be discussing later stress affects our memory and our ability to think. Our stress levels can be affected by many things. I find that one of the most significant contributors is dealing with a person in their time of illness. Dying people require a lot of time and energy from those around them. When that person passes away their survivors may find themselves overwhelmed and exhausted. They may still be in shock and this is to be expected. "No matter how many months or even years we have to prepare for the death of a loved one, when death actually occurs, the feeling of loss strikes us as never before."[7] Encouraging people to write things down helps them deal with the stress and process the experience of sharing the deceased's final illness. At the very least I find written information helpful because the onus is shifted so that when someone is forgotten it is the family who will have to deal with the repercussions. If I hear one complaint about clergy it's usually that we take it upon ourselves to read lists of names without ensuring we have all of the necessary names before us.

One of the more interesting and surprising conversations I've had with funeral directors concerns what I wear when I meet families at the funeral home. After one particular meeting a director said to me "lose the shorts". It was a hot summer day and I always dress in walking shorts and short sleeve shirts when meeting people under those conditions. People seem to appreciate the fact that I dress in a manner that is similar to what they wear as they prepare for a funeral. A pharmacist once wrote, "People want to talk to somebody who looks like them, talks like them and is a part of the community."[8] While this doesn't give us permission to dress like slobs it can encourage us to dress in a less formal and intimidating way when dealing with people focused on more deeper matters. My one regret in the example just cited is that when the director said "lose the shorts" I didn't drop them right in front of him. But I digress.

Once we've dressed ourselves properly and arrive at the meeting we may find ourselves experiencing a dilemma. What do we say when we first meet the family? Do we simply state our name? Do we offer any condolences? Do we say we're sorry? The main operating principal here is "less is more".[9] When Dr. Johnson confronted the loss of someone he knew he found that the most helpful thing to say was, "I am sorry for your loss. May I bring you some tea?"[10] Even though the phrase "I'm sorry for your loss" has been used extensively on television it need not come across as harshly. There are other, more pastoral ways of saying this. Over the years I've found it important to offer something like, "I'm sorry we have to meet this way." You'll want to develop your own statement. Regardless of your choice make sure it's genuine and warm. Nothing sets a conversation off on the wrong track like real or perceived aloofness.

When we actually sit down with the family of the deceased perhaps the first order of business is to simply find out the deceased person's full name. Sometimes mistakes are made during the arrangement meeting between the family and the funeral director. These mistakes can be passed on when this same funeral director shares information with us. I've written down names in the wrong order and things like that. I've also heard names pronounced incorrectly. It happens so it's best to clarify even the most basic information right from the beginning. When we have confirmed the legal name we should then find out which name the person went by. They could have been known by a completely different name than what appears on legal documentation. Nicknames given in childhood may have stuck or the deceased may have named a preference at some earlier point in their lives. This is usually true in smaller communities where a number of people share the same name. Ask the family if they would like us to use nicknames. Some nicknames are not appropriate for public services but some families may insist on our using them anyway.

It is then important to confirm information like service times and places. Where and when are the services going to be held? Is there going to be a burial and where will that be? Dismissing and skipping these questions could lead to disaster. I've sometimes written down one service time in my day–planner only to be corrected by the family when I've asked for confirmation. On one occasion I arrived at the funeral home in time for a ten o'clock service only to be told that the service was actually at eleven. Again, mistakes can be made and showing up at the wrong time and place could make a real mess of things.

For those occasions when the service is going to be held away from either the church or the funeral home chapel I've found it helpful to ask if the funeral home staff are going to be present at the service. Without funeral home staff we're usually the ones people turn to with questions and concerns and we're not really trained to deal with anything beyond the service itself. Something as simple as washroom locations can be an impossible question to properly answer when we're unfamiliar with the facility in which the funeral is being held.

Another question that can be asked early in the process concerns the actual cause of death. It's not that we want to be nosy but the response to this question will have some impact on what we say and do in the service. Kenneth Doka reminds us that "Grieving a suicide or homicide is different from grieving a natural death."[11] He adds, "Sudden, violent deaths, or losses in conflicted or ambivalent relationships are examples of types of situations or relationships that might complicate grieving."[12]

I officiated a service where the deceased was killed in a workplace accident. Knowing about this accident was helpful because it gave me a chance to mention an observance called the National Day of Mourning. Each and every April 28th workers around the world pause to remember those killed and injured in the workplace. This is an excellent opportunity for family, friends and colleagues to gather with other grieving people and share in another time of community and comfort and also make a commitment to help reduce the number of accidents in the workplace.

Asking about the cause of death may also affect how we approach the rest of our meeting. Relatively early in my ministry life I officiated at a funeral for a person who had died in a house fire. It was not until I had begun the service and I was lighting the candle at the front when I remembered the cause of death. While it may not be something the average person would think about it may be something that registers in some way with survivors. Suicides, accidents, and stillbirths are other situations where greater care can be taken in what we say and do. They may also affect how we order the service. They may also affect what material we either include or leave out. One small, simple mistake can derail a lot of work.

When asking about the cause of death we may have to make assurances about how this information is going to be used. There are some things that do not have to be said during the service. I was told of a minister struggling with an intense emotional response to one situation and wondering what she was going to say. Sometimes there is little for us to say. To be rather blunt, just because we think of something we want to say doesn't mean we really have to say it. There is a good reason why someone once coined the phrase about silence being golden.

Perhaps one instance where it is a good idea for the service leader to know the cause of death is in the case of a suicide. Edwin Shneidman writes, "In almost every case, suicide is caused by pain ..."[13] He goes on to add, "Pain warns us; pain both mobilizes us and saps our strength; pain, by its very nature, makes us want to stop it or escape from it."[14] When we are in a conversation with the family and friends of a suicide victim we can listen and try to understand their questions and emotions. We can also find an appropriate way to assure them that their loved one is no longer in pain. Survivors can be assured that the deceased is at peace. One helpful way to do this is by using Ecclesiastes 3:1-8 as a reading at the funeral. The power of this particular section of scripture will be discussed in a later chapter but it can also be mentioned here. Joan Chittister is one writer who has studied Ecclesiastes extensively and suggests, "If there is no other meaning at all to the book, it is surely this: life is not even, life is not smooth."[15] Life has its ups and downs. There are good things that happen and there are some tragic things that happen. Ben Witherington III suggests that Ecclesiastes "is encouraging an honest facing of the dark side of life."[16] The ancient teacher outlines the different things we experience in a frank, poetic way. For me, the important part of this reading is where the ancient teacher writes, "There's a time for war and a time for peace."

When we move beyond the early questions and basic information gathering we have to really focus on what's being said about the deceased. Listening quickly becomes our main task as we have to get the details right. If we are confused about even the most trivial thing we immediately have to ask for clarification. Canadian businesswoman and media personality

Arlene Dickinson has a sign on her desk that has one word on it: "Listen".[17] Perhaps each one of us needs this sign on our desk. Some of us need to have it smeared across our office walls or even captured at the top of the page of where our notes will be written. How many of us remember the phrase stating we have two ears and one mouth and that means we have to do twice as much listening as talking? Elaine Ramshaw writes, "… better listeners are potentially better presiders, for they know the needs of their people well."[18] She goes on to say, "… the more the minister listens the better he (sic) will be able to tailor the ritual language to the individual situation."[19] Paul Johnson writes, "He must listen well before he is ready to speak well. He must listen with his whole being — not just his ears, but his imagination, memory, empathy, understanding, faith, and love."[20]

At the very least listening is one of the ways we show survivors that we empathize with them. Empathy is that process by which we try to understand another person's experience. Paul Johnson defines empathy this way: "... one person enters into the feeling or spirit of another person to understand and respond at deeper levels of appreciation and communication."[21] It's important to point out here that "understanding" is not the same thing as "owning" or "expressing". If a person is sad we can show empathy without becoming sad as well. The people around us may be crying but that doesn't mean we have to cry with them. When defining and describing empathy, Irvin Yalom uses the phrase, "Looking out the patient's window".[22] We can look out a window and learn more about what is happening beyond the glass but that still does not mean we actually have to pass through that window in order to be helpful and effective. We also empathize when we try and figure out what people want and need. What are their commitments and priorities? What do they believe and find important? How does that affect their lives and contribute to their current state? Empathy also helps us track how people are responding to what we say and do. Facial expressions, for example, help us figure out whether or not something we have said or done is helping the situation or causing harm.

Some of us will take this to extremes and expend too much energy in the process. We will sometimes take on too much of another person's emotion and this is not always healthy. Barbara Killinger writes, "We can appreciate another person's distress or elation without overreacting, because we remain a distinct and separate Self who can only imagine another person's reality."[23] While I cannot know what exactly people are feeling when they experience a particular loss, empathy helps me bridge the gap between us and make the necessary connections. Richmond writes, "If we are to minister effectively to those in pain, we must be open to their feelings, not threatened by them, and we must do all that we can to help the feelings of anger and despair to be expressed."[24]

We do no one any favours when we allow ourselves to become too emotionally involved in the situation. We have to protect both our clients and ourselves by establishing and maintaining strong emotional boundaries. These boundaries help ensure that we have enough energy to both support the people we work with and officiate a service that helps meet people's needs. There is only so much gas in the tank. Even though our working relationship with family and friends of the deceased may be relatively brief it still takes a fair amount of strength in order to establish and maintain solid boundaries. There may be legal reasons for establishing and maintaining these boundaries. I live in the Province of Alberta and The Alberta Law Society has written, "A professional must be above taking advantage of the client's feelings and vulnerability and must suppress his (sic) own desires."[25] This is also good advice for clergy to heed.

Early in my career I was asked to officiate a funeral in which I was offered an unusual proposition. I was unmarried at the time and my parishioners were eager to begin the process of finding me a spouse. When we had completed the funeral and graveside services we adjourned to the community hall for a reception. One of my parishioners came up to me and offered to take me around and introduce me to the single women who had attended the service. While the parishioner was acting with the best of intentions I politely declined as something about the offer felt really awkward and uncomfortable. Over the years I've come to figure out why.

Funerals are simply not the time and place to initiate those types of relationships. If you're single or newly single it should become a truism that you should not be looking for a romantic partner at funerals, especially within the immediate family of the deceased.

Another way we establish clear boundaries is by effectively managing the information we share with clients. While it's important we make connections and set people at ease sometimes we can share too much information. A couple of months ago I received an e–mail message from someone experiencing the death of a member of the family. They told me the story of a recent experience with death, funerals and dealing with clergy. When asked to officiate at the funeral of the correspondent's family member, the Senior Minister promptly delegated the service to their student minister and asked him to officiate. When this student minister met with the family all he could talk about was a loss he had recently experienced and how it affected his life. This student minister's loss? His sister went off to university in another community. She hadn't even died! While it might be important to tell stories about our previous experiences with grief we need to be conscious of the fact that we are there to listen to others and try to find a way to meet their needs. There's a big difference between someone moving and someone dying. As Arlene Dickinson writes, we can build strong working relationships without sharing even one piece of personal information.[26] We cannot repeat this often enough. Our efforts are all about our clients and that's what we have to keep in mind throughout the entire planning process.

The second way we manage information is by protecting people's privacy. In each and every situation there are told things that should not leave the room. We cannot share this information with anyone else without permission and that is what confidentiality is all about. One of the reasons why people tell us these things is that they can feel relieved that they no longer carry secrets with them. Some clients will want to talk about addictions or some sort of financial impropriety. Some will want to talk about something traumatic that happened within the family in which the deceased was directly involved. It's not unusual for service leaders to hear stories about various kinds of abuse. Protecting confidentiality is important.

What's equally important is knowing when to break confidentiality. Sometimes we think that as professionals there is no way we should speak up when we know certain things. Many of us have seen too many movies in which a priest went to jail rather than share something they heard in the confessional or some other aspect of their work. There will be some situations in which we should break confidence. The main one is dealing with a threat to someone's safety or security. Conflicts between family members can reach such an intensity, for example, that one person threatens another and we find out about it. A threat like this has to be dealt with. Walter Glannon writes, "confidentiality ends where peril begins."[27]

As we make our way through this meeting we have to take a lot of notes as there is no way we're going to accurately remember everything that's said. This is the third way we manage information. This may seem like an obvious piece of advice but it's surprising how many people don't write things down when they probably should. Notes are important, especially in those situations where our schedule prevents us from going directly from our meeting to our studies and computers. We have to write things down because we'll probably forget much of what we hear. I remember a colleague who used to meet with families and not take a note during their conversation. He would wait until he returned to his vehicle before pulling out a pen and paper to record what had been discussed. While this approach may work for him it is not something I would recommend to others. I certainly couldn't do it. The human memory can only retain so much at any one time. Some psychologists have hinted that our memories can also change in even the briefest periods of time. It's for these reasons that we cannot trust the human memory. I've learned the hard way that it's best to have a planning form on hand that has been developed for this process. I've included an example of such a form at the end of this chapter. Using this form is important because we need to record as many stories and memories so that we can personalize the service as much as possible. We will also have to keep a decent list of family and other survivors so that we can keep track of everyone involved in the situation.

Given all of the questions we have to deal with and detailed information we need to collect we cannot rush the planning process. We have to be sure that we take as much time to cover as many bases as we can. Recipes can't work unless we follow each and every step and use all of the ingredients identified by the writer. Funerals are no different. Take the time to choose or suggest music that suits the person being remembered. Invest the necessary time and energy into finding the right things to say either in the eulogy or in one–on–one conversations. We have to develop a goal and follow it through.

Sometimes the deceased helps us by leaving notes concerning their wishes for a funeral. They may have read a poem they find meaningful and identified it as something they want read at their service. At the very least these notes reduce the amount of guesswork that goes into the planning process. Published resources exist where individuals can outline their wishes and include other helpful information for their survivors. One of the best I've seen so far is Kathleen Fraser's *When I'm Gone* and these may be others.[28] Mentioning one or more of these resources may be helpful for those who suddenly recognize the importance of preplanning and recording hopes and dreams for their own funerals. Barbara Okun, Ph.D. and Joseph Nowinski, Ph.D. write, "Another consequence of medical life extension is that more and more individuals are preparing for their funeral in advance."[29] One of the first people I visited while beginning a commitment as a student minister was a senior who wanted to speak with me about her funeral. When the time came for her funeral we were able to balance her requests with the needs of her family. Finding this balance was a powerful experience. While considering the wishes of the deceased is important, it is also helpful to consider the needs of those left behind.

In finding balance and addressing the needs of mourners another question that can be asked at this meeting is: "How can we keep this person's memory alive in the minds and hearts of loved ones?" Is there a song we can listen to or even sing? Is there a Bible reading or poem that can help stimulate the memory making process? Are there photos or other mementos that we can look at or video segments we can watch? Is there a certain prayer we can offer? Some families, regardless of whether or not they are religious, may ask for something like the Lord's Prayer. For many, the words alone bring comfort. They offer assurance for people experiencing a chaotic time.

One quick exercise I do with families, for example, is simply ask them to find a word to describe the deceased. Were they friendly and outgoing? Were they quiet and reserved? Were they helpful and generous? This one simple exercise helps me gather a lot of information. This information can be used throughout the service to help give depth and context to what is being said. If the deceased is quiet, for example, then mention can be made of his or her "quiet approach to people". There may be a story of how his or her quiet nature affected life around the house or workplace. These are all things we can use.

But not all questions concern the life and legacy of the deceased. People I meet with usually ask me how long a service is going to be. The best answer I can offer them is "it depends". The family may not find this answer very helpful but it is an accurate response. A lot depends on what is discussed at the preparation meeting. For me, the ideal length of a funeral is between 30 to 40 minutes. Given the emotional intensity of the experience it is extremely difficult to endure much longer than that. I've heard of services lasting two or three hours and that is simply too long. If people want a service to go longer than thirty or forty minutes they have to work hard to ensure that listeners don't "drift off" or "zone out" completely. Listening to a presentation like a funeral is hard work and one of the reasons for this is the emotional intensity of what we're going through. Carmine Gallo argues that one of the main reasons for this is our need to remember what's said. We're trying to add items to our personal memory banks and these are things we'll want to review at a later opportunity.[30] When we offer too much information to a person we increase the possibility of overwhelming them and that isn't helpful.

The responses to many of the questions we ask may surprise us. The thoughts and ideas we hear may challenge us in ways never experienced by our predecessors. They may cause discomfort or force us out of our safety zones. As we mentioned in the previous chapter, people are moving away from the traditional services experienced by previous generations. They're moving away from the music, prayers and symbols that once went into the service. Even the most religious individuals and families are creating their own rituals and traditions. They're showing more of a willingness to customize the service and try new things. They're selecting different types of music and readings. They're finding poems that capture the intense emotions they are experiencing. They're incorporating things like the presentation of symbols such as eagle feathers to the survivors of the deceased.

We cannot be afraid to move beyond traditional limits and expectations ourselves. Froma Walsh and Monica McGoldrick tell the story of a woman who wanted to be a pallbearer at her grandmother's funeral service. Her grandmother lived to be 100 years old and held an important place in her granddaughter's life. When the granddaughter expressed a desire to be one of the pallbearers she was met by friends and family members offering reasons why she couldn't. One family member told her that there were only supposed to be six pallbearers and another told her that they had already been selected. The granddaughter challenged these traditional expectations and became one of twelve pallbearers at her grandmother's funeral service.[31]

When exploring different ways of celebrating the life of the deceased family members may feel pressured by organizations and professional associations to go in directions they do not feel comfortable in going. Police and fire departments, for example, may want to run a service in a particular way and they have the hard experience on which to build such a tradition. But these regimented services may not be what the family needs at a particular time. Whenever we find ourselves in a situation in which there is conflict between the needs of a family and the needs of a wider group we have to move to the side of the family. Their needs take priority. Paul Irion writes, "People need to be free to use as much or as little established ritual as they wish."[32]

Because individuals and families may want to "explore their options" service leaders may want to acquaint themselves with how different traditions "do" funerals. The Quakers, for example, begin their services with a time of silence. People then take turns recalling the deceased, sharing memories and talking about what the life meant to family and friends. What did we learn? How did this person change us?[33] I like how this silence helps set the table for the ritual that follows. I still incorporate this approach into some of the services I lead, especially when the gatherings are small.

Knowledge of different traditions helps give us resources from which we can draw upon when we experience surprises. There are challenges and problems over which we have little or no control. We have to respond to these in creative ways. One morning I was scheduled to officiate at a graveside ceremony and woke up to find the temperature a very chilly minus 30 degrees Celsius. That didn't even include the wind chill factor. I didn't know what else to do so I bundled up and went off to the funeral home expecting to officiate at one of the quickest graveside services a person could spit out. When I arrived at the funeral home the funeral director informed me that the family had requested a change to an indoor service. I was probably the strangest–dressed service leader anybody had seen but we all rose to the occasion and accomplished the task at hand. We were able to do things like add a candle lighting and some music at the last minute.

It's even appropriate to welcome moderate amounts of humour into our meeting with the clients and the service itself. This may be surprising to many. When we think of grieving we often experience such as sadness, shock, fear and regret. We aren't always prepared for the laughter and smiles that often accompany the loss of a loved one. What may surprise readers even more is that laughter and humour have always been an important part of the human response to death. African societies, in particular included laughter and humour in their funeral rituals.[34] At the very least it's another way we can release our emotions. Sam Barry writes, "We laugh to relieve stress; we laugh in response to the absurdity of people offering pat answers to life's dilemmas; we laugh to ward off our fear; and we laugh at happy memories."[35] Humour also bridges differences on those occasions when we don't agree with one another. In other words, to borrow some terminology from scholar Scott Weems, laughter is a "psychological coping mechanism" and "a process of conflict resolution".[36]

I learned this first hand a number of years ago. My grandmother died and I remember this one get together where people were in tears as they talked about her. As the conversation developed, however, something changed. This change came about in that one instance where someone said, "Remember when she almost set fire to the barn?" In that one moment tears became mixed with smiles and laughter. I learned at that very moment the power of those simple words "remember when". I also learned from this experience that humour doesn't always come in the form of jokes. It's important to learn how, to borrow a phrase from public speaking guru Carmine Gallo, "how to be funny without telling a joke."[37] This is a skill that will also apply to the presentation of the funeral itself but we'll address that in future chapters. For both our meeting and the service itself humour "lowers defenses, making your audience more receptive to your message."[38]

For the planning meeting the type of conversation that needs humour the most is perhaps the one with the most conflict feeding it. In an essay entitled *She Laughed Until She Died* Victoria Zackheim describes the place that humour has had in her experience of loss and grief. She writes, "Humour softened the anger, opening a door that allowed us to step through and repair some of the damage."[39] This "appreciation" of humour as a response to loss is nothing new. In 1910 Canon Scott Holland said, "wear no forced air of solemnity or sorrow ... laugh as we always laughed at the little jokes we enjoyed together."[40]

There are definitely times and places during a funeral itself when humour is appropriate. In fact, some cultures have encouraged it. The Dahomey people in Western Africa, for example, consider humour a critical part of their funeral. Dahomey funerals are celebrations where people drink, and dance, and sing throughout the night. Friends and family also tell raunchy stories about the departed. These stories are told to help people deal with the intensity of their grief and they help appease the spirit of the departed.[41] These stories also inspire people to move on and live in new ways. An ancient people known as the Getae, according to Herodotus, buried a person with "laughter and rejoicing."[42] Humour also brings people together and strengthens the bonds that hold communities together. Humour also helps us deal with tension and conflict.[43]

Not all humour is appropriate, however, so we have to be careful. I've been asked to read through eulogies and have found myself recommending changes. It's not something I enjoy doing but there are occasions when it's a necessary move. I've asked people to remove off–colour stories and jokes as not everyone shares the same sense of humour. I've also been surprised by eulogists going "off script" with stories and memories they think are funny. Not everybody feels like laughing. The best humour is mild and heart–warming. Perhaps Scott Weems explains this need for caution when using humour and laughter at times such as funerals best when he writes, "People have different thresholds for what they find offensive, and they vary widely in their responses when that threshold is crossed."[44]

While walking this line is difficult, it is a critical balance to have when collectively building memories of the departed. In his song *Changes In Latitudes* Jimmy Buffett sings, "If we couldn't laugh we would all go insane." Perhaps there's a chemical reason for this. Scott Weems explains that when we laugh a chemical called Dopamine is released in our brain and we feel good as a result. This is why Weems calls Dopamine our brain's "reward chemical".[45] This is definitely true when it comes to funerals. David Switzer once wrote that one of the most important responses to any crisis is the appropriate dissipation of emotional energy.[46] Laughter is an "appropriate dissipation of emotional energy." The key word is "appropriate".

"Dissipation" is good too. Because of the stress experienced when someone dies pressure that continues to build within a person can lead to many different physical symptoms and conditions. Throughout recent history scholars have made the connection between the intensity and stress with physical illness.[47] Grieving survivors have developed everything from cancer to auditory hallucinations[48] Emily Dickinson, for one, observed that hallways and buildings aren't the only things that can be "haunted". She once wrote that our brains have "corridors" that can be haunted as well.[49] Ghosts can haunt our thoughts and memories as well as our attics and spare rooms.

Our clients may not be willing to admit seeing or hearing things but they shouldn't be too concerned. Scholars such as Oliver Sacks reassure us that hallucinations can happen when we experience grief and bereavement, especially when we lose someone we have been close to for a long time. When we lose a spouse, for example, we experience a "hole" in our lives and the brain often tries to fill the gap with visual and auditory stimulation.[50] Robert Graves experienced loss on an incredible scale while serving in the First World War. Most of the people he served with were either killed or wounded in the fighting. In his memoir *Goodbye to All That* he recalls that he could see the faces of those he lost whenever he walked through a crowd in those early years following the armistice.[51]

When I was a student minister I visited someone who had just lost their spouse. He told me that one night while he was sitting in his chair watching television his wife appeared in the middle of the room. She continued standing there for a few seconds and then faded from sight. We shouldn't be too worried about this. Hallucinations occur more frequently then we may think. One study suggests that up to half of those who lose spouses experience hallucinations.[52] Sacks suggests that hallucinations in general are "an essential part of the human condition."[53] He tells us that hallucinations are a familiar part of spiritual practices in numerous cultures.[54] They're also another way of remembering and processing.

One of the things we may be processing is guilt. What is guilt? It's one of those churchy words we hear all the time but what does it really mean and how does it work in our lives? A notorious 19th Century writer by the name of Cora Pearl once wrote, "Between what one ought to do and what one does there is always a difference."[55] This difference leads to an emotional response we can call "guilt". Guilt can develop in situations such as neglect and suicide. We may come to believe, for example, that it was something we said or did that pushed a person to act in a lethal way. Hooyman and Kramer write the following about guilt: "Guilt is most likely to be salient in instances of suicide or sudden death, when people had no chance to say goodbye or felt they could have done something different to prevent the loss, or when things have been left unsaid."[56] Finding the right thing to say when addressing a person's experience of guilt can be tricky.

Throughout the planning process one of the challenges we face when communicating with grieving individuals and groups is the risk of creating hostility. Without intending to create problems something we say or do can set off a shocking and intense response. Johnson writes, "Hostile reactions are often quite marked, to the surprise and distress of bereaved persons, and may be directed against the physician or nurse for neglect of the patient, or take the form or suspicion of foul play and bitterness against the insurance company, undertaker, or attorney for not doing more on behalf of the survivor. Hostility may be self–directed, leading to despair or suicide."[57] One way of preventing a hostile reaction from a family is to do simple things like speak clearly and ask for clarification whenever necessary. People would rather say something more than once if it prevents a more public mistake when the service is in progress.

While we do not need to include mention of hostility and conflict in the actual service it is important to know about it. Funerals are intense so it's natural for conflict to be a natural result of this intensity. In some ancient cultures this conflict was channeled into taunts and challenges. Others saw funerals as a time to "settle grievances".[58] When it comes to conflict in our own day we can remember the Boy Scout motto: "Be prepared". Some conflict can be dealt with in a relatively brief and decent way. There is also conflict that has to be left until after the funeral. Regardless of how the conflict develops and is resolved we can remember something Garret Keizer has written in a recent article. He writes, "except for a few psychopaths, most people on most days are doing the best that they can."[59] These are words I carry with me whenever I deal with conflict in my work. Regardless of how things develop and who's involved our task is to officiate a funeral and not mediate deep and festering divisions within a family or social circle. I've told more than one family that they have to focus on the funeral service and to consult legal counsel when the service is complete. Once we've reviewed the risk of potential conflict we can discuss other parts of the service.

We shouldn't worry if there are people who do not respond well to our planned and impromptu services. Not everybody will like everything we do in the service. People's comfort levels with different elements of the funeral will vary. Not everybody will be comfortable with the deceased present in the room during the funeral, for example. Bill Sucharsky says, "It's hard to celebrate someone's life at the service when his dead body is sitting there in the room."[60] Others will need to be present with the body, however. We'll address the feedback we receive following the service in a later chapter on evaluation. But for now, any planning process has to find a balance between facing reality and acknowledging the grief that is filling our lives as a result of this incredible loss.

In the course of our meeting we may want to find out from either the funeral director or family members themselves whether or not the service is going to be private or public. Circumstances may dictate which of these two options the family chooses. If they choose a private service it is important to respect their wishes and not reveal the time and location of the service to anyone, including friends and other family members. I remember hearing about one clergyperson who was asked to officiate at a private service for a member of her congregation who had died. Even though it was clearly stated that this was to be a private service she still invited a number of parishioners who had known the deceased. The family of the deceased were enraged at this breach of etiquette and felt that her invitation did more harm than good. If family and friends request a private service then we have to ensure that the service remains private.

One reason for holding a private service is to avoid media attention. Some deaths can have a fairly high profile and find their way into the media spotlight. Even in some public settings family will have concerns over the presence of the media. Some news agencies and other media outlets may want to cover the funeral itself. It may be helpful to discuss these possibilities with the family and determine their level of comfort. It would also be helpful to consult the funeral home and find out how their staff will be responding to the media attention. Some funeral homes may have a policy concerning these sorts of things. The family can set limits on how the media interacts with people gathered for the service. Reporters can be welcome into the service space or they can be asked to remain in the parking lot for the duration of the service. The same requests and permissions can be granted of camera operators. We can give the family permission to respond to media requests in any way they see fit.

Helping families know what they can and cannot do may require some tact and that may not come easily. It's an important skill to develop, however. It may save both ourselves and the family a lot of potential embarrassment. One family asked me to wear a red clown nose during the funeral of someone having a unique sense of humour. While I politely declined I did try to offer alternatives in order to honour the spirit of this request. Discussing alternatives helped me make some choices at a recent funeral for a young child. The child loved wearing wild and vivid colours and the parents asked if I would wear something colorful. I really only have two shirts that match that description so brought them both to the service. I asked which one they would like me to wear and they chose the wild tie– dyed one. The funeral directors working the service were a little shocked when they saw what I was wearing but everybody else thought it was more than appropriate.

Discussing possibilities and offering alternatives helps us be clear and direct with families. Honesty is an obvious and important value that accompanies this skill. It's critical that the family see us as being genuine and legitimately concerned about what's going on in their lives. And they know when we're not being honest with them. Therapists as diverse as

Rollo May and Sigmund Freud discuss the human ability to see through dishonesty and insincerity. They know when we're lying or "BS–ing" them. This suggests that we have some sort of instinct for BS–detecting.[61] Carmine Gallo states this more bluntly when he writes, "People can spot a phony. If you try to be something or someone you're not, you'll fail to gain the trust of your audience."[62]

This commitment to honesty has to be reflected in our service materials. A frequent complaint about clergy it's that we pretend to know the person when we really don't and that can all but destroy our credibility with those attending the funeral. Bluffing, in general, is never a helpful practice for any public speaker. Peter Urs Bender writes, "Do not ever bluff or pretend that you have things in common with them when you really do not. It will show."[63] When we gather a person's history it is important to reassure survivors that we are not going to pretend we knew the person well or even knew them at all. Carl Rogers once addressed a group of university students and told them, "In my relationships with persons I have found that it does not help, in the long run, to act as though I were something I am not."[64] It is important to be genuine, clear and honest.

This clarity may not be appreciated all the time, however. It may be counter–productive to tell people that we haven't met the deceased or even met with their friends and family. While it may be the honest thing to say it does build a wall between the service leader and the gathered mourners. It's best to avoid saying these kinds of things and focus on straightforward statements like, "Jane Doe was an extremely generous person who would give you the shirt off her back. One day, while she was …". We don't have to disclose how we first heard this story or how we know about her generosity. The important thing is that mourners hear about it and learn more about the life and character of the deceased. It is possible to be honest and silent at the same time.

At some point in the conversation it may become apparent that an individual or group of survivors has issues above and beyond what we are dealing with in the planning meeting. While I have already mentioned legal referrals I'll say here that we may need to make suggestions regarding mental health referrals as well. Paul Johnson offers this definition of counseling: "Counseling is a responsive relationship arising from expressed need to work through difficulties by means of emotional understanding and growing responsibility."[65] If we have a hunch that someone would benefit from this kind of interaction then we can find a diplomatic way of raising the issue with him or her in private and invite him or her to make his or her own decision. If they cannot find a counselor themselves we can perhaps suggest some names. Funeral directors will often have a list as well. The funeral home may even have someone on staff who can speak to a group or individual and ensure that they find the assistance they need.

One thing we must avoid in these meetings is the temptation to fix many of the problems we hear about. This may be extremely difficult for those of us with a background in the so–called healing and helping professions. We'll hear about problems with the deceased's Will and bad behaviour displayed by people connected to the situation. We may hear complaints about almost everything under the sun. It's important that we listen to these concerns but we also have to be clear about our own abilities and competencies. There are some problems that are simply beyond our scope. One widow I was working with began asking me about terms of a car loan she and her spouse had taken out. I suggested she speak with her bank's loans officer and she appreciated the suggestion.

It's important that we focus on the funeral, itself, and invite friends and family to confront problems and challenges in other ways. This means we have to focus on even the smallest details of the service and not allow distractions to interfere with our work. Even something as simple as announcements is important. This may sound like a trivial detail but I always ask whether or not there is going to be a reception as that is one of the announcements I make at the conclusion of the service. If the reception is away from the site of the funeral service we may have to give directions at the close of the service. We could also suggest to the family that they provide maps for people to use when making their way to the reception location. Funeral homes often provide the officiant with a list of announcements and other important information to be relayed the congregation before the service comes to a final close.

When it comes to the amount of information gathered in the preparation process it is always better to have too much material. This gives us the ability to focus on those stories and points that deal best with the service we will be offering. If we hear three stories dealing with a person's approach to life then we can choose the one that we deem most appropriate and that we hope will garner the best response. While it would be nice to share all three stories but this would add length to the service and increase the risk of boring listeners.

Near the end of our meeting we can open the floor to any questions people may have. This is an opportunity for people to ask for clarification and permission. They may want to know things like whether or not children can attend the funeral. They may want to know if they can tell a funny story or sing a nonreligious song. Each and every question is important and deserves our complete attention and utmost respect.

We can also be meeting with families where the shock has begun to wear off and confusing thoughts and feelings are emerging. Joan Didion uses the term "Magical Thinking" to describe much of what we experience following someone's death. When describing her response to death she said, "I was thinking as small children think."[66] These thoughts and emotions present their own problems. They may lead to strange requests and even stranger conversations. Patience is definitely a virtue when letting meetings run their course.

It's because of things like shock that we have to draw the meeting to a close in a particular way. One of the things we can do as a way of drawing the meeting to a close is review the order of service with them. While there may be a standard order (I've included mine as an example at the end of this chapter) we frequently use, the family may ask for changes, additions and deletions as needed. This part of the meeting gives us a chance to bring both sides together and build a service that works. This review may raise new questions and issues. It may put minds and hearts at ease. People often feel better when they know that they've been heard.

Reviewing the order of service with them offers assurance that we've heard what they've had to say and have responded accordingly. Once we have reviewed the order of service we can gently remind the family of the importance of balance and moderation. Plutarch once talked about the importance of getting enough sleep, exercise, and eating the proper foods. People can get so caught up in details and arrangements that they don't always eat or get enough sleep. He claimed that this was the key to achieving good health and it is wisdom that has stood the test of time for over 2000 years.[67]

When the meeting is complete we can move to our studies and begin the work of actually assembling the service. This part of the preparation process will take some time as well. Bender writes, "It takes time and practice to organize your thoughts before you speak."[68] It also takes time to write and edit our materials. When our service material is complete it's critical to proof read what we have written once again. This can happen while we're rehearsing as some words and phrases sound better when they are read aloud. All of our notes have to be reviewed for mistakes. One pastor told me of the time when he had written a bulletin which included the titles of hymns the congregation would be singing. One of the hymns was supposed to be "It is Well With My Soul". When the service began the pastor suddenly realized that the bulletin contained the words "It is Hell With My Soul". This one little mistake affected the rest of the service and the relationship between the pastor and the family. We have to give our service material that one final review prior to actually leading the service.

As we prepare the service it's important that we rehearse we have to make sure both the delivery and content of the service are appropriate to what we need. We need the opportunity to review the content of the service and change words and ideas wherever possible. We also need the opportunity to practice whatever gestures we feel are important to the delivery of the service. Rehearsing every part of the funeral beforehand is critical to ensuring that the funeral will be effective.[69] While it's normal to mess up our lines when we're public speaking, rehearsing our material minimizes mistakes and helps make our presentation smooth. As Arlene Dickinson states, when it comes to public presentations there are no "do–overs".[70] The funeral service is high–intensity, so mistakes can sometimes have a serious effect on listeners.

To help me rehearse my services, a former parishioner gave me a wonderful gift several years ago. It was a small, hand–crafted podium that I could fit in my basement office space. I use this podium all the time to rehearse almost every funeral I'm asked to lead. Any athlete or musician will tell you how important constant practice is for any activity. Stretching and other warm–up exercises are standard in almost every sporting activity. The same is true with any public speaking commitments, including and especially funerals.

While it is considered ideal to speak without a text this is not always possible or recommended when it comes to leading a funeral. Given time and energy constraints, for example, it is not always possible to commit service material to memory. I was once asked at the last minute to include the Lord's Prayer in a service I was leading. It's one of those prayers I say all the time so I simply wrote "Lord's Prayer" in my service notes. When it came time to recite the prayer during the service my mind went blank and I struggled to finish the prayer. I now type out the prayer whenever possible. Copies of it are also taped on the inside covers of my day–planner and Bible.

Perhaps the best alternative is to review the text of the funeral at least twice so that we are familiar enough with our material we can make the necessary adjustments whenever necessary. When rehearsing the funeral it may be helpful to make notes on the pages themselves. These notes can help us remember gestures we would like to make and identify words that need some emphasis. Gestures can communicate things that words cannot. Our body language can affect how people hear the words we speak and can often negate whatever it is we have to say. One professional public speaker has written, "Good eye contact helps you to carry your message individually to each person in your audience."[71]

If we are relying on a text then it is critical we print this text in large enough font that we can see it from a distance and in almost any lighting conditions. Many venues are not properly equipped for services such as funerals so we may be using equipment that is far from ideal. The lighting may be poor or the podium may be too small for our use. Printing our notes in a large font is critical in each and every situation.

If we are using rented or borrowed equipment it is important to make sure the equipment is going to be where the funeral is going to be held. It is also important to check the equipment and make sure it is functioning normally. If it doesn't work then we have to find alternatives. There is nothing more awkward then trying to get a computer projector to work in the middle of an emotionally charged service. The same is true for Skype connections. Problems are too disruptive to the flow of the service.

It's also helpful to arrive at an unfamiliar location earlier than usual. This gives us a chance to check out the service space and ensure that any equipment we're using is properly located and set up. This also gives us a chance to find the washrooms and other important locations. Arriving earlier also gives us a chance to meet with the funeral directors and deal with any problems and questions they may have. For the purposes of a funeral directors and clergy have to work as a team. A failure to do so can lead to trouble. According to Rollo May the height of arrogance is the notion that we can succeed by ourselves[72] and when it comes to funerals that is certainly the case. We have to work together in order to be effective.

Sometimes we may be tempted to skip the rehearsal part. Let's face it, we're busy people. However, funerals are too important for us to cut corners. Even in those times when we're familiar with our text and materials we need to review them and practice. I used to play baseball when I was growing up and every spring brought the same reality: training camp. Our season would begin with several practices where we would go through the same drills over and over again. The constant work would be painful and boring but we knew it was important to work our way through even the simplest plays. The constant practice helped us develop our skills and prepare for the season ahead. We have to practice and rehearse our materials, even when we think we know it off by heart. Gail Vaz–Oxlade writes, "... you must be willing to commit the time and effort necessary to practice and become good at what you want to do."[73]

When we're practicing and reviewing our material we have to be careful and pay attention to every piece of material because a part of effective preparation is sheer vigilance. Be aware of everything that is said and done. Sometimes even the smallest details are critical to the effective funeral. Anthony De Mello once told the story of a student who once traveled through a rainstorm to meet his master. The master asked him, "On which side of your sandals did you place your umbrella?" The student was humbled to say that he did not know.[74] As a result of this lack of awareness the student had to go back and begin his training all over again.

We also have to be vigilant about what we are experiencing throughout the meeting and overall preparation process. These meetings may be difficult depending on our personality types. Introverts may find these meetings extremely taxing and should manage their time and energy accordingly. Even though the circumstances may be quite difficult the extrovert may gain some energy and that will help build some momentum towards the service itself.

Vigilance also extends to our grasp of what people want us to say and do at the funeral. There will be times during the meeting when questions will be asked about elements of the service or the order itself. We cannot be afraid to share appropriate amounts of information that will help answer these questions or send people in directions where they can find things out for themselves. These are important teaching moments for surviving friends and family.

Vigilance and listening also help us identify and encourage people who may be willing to participate in the service. It can be something as simple as lighting a candle or reading a poem.[75] A family member may want to share a memory or a story. Some may even want to sing something they have written or offer a more detailed eulogy or tribute. While next of kin may want to simply remain in their seats some may want to be more active and both choices can be honoured. Our vigilance will help us figure out who is who. This is consistent with our roll as leaders and facilitators. We can provide space and opportunity for people to share their message or use their talents.

One goal to keep in mind as we prepare and write the service is to offer hope to the loved ones left behind. According to Dr. Steven Girali, there are two key words to keep in mind when helping people with their grief and they are hope and comfort.[76] These are the important words we should be using. Help them understand the grief they are experiencing and give them some idea of what the journey they have begun will be like. Help people see the importance of connections and relationships. Help them see the need to build new bonds, intensify the connections that remain[77] and rebuild their lives in a helpful, life–giving way. Above all, offering hope helps us address the fear that can develop when we lose someone close. Beverly Raphael refers to the bonds between individuals as being "the essence of human existence"[78] so these efforts to resolve our fears, rebuild and re–establish connections are critical. One of the reasons why we make these particular efforts is because we never know how our individual grief journeys will develop and turn out.

This uncertainty about how our preparation is going to be translated into our service materials has to be factored into our thinking. A military theorist once said that the greatest plans never survive the first contact with an opponent. After this first contact leaders must adapt to what is happening in the field.[79] There will always be last minute changes to a service. We have to respond with flexibility and understanding. Things can happen quickly when it comes to planning for and preparing a funeral.

There are many different ways in which we can be flexible. I was told of one service where the family didn't want any music during the service. The pastor reviewed some alternatives and members of the family read poems instead. As we make our way through the planning process and actual funeral we have to be ready for anything. Sometimes even the smallest changes can throw us off track and that isn't helpful for the family. It's also important to tell people that when it comes to funerals there really aren't any rules.[80] This helps the family adapt to problems and challenges in creative and helpful ways. It also helps us deal with the more unpredictable things that can block our way.

One of the things that contribute to the service's "unpredictability" is the mental state of the people we are working with. While we've already discussed a person's potential need for counseling it's also important to remember that not everyone needs professional help. People will still be experiencing shock at what has happened and this is a natural response trauma and loss. Bozarth–Campbell writes, "Shock, in physical injury, is the body's way of protecting us against the reality of hurt, lest the pain of the hurt be too great to bear. Just as the body can numb itself, so can the human heart."[81] In terms of the stress people find themselves experiencing Malcolm Gladwell writes, "Stress wipes out short–term memory."[82] This potential memory loss is why I recommend that families find or purchase a notebook and use it to keep written notes, questions, and other important information. When the shock wears off they have a record that may help them sort through what has been happening to that point.

As I have said before, it is impossible to cover all of the bases when dealing with families, friends, and colleagues of the deceased in such a relatively brief period of time. Some things will take time to develop and show themselves. One quick caution: because the loss is so raw it is almost impossible for us to tell whether or not a person's grief is healthy. George Bonanno claims that it takes a minimum of six months before something like a "prolonged grief reaction" can be diagnosed.[83] For the most part, this is beyond our ability to respond. Illnesses such as depression take time to manifest themselves. They require medical assessment and attention and this doesn't happen quickly. While the death of a loved one can trigger depression it is not something that instantly happens.[84] Klein and Wender write, "In normal grief or bereavement, a person manifests symptoms very similar to those of biological depression, but there are some differences." They go on to add, "In some instances prolonged grief may merge into biological depression."[85]

Someone once said, "It's OK to remember, but not to dwell."[86] Survivors wonder how they can deal with their grief. While there may be little time to properly deal with this important question there are a few simple possibilities we can offer. We can talk about the importance of caring for ourselves. We can get out and meet people. We can exercise by doing simple things like walking. We can focus our time and energy on family, friends, and even pets.[87] People don't have to do all of these things at once. They can take their time. This is a journey that will have to take time. How many of us have heard the phrase "The longest journey begins with one step"? That piece of ancient wisdom applies here as well.

Our suggestions concerning self–care have to be simple and practical. This includes any thoughts we may offer on how a person's grief may proceed. Try to avoid getting into detailed theory about steps and stages people are believed to experience when grieving. The work of Elizabeth Kubler–Ross has been valued in recent decades but many are beginning to rethink these stages and find new ways of understanding how we respond to loss. This response is now being described in many ways. Doreen McFarlane suggests that individuals and families experience three kinds of grief when they experience a death. They grieve for the individual they have lost and they also grieve for those having gone before. We are also reminded of our own mortality so we grieve for our own impending deaths.[88] McFarlane also writes, "So to some degree, there is more than one death you are talking about ..."[89]

Grief may be difficult and intensified in situations where there's been a tragic death. In traumatic cases it is helpful to reinforce the importance of things like relationships. Judith Herman writes, "Recovery can take place only within the context of relationships; it cannot occur in isolation."[90] She adds, "Traumatic losses rupture the ordinary sequence of generations and defy the ordinary social conventions of bereavement." And "Since many of the losses are invisible or unrecognized, the customary rituals of mourning provide little consolation."[91] When dealing with the survivors of a tragic loss it may be helpful to use the marathon metaphor when helping them understand the long–term grief journey they'll be facing.[92] Their grief will not be quickly resolved. Navigating the twists and turns of the road ahead will take a lot of time. Those of us who grieve have to pace ourselves.

Bonanno writes, "When we are sad, we are more likely to turn our attention inward, to reflect, take stock, and recalibrate to the reality of the loss." He goes on to write, "All emotions, including sadness, are designed to be short–term solutions."[93] Sadness eventually gives way to other emotions in an effort to establish balance in our lives. These transitions happen in their own time. When it comes to grieving and the timeline many people try and apply to the process, Comte–Sponville writes, "Mourning is not a race."[94]

Regardless of whether it's in conversations with clients or writing out our service materials we have to pay attention to things like language and terminology. There is a difference between producer and product. As we try and teach our children from an early age, once we say something it's impossible to get it back. How many of us remember the toothpaste tube illustration? This is where we push some toothpaste out of the tube and invite kids to shove it back in. When we write or say something we literally cast it out into space and people beyond ourselves try to figure out what it means. If they respond to our words in a negative way our thoughts and intentions become irrelevant. Even the most mundane words can be problematic if used in a situation in which listeners are in a highly stressed state. This is why scholar and therapist Paula Caplan cautions against the use of words such as "normal" when describing people's situations.[95] We can tell people that their response to a situation is understandable. We can use words like "common" and "frequently". When people know they are not alone in an experience they are free to pursue their journeys with a reduced chance of complication.

It's often difficult to know what to say both in planning meetings and at a service. Structures need building materials and the same is true of funerals. Pastors and celebrants officiating for the first time may have a hard time finding resources that are helpful and appropriate. Some pastors will rely on denominational resources while others borrow from trusted colleagues. Regardless of the source, however, celebrants and clergy have to be careful and adapt these resources to their particular circumstances. Not all denominational resources are created equal. Within my former denomination there are dozens of publications and websites designed to help us prepare a funeral. Some are safe and traditional while others help us experiment and innovate. We cannot be afraid to try using material from denominations beyond our own.

Also, when I refer to resources I'm not simply talking about "information". I'm also talking about things like time and energy. How can we be compassionate when we're juggling funerals and other critical commitments? We have to find a way to manage our time, emotional, and energy resources.

When we know both the people and our material we can relax and know that there is an extremely strong possibility that the service will be helpful and touch a lot of people. The funeral will still be a lot of hard work but we can know that everything is in good hands. As I have already said, it's not about us. The service is for the deceased and surviving family and friends and as long as we have them in our minds and hearts everything will be fine.

When the planning meeting is complete and our materials are ready there are some follow up things we may need to take care of. We may need to contact the funeral home with some follow–up issues, questions, concerns, and information for example. We may have needs and requests that are particular to the group or family we were speaking with. The funeral home may be wondering which songs will be played during the service or who will be doing the eulogy or other tributes. Service folders take time to finalize and print and office staff at the funeral home sometimes gets panicky. We may need to phone the funeral director with concerns. Sometimes we hear things that may threaten to interfere with the smooth flow of the service. Conflict between groups and individuals may flare up and cause trouble at the service. While these events are rare it is important to raise the possibility with funeral home staff and management. If I think there is a chance for trouble at a service, for example, I ask for at least one or two experienced funeral directors to be present at the service. These directors will be able to help the service leader plan for dealing with any disruptions. Sometimes all it takes is some advice or a story or two. Sometimes active responses to potential threats have to be planned ahead of time. Prior to one service I led I spoke with the directors about how we were going to deal with at least one person we knew may cause problems. We spoke about verbal cues and warnings. We talked about how clergy have previously dealt with disruptions. At one point we discussed the possibility of contacting the police if the situation warranted. Luckily, most threats do not materialize but it is helpful to transmit concerns and knowledge of potential problems to funeral home staff and management. Sometimes preparations, alone, are enough to ensure a smoothly run service. As the old saying goes, "Plan for the worst and hope for the best!"

Preparing a funeral continues well beyond the meeting with the family and our work in the study. Preparation will continue right up until the funeral actually begins and the kind of technology we discussed above is one of the reasons why. People will often prepare special music and slideshow tributes for the service and that means they'll be bringing things like CDs and memory sticks with them to wherever the funeral is going to be held. We have to help ensure that these memory aides work with the equipment at the funeral location. I've seen too many people arrive at the church or funeral home with a CD, for example, that will not work with the available player. This is heartbreaking. The best way to keep this from happening is to encourage people to bring their CDs and memory sticks to the funeral location one or two days prior. If they don't work then family and friends can find another way to bring their tribute to the funeral location.

Someone who can help us with this pre–funeral preparation is a funeral host. In my last pastoral assignment I noticed that the congregation had wedding hosts to help people getting married but there wasn't anyone assigned to help with funerals. Asking people to "host" a funeral seemed to be a sound way of involving lay people in the life of their congregation and it also promised to help reduced the stress on the service leader. I was lucky in that one parishioner did agree to help out and for me it made all the difference in the world. In my previous congregations the minister was responsible for ensuring that everything was ready and that the necessary people were in their assigned jobs. This was a lot to deal with in such a brief period of time. There are simply too many bases to cover in that situation. Wherever and whenever possible funeral hosts free us up to assist both family and funeral directors in any way we can. Funeral hosts also allow us to complete our personal preparations for the service we're about to lead.

One other way we help prepare for the funeral is to help ensure that the funeral location is set up so that we can hold the service in what we can call "sacred space." Where will the funeral be held? What will it look like? What equipment or other items will we need to help make it "sacred space"? Will we need a table for candles and photos? Will we need separate podiums and microphones for the different speakers? Will there be enough room for a casket or urn? We are one of the key people helping to ensure that the sacred space looks decent and that everything works. This can be as simple or complicated as the situation requires. Back in 1993 Time Warner's CEO Steve Ross passed away and his spouse, Courtney chose to have his funeral at an art gallery on Long Island. She completely renovated the place. The walls of the gallery were painted, carpet was installed, and a stage was built. And even though this was an art gallery Courtney brought in a specially–selected painting for the wall behind the celebrant.[96] While this is an extreme example few of our clients could manage, it does remind us of how important it is to ensure that the funeral location is properly equipped and decorated.

Regardless of the amount of life experience we may have, these are a few things we can keep in mind when helping people deal with death and prepare for the funeral ritual. Through the years a number of clergy have told me that their work is informed by words included in the physician's Hippocratic oath. These words are "do no harm" and they should be foundational to everything we say and do. William Baird, Sr. and John Baird suggest that the funeral service is not the time to convert people.

They write, "The ethics of attempting to do so would be very questionable."[97] They go on to write, "People in sorrow and under the emotional stress of grief are not able to make the kind of decision that conversion involves." In other words, if you are religious don't even bother trying to use the funeral event as an opportunity to encourage others to buy into your beliefs. It's unethical and it only causes harm. The Bairds write, "He (sic) has no right to judge the departed, and he has no right to demand a decision from those left behind."[98]

Actually experiencing someone's death is rare. The way our society is structured and has been operating, death is something that happens in hospitals and hospices. No matter how hard we try to change this, for the most part, death is something that happens behind walls and doors. Northcott and Wilson suggest that a person's "Contact with death may be limited to attending a funeral or memorial service."[99] When it does happen, however, and we're asked to lead a funeral it's important to approach the situation with all of the skill, empathy, compassion, and professionalism we can muster. This begins with the planning of the funeral and once again, there is no room for adventure.

Sample Order of Service

The following is a sample of an order of service I frequently use. It covers most, if not all of the bases I've mentioned in *Dead Reckoning*.

Welcome and Introduction
Candle Lighting
Opening Prayer
Special Music
Readings (scripture, poetry, etc.)
Tributes and Eulogies
Slideshow Tribute
Meditation
Special Music
Lord's Prayer
Committal
Closing Blessing
Announcements

Funeral Service Planning Form

Date of Meeting:

Deceased's Name:

Date of Birth / Date of Death:

Age / Cause Of Death:

Service Time and Place:

Staff Contact:

Family Contact (#1):

Phone Numbers:

Family Contact (#2):

Phone Numbers:

Candle Lighting:

Music:

      1)

      2)

      3)

Other Music:

Eulogy / Tribute:

How Religious?

Announcements:

Biographical Notes: (birthplace, work history, hobbies, interests, etc.)

One word to describe the person:

Phase Two: Warm-Up

In a previous chapter we discussed the different aspects of Jon Stewart's bold statement that memorial services were not "shows" as we understand them today. There are a couple of ways in which we can approach both sides of this argument and we have covered some of those bases already. In this chapter I will address one more reason why a funeral is like a show. The type of show I'm referring to here is the talk show. We see them all the time and we could probably list many of the more prominent hosts and hostesses off the top of our heads. They all have their unique approach to what they do but each respective show tends to follow a tried and true formula. My favourite part of the talk show is when the host or hostess stand before the camera and audience cracking jokes and making observations based on the events of the day. They often enhance their comments by adding lists, graphics, music and videos to their performance. This segment of a talk show is often called the "warm-up" and that's why I've borrowed that term as a label for this next phase of the funeral.

When it comes to funerals the warm-up phase allows the respective leaders to establish a rapport with the audience. We bring people into a place or zone where they can be more open to what they hear and experience. We build a level of trust with listeners. We have a chance to explain what's going to happen. We can even introduce some of the people participating in the service. Music people, for example, are often under-appreciated and welcome a simple thank you either at the beginning or end of the service. Public-speaking experts such as Peter Bender agree with the need to build strong connections with the audience and suggests that we do this at the beginning of our service.[1] The warm-up phase may be relatively brief but it is critical to the overall effectiveness of the funeral. It's like the first notes of a song or the first words of a book. If we mess these up we risk losing our listeners for the rest of our time together.

It's been said that the most important part of any book is, indeed, the opening sentence. This is what grabs our attention and drops us into the narrative. It's a kind of hook or nudge that moves us into the early part of a story. We've heard people claim that a particular book is one they "can't put down". That book probably begins with a sentence that really snares the reader. This is a tremendous challenge for the writer. A number of things have to be established in a relatively brief space. According to scholars like David Lodge, the first few pages of a book introduce us to people and locations.[2] We learn about things like time and place. We get a sense of the atmosphere and mood. Most important of all is that we begin learning more about the characters populating the story. From all of this introductory information we ultimately decide whether or not we're going to continue reading the story or book.

This principal applies to any public action or ritual. Aristotle once described the plot of a story as being "the arrangement of the incidents" and the warm–up is the first "incident" in a series of components we'll be experiencing in the funeral.[3] Keith Watkins writes, "The beginning of any social drama — including services of worship — influences much of what happens thereafter. The opening words and sentences identify the participants and determine their roles; they also introduce purpose and intentions. Therefore, the beginning of a ritual needs to be planned carefully and conducted skillfully."[4] We live in an age when we are seldom granted more than one chance to make a strong first impression. The first moves of the funeral will help our listeners decide whether or not they're going to engage with what we have to say or offer. If we cannot manage an effective opening sequence then what follows loses a lot of power and effect.

One of the challenges we face when trying to make an effective first impression, however, is that we cannot use the same kind of gimmicks the talk show hosts use during their routines. We can't use lists or raunchy graphics. We can't always kid around with the music people or audience.

While we can describe ritual by using words like "drama" we should avoid using words like "entertainment". While the so–called "warm–up" segment is a critical part of any talk show, funerals are far from being "entertainment". They're completely different animals that way. Brian Spinks once said, "… although it is true that liturgy is performance, it is not primarily to entertain us."[5]

If the warm–up phase of the funeral isn't supposed to be entertaining then what are we supposed to accomplish? For me, the two main goals we should be striving for in the warm–up phase are information and connection. When we inform our listeners we name the deceased and lead them into the funeral ritual. We can do this by telling a story about the deceased's life or offering some historic pieces that help build a foundation or base for what is to come. When we connect with our listeners we establish a bond that helps us make our way through the rough waters that await as we proceed through the funeral.

Perhaps the most important opening steps occur prior to the actual service itself. Some families choose to view the body of the deceased prior to the service in what's traditionally been called a "visitation". This is a variation of what used to be called a "wake", which is an opportunity for surviving family and friends to spend time with the body of the deceased. Wakes would be held during the evening and they could go on for extended periods of time. Historically wakes were also an opportunity to make sure the person was actually dead. One young Egyptian man had a heart attack and didn't wake up until his friends were bathing his body for his funeral.[6] Today wakes and visitations can be a little different. Things may happen that we may find a little different and perhaps even questionable. One family was telling me that at one wake they attended people would approach the open casket, pull out their cell phones, spin around and take a "selfie" with the deceased. Regardless of what happens during this period, spending time with the body helps prepare us for the service ahead. It helps set the tone and atmosphere. It helps us focus our thoughts and energy. This allows us to be in a more receptive frame of mind when the service begins.

When the visitation is complete and we're certain that the person is really dead and prepared for burial the casket is closed and the service begins. The advantage of having a visitation, or a wake at some point prior to the service is that it helps establish the reality of death for the mourners and, as we have already discussed, this is one of the main reasons for having a funeral in the first place. Therese Rando writes, "If the necessary grief process is to commence, the reality of the death must be acknowledged."[7] In those cases where cremation has been requested the viewing of the body, or "visitation" can happen at the crematorium prior the actual cremation. The same principal applies here as well. Viewing the body of the deceased may be difficult but it helps people experience the reality of the death. There is a power to this kind of visual that cannot be expressed in words. This is one of those times when it's best that people "see it to believe it".

When we move beyond our encounters with the deceased and the open casket one of the more common ways to begin a service is called the "processional" and that's usually when we bring the coffin and family into the sanctuary space. We normally do so accompanied by an appropriate piece of music. We are physically, psychologically and emotionally moving from one world to another. We are moving from busy lives to a moment in which we shift gears and reflect on life in a deeper way. This is a powerful and physical way of showing that "separation" is taking place. This opening part or warm–up phase of the service is what Arnold Van Gennep would call the "rite of separation".[8] The first part of the funeral service acknowledges the separation that has occurred between the deceased and the surviving friends and family. We are being separated from the people and reality beyond the doors of the funeral home or chapel or any other space being used for the service.

This separation can be marked in different ways. For one thing we can stand when the family and casket enter the worship space. As the processional begins it is always helpful for someone to ask that people stand as they are able. A couple of years ago I attended a funeral in which the lead director simply offered hand gestures when indicating the places where we were to stand and sit down. Few of us knew what this hand gesture meant and there was a fair amount of confusion resulting from this. Perhaps words are best when it comes to instructing and moving people. I use verbal instructions and invitations whenever possible. I use the words "as they are able" because physically challenged people may be present and they are not always in a position where they can stand upon request. I lead one service where most of the young people in the congregation were in wheel chairs so avoided the invitation to stand altogether.

So how can we begin the actual funeral in a helpful way? How can we move people from their everyday lives, routines and busyness and warm things up, so to speak? One of the first things we can do is simply name the person who has died. This, alone is a powerful act. Peter Ellis writes, "Until something is named it remains unknown, without place or purpose."[9] This same notion applies to people. We can use the legal names and then tell people what they normally went by. It's also appropriate to use the name the deceased was known by throughout his or her life. As I have said in a previous chapter it's best to consult the family of the deceased and confirm that it's appropriate for us to use the more familiar name they used throughout their life. At the very least this helps ensure that we continue to grow a healthy rapport between ourselves and those attending the service.

The beginning of a funeral is important because it is the first opportunity to acknowledge death and confront it from the very beginning of the funeral service. Not everyone has a chance to view the body prior to the beginning of the service so our opening words can move everyone to the same page. Once we are all at the same point we can proceed. This is important for people who are nervous about attending a funeral. People are often nervous because they don't know what to expect. They may be confronting fears about their personal death for the first time. They may have either heard stories about funerals gone wrong or they're anticipating a service that will be extremely ideological or religious. The leader can do some simple things to put people at ease and we'll be exploring some of these ways in this chapter.

The warm–up phase helps us burn off some of the nervous energy we bring to the service. I use the word "some" carefully and intentionally. While extreme amounts of nervousness can be counterproductive[10] we cannot be afraid of some butterflies prior to beginning a funeral. Italian tenor Enrico Caruso once wrote, "The artist who boasts he is never nervous is not an artist — he is a liar and a fool."[11] Arlene Dickinson echoes this sentiment when she writes, "… a bit of stress increases efficiency and improves performance."[12] Healthy amounts of stress and nervous energy can fuel us and drive us towards a successful experience. This energy can help us carry out our plans and respond to mistakes and surprises along the way. It can also help us keep on track through some of the more routine parts of the service. If we're not careful we can tune out just as easily as any of our listeners.

When we've welcomed people, acknowledged the loss of the deceased and gone through our introductions we can take care of some housekeeping. We can include something as simple as a request to turn off cell phones, even though this may lack drama and it hardly tells us anything about the deceased or the service itself. A simple announcement can reduce the chance of disruptions and enhances that sense that we are experiencing a sacred moment.

One time I forgot to make this cell phone announcement and just prior to the graveside service someone's phone rang. We were moving the casket from the coach when we heard this loud rendition of "When the Saints Go Marching In" and the timing couldn't be more perfect. That was the only time I didn't bother getting angry about an interruption like that. To this day I remember that phone call whenever I ask people to turn off their devices.

Nobody wants to be listening to the funeral and be shocked out of his or her seat by a loud ring tone. It does help establish a mood where we remind listeners that we are in a special place for a brief, yet critically important period of time and it's a place where we cannot or should not be interrupted. Honouring and remembering the deceased is perhaps the most important thing we can do. Cell phone calls and "Tweets" can wait. This is why voice mail and power buttons were invented.

If we actually knew the deceased while they were alive then it may be helpful to include some personal information at the beginning of the service. We can tell a brief and appropriate story or anecdote of how we met and we can also thank people for traveling to the service. While we will be reviewing the person's history later in the service, it may be helpful to make some links and give listeners a sense of what they'll be hearing and learning as the service unfolds. Listeners often find comfort in knowing that the service leader has made an effort to learn about the deceased and share this knowledge with the congregation. It's often disconcerting to know that the leader is a stranger dropped into the pulpit to do a job without knowing the deceased.

Sometimes all it takes to make the necessary connections is one simple sentence. We have to ensure that our opening words and anecdotes are as concise and to the point as possible. A family once told me that the deceased was extremely generous and put others before herself. I opened the funeral service by saying, "All her life Jane put others before herself — well, this morning we put Jane first and celebrate her life among us."

On the other hand I have also been asked to officiate at services where the deceased was not fondly remembered. I've had people describe the deceased as being a "bastard" or "son of a bitch". In these situations family members have been honest in saying that they are happy the person is dead. This makes an introduction difficult. While we can sometimes get away with our usual service resources in these situations, it is also important to pay particular attention to some of the wording we use. Friends and family may not respond positively to our use of words like "love" and "caring". God may love the departed but we shouldn't be forcing the survivors to relate to them in the same way. God may love someone but that doesn't mean we have to like them or praise them when they don't deserve it. It's impossible to force people into emotional states they do not want to assume. It's best to be diplomatic and find the safest, most diplomatic words possible.

As I have previously mentioned verbal instructions and introductions are an important part of the warm–up phase of the service. This is true throughout the entire service as well. Clergy will sometimes offer a prayer or meditation and then sit down without introducing the next part of the service. The next person to participate in the service will have to be attentive for when they are expected to approach the front of the chapel. They also have to introduce themselves and say something about the part they are to play in the funeral. I have found it helpful to invite people to come forward by name. This takes the guesswork out of what we're doing. By introducing and explaining as much as possible we allow mourners to focus on the actual content of the service. This is far more important than trying to read the service leader's mind.

Part of our work as service leader is being a tour guide of sorts. It only takes one or two sentences to give people a sense of what is happening and why. A friend of mine once told me of a graveside they attended where the officiating minister asked them to take a stone from a basket and place it in the ground with the urn of the deceased. She said they had no idea why they were doing it or what it meant. When we ask people to participate in a service we need to explain what we're doing and what it means. If we ask people to place rocks in the ground we need to say things like: "Please take a stone and pray over it and place the rock in the as a sign that our thoughts and prayers go with the person on their continuing journey."

Funerals are foreign territory to so many people that we have to walk them through the service in almost the same way you'd lead them through a museum. People seem to appreciate it when we introduce the different elements of the service and explain why we're doing things. Sometimes all it takes is a word or sentence to help people get their bearings. Perhaps the biggest reason for doing this is simple continuity and order. Hearing a consistent voice also helps maintain a flow to the service and eliminates as much guess work as possible on the part of participants.

Not every piece of information is helpful at the beginning of the service, however. Something you may not want as a part of the warm–up phase of the service is a slideshow tribute. While we will be discussing these in a later chapter it is still important to mention a couple of things here. A couple of years ago I attended the funeral where the service began with a slideshow tribute. One of the things I learned is while the slideshow tribute is important there are places in the service where it is more helpful than others. I encourage families to have the slideshow tribute follow the eulogy and other spoken tributes later in the service. This way people can see the photos and reflect on the words they have just heard. It can be a powerful moment when all of these things come together. While having the slide tribute at the beginning of the service can be helpful it can strike people as being out of place and it could affect how the rest of the service is experienced and interpreted.

Instead of beginning the service with loud music and projected images, traditional religious services can begin with simple phrases or sayings drawn from scripture. Less traditional and religious services can begin in a similar way although with very different content. In this case thoughts can be drawn from philosophy, classical literature, and poetry. I've included some samples here and you can add whichever ones you come across in your personal reading.

> "When parents die…they take with them a large portion of the past. But when children die, they take away the future as well. That is what makes the valley of the shadow of death so incredibly dark and unending." *The Rev. William Sloan Coffin.*

> "One should not develop a taste for mourning, and yet mourn we must." *Jacques Derrida.*

> "Speaking is impossible, but so too would be silence or absence or a refusal to share one's sadness." *Jacques Derrida.*

"None of us is the only member of the human race. There are others around us and we exist in association with them." *Alfred Adler in "What Life Could Mean for You".*

"There's only one thing worse than speaking ill of the dead — and that is not speaking of the dead at all." *Anonymous.*

"There's a saying in Africa that every time a very old person dies it is as if a library has burned to the ground." *Alex Haley, Author of "Roots".*

"They (Dene elders) would say I don't want you to be rich, happy or famous. I just want you to be a good man." *Paul Andrew in "Remembering Peter Gzowski" Ed. Edna Barker.*

"For all things come from earth, and all things end by returning to earth." *Xenophanes of Colophon, moral philosopher.*

"Life changes fast. Life changes in the instant." *Joan Didion.* Note: Use for sudden deaths.

"If winter comes, can spring be far behind?" *Percy–Bysshe Shelley.*

"I was not; I have been; I am not; I do not mind." *Epicurus.*

Try to include at least one or two simple texts. However, using too many quotes to open a service may make it more difficult to establish an overall flow for the service. I was hesitant to use the above quote from Epicurus as it seems to trivialize his sensible and decent approach to life. This saying, however, can be a helpful part of secular services[13] so I've included it as an example.

For individuals who are more traditionally religious and have a strong Christian faith here are some Bible readings that can provide both opening sentences and ideas for readings and sermons.

Psalm 46:1-7 God is our refuge and our strength, a very present help in time of trouble. Therefore, we will not fear though the earth should change.

Romans 8:31-39 Paul writes: "For I am convinced that neither death nor life ... will be able to separate us from the love of God in Christ Jesus our Lord."

Isaiah 43:2 "When you pass through the waters, I will be with you; and through the rivers, they shall not overwhelm you; when you walk through fire you shall not be burned, and the flame shall not consume you."

Psalm 91:1-6 "You who live in the shelter of the most high ..."

2 Timothy 4:7 "I have fought the good fight, I have finished the race, I have kept the faith."

Revelations 21:1-4 "Then I saw a new heaven and a new earth; for the first heaven and the first earth had passed away, and the sea was no more ... he will wipe away every tear from their eyes. Death will be no more; mourning and crying and pain will be no more, for the first things have passed away."

> Zechariah 8:1-8 God offers a vision of the future
> Kingdom in which people will share in a public park type
> atmosphere. Cemetery is a place of rest and waiting until
> that time when we are called to share in this time and
> place of caring, community, and love.

Some clergy will want to read one or more of these texts as they lead the casket to the front of the chapel or service space.

Perhaps the most important scripture sentences we can offer come from the Gospels. One in particular comes immediately to mind. Preacher and scholar N.T. Wright once asked his congregation if they knew "the most frequent command in the Bible". After suggesting some possibilities Wright settled on his answer: "The most frequent command in the Bible is 'Don't be afraid.'"[14] Beginning the service with "fear not" sets a tone that is both comforting and spiritually in tune with many of our listeners. It may also help establish material we'll be using later in the funeral.

Worship leaders can review each and every recommended quotation, sentence and text in an effort to personalize the service. Don't be afraid to ask the family if the deceased had a favourite reading. If the reading is brief enough we can include it here while more extensive sections of scripture can be used later in the service. Using scriptural verses has its advantages over more lengthy readings. Paul Irion writes, "I propose the use of verses rather than chapters because so often in the same Psalm or chapter a great variety of thoughts may be contained some of them helpful, others harmful, in the particular situation."[15] Perhaps the best example of this is John 14. People like the idea of God preparing a place for them in heaven but the other parts of this chapter may not be as helpful. This is why I always tell people that I'll be reading "selected verses" from the chapter. Preaching on John 14 in its entirety is something perhaps best done during a regular weekly worship service.

For the more justice–oriented a person we can quote lines from writers such as Wendell Berry. Berry once wrote, "we hurt and are hurt and have each other for healing."[16] This is a powerful statement reinforcing the importance of relationship and community. It also says something about the deceased's beliefs. This line can be used later in the service. We can use lines like this in our messages, for example.

When we move past the opening sentences, the following can be used as a "Welcome and Introduction":

"We would like to welcome you to this place this afternoon as we remember and offer thanks for the life of ——. Family and friends knew him/her as ——. —— recently passed away at the age of —.

In many ancient languages the word "mourning" means to care and to remember. So we have gathered to offer our condolences to ——'s family and to share with them our strength and our support. We have gathered to remember and say "Goodbye" to a loved one, a friend, and a neighbour."

There are occasions when no one attends a service. In these situations I prefer to make one minor change and use the following variation of the above introduction:

We would like to welcome you to this place as we remember and offer thanks for the life of —— —— recently passed away at the age of —.

In the ancient languages the word "mourning" means to care and to remember. We have gathered to acknowledge Loretta and name her as one who has walked among us. Loretta's journey among us began in —— and it continues to this place where we have gathered to remember and say "Goodbye" to a loved one, a friend and a neighbour.

We can mention here the location of where the person was born. We can say something like, "John Doe's journey among us began in —— . Their journey continues to this place where ——" As Canadian performer Tom Cochrane sings, "Life is a highway". Life is a journey that takes us from one place to another and this is a notion that is easily captured in a funeral especially when using the words I've just shared here.

We can create our own introductions or we can borrow from others. For example, I find the following words from William and John Baird extremely helpful: "This is not a "last" tribute, for the most beautiful memorial left by anyone is not carved on stone, not even in a service such as this. It is the memorial left in the hearts of those who knew and loved him (sic)."[17] When we do borrow material from others writers or colleagues it is important to acknowledge our sources whenever possible. Do not publish anything without the appropriate end notes and footnotes. While listeners may not ask us for references they're good to have in case we ever decide to publish our service materials. Denominations will sometimes request submissions whenever they offer a new or renewed service resource for particular occasions. If and when we respond to these requests it's best to have our materials in order.

One thing we can include in the warm–up phase of the funeral is a personalized candle lighting ceremony. A number of years ago I attended the funeral of a friend and at the beginning of this service the minister lit a candle. This was a very powerful moment for me so I made a decision then and there that I would include candle lighting elements to each and every service I lead from that service forward. Clients and funeral directors have spoken positively about this part of my services.

Hooyman and Kramer write, "Rituals usually involve objects that have a symbolic value, such as a candle, letter, song, or picture."[18] Of all of these items listed here I find that candles are the most powerful. Padre Kenneth Best experienced the power of candles in particular when he officiated his first funeral in Cairo during World War One. Due to the dangers of burying soldiers near the front most funerals happened at night. This meant that clergy read their services either by candlelight or moonlight. The service Best mentions was held on a late October night in 1914 and candles offered enough light so that the soldiers could carry out their duties. We can only imagine how these small points of light played against the darkness and shadows. According to Best the effect of the candlelight was both "impressive and memorable".[19] This was a powerful way to begin a ministry and it can also be a powerful way to begin a funeral.

Not everyone has been in universal agreement about the value of candle lighting, however. Reformation theologians such as Johann Eberlin have suggested that candles at a funeral have been a dramatic touch for the survivors and, to quote Eberlin himself, "of no use to the dead."[20] They may be "of no use to the dead" but they do have an effect on the ritual experience of mourners. Eberlin and his cohorts may have dismissed the importance of candles at a funeral but I have found them pastorally important to the marking of a key transition.

It's because of this pastoral effect that I begin each and every one service with a brief candle lighting. It's one of the ways we can acknowledge the reality of death and the changes this loss brings about. When someone dies we often think of him or her as "ceasing to exist". We may think that we'll never see him or her again. What we often forget is that the person lives on in ways that are not always physical and a candle lighting ceremony recognizes this. This is why one of the most important things we can do when lighting a candle at the beginning of the service is to name the changed relationship the deceased has with the survivors. The candle can be a symbolic reminder of the person's life and it can also remind people that this person continues to live on in a new way. This can be interpreted both in religious and nonreligious ways. A religious person can be assured that the deceased is with God. A nonreligious interpretation could be that the person lives on in minds, hearts, words, actions, etc.. We can use both interpretations. A person could even apply their own interpretation on what this candle means to them. For me, a helpful way to introduce this candle lighting is by saying the following:

"Throughout history people have lit candles to bring light and warmth into their lives. The light of a candle can chase away the shadows that haunt our world. The light of a candle can also help us find our way through unfamiliar places.

As we begin our time today I would invite —— to come forward and light this candle here at the front. As we share this service may this candle be a symbol of John Doe's continuing presence in our lives. John lives on in our stories and in our thoughts. He lives on in our laughter and in our tears. He lives on in our words and in our actions."

This can be adapted to meet many different situations. I recently officiated a service for a still born baby where I replaced some of the above with: "She may not have had a chance to live among us physically but we believe and can be assured that she continues to live among us in spirit." What may seem like a slight adaptation to us can be a significant statement to a grieving family.

I normally ask a member or close friend of the family to light the candle. This helps personalize the service and it can include someone who has not yet been able to find a place in the service in which they can participate. Not everybody feels that they are able to speak at a funeral and this is a good opportunity to offer someone a nonverbal way of participating and contributing to the service. It can be helpful to have a young child light the candle. There are a number of reasons why this can be extremely important for the child. Claudia Jewett suggests that participating in the funeral helps a child develop a healthy approach to loss and grief.[21] The feeling of inclusion helps them build stronger ties to both family and community.

So often we try to protect children from death and funerals and this can be confusing later in their lives. A friend once told me a story of when she and her young son drove by a cemetery. He noticed something happening in the cemetery and said: "There are people in the graveyard. Why are they there?" The mother responded by telling her son that they were probably visiting. "Who are they visiting?" the son asked. The mother said, "They're visiting the people who have died." The son thought about that for a moment and suddenly blurted out: "Do they dig people up so that they can talk to them?" Children need information and the best way to get that information and to have as many questions addressed as possible is to attend the service when appropriate and participate when possible. Again, lighting the candle is one way they can do that.

The candle can be provided one of two ways: Either the family can provide the candle or the funeral home can provide one. One advantage of the family providing the candle is that they can take it home with them and light it at major family functions. These occasions can be major holidays such as Christmas and Thanksgiving. The candle can also be lit for special birthdays and anniversaries. I officiated at one funeral where the child of the deceased was getting married within days of her parent's funeral. She took the candle from the funeral and set it on a small table at the front of the church where the couple were celebrating their wedding. The same person lit the candle on both occasions. The candle was lit prior to the wedding and remained so throughout the ceremony. A couple could add to this by placing a small picture of the deceased parent beside the candle.

When it comes to taking things home following the service, flowers and food have their place but they really don't last very long. A candle can be a present and more enduring reminder of what is happening in their lives. This same candle can also be a reminder that the strength and meaning of the original funeral ritual can carry on long after the closing blessing or dismissal. This ritual strength can be experienced when the is lit in private moments when a surviving spouse, parent, or even friend wants to pray, meditate, or simply remember their departed loved one. Grieving people don't always know how to handle the emotions that are generated when a loved one dies so this candle can help them with this process. Lighting a candle can help them through difficult times when they aren't really sure what's going on. The grief process can bring about some strange experiences and something like a candle can help us reflect and think about what's happening in our lives. It's not unusual, for example, for grieving people to speak with the dead. The candle may help them focus their thoughts and words so that they can say what they need to say. The same is true if the person is trying to write a letter, draw a picture, or work on a scrapbook.

Another advantage of inviting the family to purchase a candle is they can select a style and colour that suits them. They may even wish to purchase a scented candle that can also be used on those future occasions when the candle is relit. Perhaps the main reason for doing this is that scent is a powerful trigger of emotions and memory. If the family is at a loss as to which candle they can purchase they could even bring a candle from the home of the deceased. There may be a favourite candle the deceased has used from time to time. They may have even made the candle with their own hands.

There are different ways we can adapt this simple candle lighting ceremony to a variety of situations. There may be more than one person who wants to light a candle, for example. In this case there can be more than one candle on the table at the front. There may be more than one person who would like to have a candle lit, as they may need something like this to help them through their future grieving. Lighting the candle within the service may place a special meaning on this candle so that the grieving person can see it as some sort of blessing. The service leader will simply have to alter their notes to include this change.

Service leaders can tailor this candle lighting to different situations. One of the most difficult situations we can experience, for example, is the death of a baby. One thing we can do is invite one of the family (perhaps the mother herself) to come forward and light a candle. We can then invite others who have experienced a similar kind of loss to come forward and light a candle as well. Give people time to come forward and complete this gesture. This helps show the grieving parents that they are not alone. Please note: Ensure that there are enough candles available for this to happen. This may be best accomplished in a church context, as funeral homes don't always have the inventory necessary to provide the necessary candles, holders, etc..

In a recent regimental service I led the size of the candle was important for one very practical reason: the service was held in an arena and it would have been extremely difficult to see one of the smaller candles I normally use. The only candle we could effectively use was a large Christ candle from the local Roman Catholic parish. A colleague of mine had a pickup truck and went to speak with the local priest. The priest was more than willing to loan us the candle and even helped us load it onto the truck. Lighting this large candle before a gathered congregation of over a thousand people was a powerful moment. What made this moment even more powerful was the quiet and easy piece of music playing in the background while we lit the candle.

At any point during the warm—up phase of the funeral we can have music guiding us and accompanying us on our way. This music can be dramatic or it can be more reflective. While we will discuss music in more detail later I will say a few things as we address the opening moves of the funeral. For one thing, we can have music playing when we make our way into the funeral space with the casket, urn and/or family. We can also play music while someone comes to the front and lights a candle or offer an opening word. Music is an important part of our emotional and spiritual entry into the service time. It's one of the key elements that helps us prepare and engage and there are a couple of strong reasons for this. Michelle Robinson writes, "At the beginning of worship people seek rapport, a sense of safety and reassurance that makes them feel 'at home'".[22]

Whether it's candles or notes or music, ensuring that we are ready to begin the service is important. Now that our listeners are "warmed up" we can move into a more inspirational phase so that they may think about deeper matters.

Phase Three: Inspiration

Every Halloween I find myself thinking about the same prayer. It's an old Cornish prayer that says: "From ghoulies and ghosties and long–leggity beasties, And things that go bump in the night, Good Lord, deliver us!" Prayers have been a critical part of almost every spiritual occasion since the very beginning of human history. Even in some of the most nonreligious situations prayer often provides a spiritual element listeners may find inspiring. It's inspiration like this we'll be discussing in the next few pages. "Inspiration" includes prayers, music and readings. For me, these are the three most focused and intense ways of building a bridge between human and divine. It's also a healthy way of developing our personal spiritual lives.

A number of years ago I was asked to officiate at a so–called non–religious funeral. The family made it clear that they wanted no religious content whatsoever. The deceased wasn't a churchgoer and they wanted a service that reflected that reality. So I gave them what they wanted. The service was stripped of anything that even remotely referred to God or Christianity. We read some poems and talked about his life. We listened to some of the music he found meaningful and swapped stories about how he touched so many lives. Everything worked according to the family's wishes. At least I thought I was being consistent with the family's wishes.

At the conclusion of the service I was approached by the family members I had originally met and worked with. To my surprise they were not happy with how things had developed. The first words out of their mouths were, "Are we at least going to have a prayer at the graveside?" This family had made it clear that they wanted a non–religious service and yet there they were asking for a prayer. Perhaps I was more focused on the letter of their request more than the spirit. Perhaps I should have gambled and included a prayer. It's difficult to know what the right answer is.

When we do include a prayer we have to be careful about its tone and content. Peoples' experiences with religion aren't always positive. One of the reasons for this is the content and intensity of prayers they've heard at previous funerals. I asked one family about whether or not they wanted a prayer included in the service and they responded by telling me that it would be alright but I was not to "pray too loud". This suggests to me that people want prayers in a service even though they don't always understand what they're asking of us. This is an opportunity for us to explain prayer to mourners and explore some possibilities with them.

So how do we explain prayer to survivors and include them in our services? Perhaps we need to begin this part of our discussion with a definition and move out from there. What is prayer and what does prayer do? Simply put, prayer is that form of communication that helps us touch a bigger and wider reality. Pat Schneider writes, "To pray is to open oneself completely, into the Presence that is beyond our ability to name."[1] She later adds, "Prayer is, for me, an intentional openness to the presence of mystery in my life."[2] For those of us who are Christian this presence is God. Paul Radin offers this about prayer: "Prayer, in its most general form may be described as consisting of two parts: first, the statement of certain wishful thoughts; and, secondly, the enunciation of the facts of everyday life."[3] Radin suggests that, in terms of length, prayers can range from a simple, yet heartfelt cry for help and a full day's recounting of a problem or situation needing a particular god's attention.[4]

This may seem overly general and obvious to most readers but it does speak to a spiritual element deep within human nature. This spiritual element emerges at times such as death, grief and leave–taking. This may come as a shock to many when they begin the grief journey. It is perhaps for this reason many people request prayers when they normally wouldn't in other situations. Paul Radin once wrote, "… all people are spontaneously religious at crises …"[5] This may have something to do with the general nature of a crisis. Above all, a crisis is an experience that is often overwhelming and shocking in a way that is well beyond our norm. We do not always know how to initially react to something so big happening in our lives. We often react by relying on what we can call a default response. We turn to prayer and spirituality when nothing else makes sense. Grieving people may find themselves responding in this way.

With this in mind, there are two types of prayers we can use in a funeral service. The first type of prayer is religious in nature and can usually be found in denominational resources and books found in most Christian bookstores or on websites. These prayers are based on both scripture and the teachings of our respective traditions. They are often based on traditions that date back centuries and have been a comfort to many throughout these years. They can also be based on the experience of those writing the prayers and other service materials. For those of us who rely on these prayers in services we can either read them word for word or adapt them to the circumstances of each and every service. It's usually best to adapt them whenever possible. People want personalized service materials and it's more than appropriate to make whatever changes we feel to be appropriate. We can thank God for the lives of the deceased and pray for their families and friends, for example. We can ask God to be present through the grief, difficulties, and challenges. We can name the presence of trauma and tragedy without getting into specifics. At the very least we should mention the name of the deceased in whatever prayer we write or use for the occasion.

Religious scholars such as John Macquarrie tell us that the content of our prayers don't always have to be Christian.[6] These non–Christian, or nonreligious prayers are our second type of prayer. Non–Christian prayers can be just as powerful as Christian ones. One of the examples that stands out for me was from the state funeral for the Honourable Jack Layton.[7] At the beginning of the service the National Chief of the Assembly of First Nations in Canada, Shawn Atleo, offered an Aboriginal blessing to bring heaven and earth together and create a sacred space in which the service could be held. With words and movement he created a spiritual experience that was beyond any one particular religious tradition. It was powerful and that's what counted. It's this powerful experience that spiritual people around the world try to capture when they lead a funeral service or ritual. Geoffrey Parrinder tells us that Taoist followers, for example, are urged to "pray for the souls of the dead, who, through the merit of the living, might finally gain release from the underworld and entrance to paradise."[8]

Many service leaders may want to address these situations by writing their own prayers. Perhaps they've reviewed the various denominational resources and have found little, if anything they can use. This seems to be a reality many of us have experienced. If we do write our own prayers there are a couple of things we can keep in mind. For one thing, it's important to name the deceased and, where appropriate talk about the difficulties and trauma people may be experiencing. Include the friends and family of the deceased. If people are put off by religious language we can easily make helpful substitutions. We can address our "Creating Spirit" and talk about things like heaven with more neutral language. Clergy may be leery of toning down the God–talk but it may be more helpful than needlessly offending and antagonizing people and having them turn off to the rest of what we have to say.

We have to find and maintain a decent balance when it comes to writing prayers. This may not be easy. We may feel as if we're selling out our beliefs and faith commitments. We may feel as if we're watering down God's message. In response to these potential concerns I would suggest that we take a moment and try to visualize and think about the people gathered for the funeral. Who are they and what do they believe? What do they need to hear? In a previous chapter we discussed the importance of listening. Listening to the needs of the family help us determine which type of prayer to use. Listening will help provide content for the prayer and give us a sense of where we need to go with our service materials. Elaine Ramshaw states that when listening feeds our prayer "it can be a way into the need, rather than a way around it".[9]

As we write our prayers we can be mindful of how difficult it can be to express our thoughts, feelings, and experiences in words. There are times when we may need to acknowledge that words are simply impossible to find. Death is one of those realities that can literally leave us speechless. It's for this reason that it may be necessary to include periods of silence in our prayers. John Keats once wrote, "Heard melodies are sweet, but those unheard are sweeter."[10] People may appreciate our silence and use it to offer their own personal prayers. Thomas Merton tells us that when we pray we have to go beyond thought, words, and imagination. We have to pray "out of the very roots" of our being.[11]

Words alone, however cannot begin to describe what we're going through when we experience a funeral or the grieving process itself. As I have mentioned previously, there is also a place for silent prayer and reflection. Where these periods of silence are placed is up to you. We may want to include times of silence in each and every funeral. In less than religious situations we may want to use a term such as "silent reflection", "silent goodbyes" or something like that. Betty Jane Wylie says it well when she writes; "There is something awe–inspiring, silencing, and shattering about emotional pain that does leave one at a loss for words."[12]

One type of prayer that comes from the "roots" of our souls is the lament. Laments are those times when we literally "cry out" to a higher divinity. Crises in our lives generate a tremendous amount of emotional energy and that energy has to be released in some way. We frequently experience laments throughout the Psalms. Perhaps one of the best examples is Psalm 105, in which the Psalmist writes, "Lord, hear my prayer, and let my cry come to you. Hide not your face from me in the day of my distress." There's a lot of raw emotional energy that's pumped into Psalms such as these. This is what makes them so effective and powerful.

Historically, laments were an important part of the ancient ritual meals we discussed in a previous chapter. One of the main things they helped accomplish was the assignment to memory of what the deceased had accomplished in their life. It was hoped that this memory would live on in family and community as listeners tried to move on with their lives.[13] In his recently published book entitled *Racial Justice and the Catholic Church*, Bryan Massingale writes, "Lamentation is an expression of complaint, grief, and hope rooted in a 'trust against trust' that God hears the cry of the afflicted and will respond compassionately to their need."[14]

Another way laments work is to inform. Historically people didn't have access to the communication technology we have today. They couldn't just pick up the phone or post something on a social media page. They had to spread the news by crying and screaming it out. According to Ian Hogbin people lamented in order to let others know that someone had died. It was also a signal that all work had to cease until after the funeral.[15]

The one challenge ancient service leaders had to confront was the sheer chaos this public lamenting could cause. As we've already discussed, grieving can push us to release some powerful emotions. When we're not used to dealing with these powerful responses we may find ourselves acting out in dangerous and inappropriate ways. When taken to extremes laments could seriously and negatively affect the overall ritual process itself. Service leaders had to find some way to bring order out of chaos.[16] Laments and prayer help us do this.

While prayer can be helpful it can also be abused. As I have already mentioned I constantly hear about services in which the service leaders tries to focus his or her efforts on converting the gathered congregation to a particular set of beliefs. The term I use to describe this is "hijacking". The service leader takes control of the service in a way that sends it in a direction contrary to where family and friends would like it to go. The minister has a brief moment where they can steer the ship anywhere they want and going "off course" like this is completely inappropriate. Many clergy are unaware of the cost of such an action. One young father told religious scholar Diana Butler Bass that such a funeral ended his commitment to the church. His infant son had died and the pastor leading the funeral made the astonishing claim that the death occurred because the parents "hadn't prayed enough" and that "a lack of faith" killed the child. The young father said that he "walked out that day and never returned."[17]

It's both inappropriate and unethical to force our views onto others, especially in such difficult circumstances. People will respond by tuning out and walking away. They will "vote with their feet" both literally and figuratively. The one question that can be asked when writing or adapting a prayer is, "Whose needs are being met here?" Are we meeting the family's needs when we try and convert them? Is that what we're supposed to be doing when leading a funeral? I would say "no" to this. As I have said in a previous chapter we cannot force our beliefs onto others. We cannot, to quote a colleague of mine, "preach a person into heaven". It cannot be said too often that the funeral focuses on the life of the deceased and "is not about us". The prayers we offer and the overall funeral itself is about the deceased and gathered survivors.

While it is important to have a number of prayers and resources available for these occasions, reading from a book and filling in the names where appropriate can come across as being distant and cold. Only original and/or adapted prayers can address particular needs and situations.[18] They may simply require some minor alterations to help make them apply to a particular situation. Many service leaders have four to five prayers they use on a regular basis and, providing the necessary alterations are made, there is nothing inappropriate with that. Even the best pitchers in professional baseball have two or three regular pitches they rely on throughout a game. They may even add a new pitch or two as their career develops. I frequently use the following two prayers in services:

"Loving God, you are with us through all of the seasons of life. You are with us when we are born and you are with us as we grow and build our lives with family and community. We ask that you be with us in our songs and in our hearts. We ask that you be with us in our words and in our silences.

We ask that you be with us as we offer thanks for —— and the life that he/she has shared among us. Help us through this difficult and challenging time. This we ask in your name. Amen."

Or:

"Creating Spirit, we bring our emotions, stories, and experiences before you as we gather for this time of remembering and reflection. Bless each one of us with your caring presence this day. Be present as we give thanks for ⸺ and the life he/she has offered so many. Move among us as we make our way into the difficult days and weeks ahead. Amen."

One type of prayer I do not usually include in any of my services is the so–called "prayer of confession". Even in religious services held in churches we do not attend funerals to dwell on our own sins and shortcomings. The only time confession may be helpful is when we've done something to the deceased that needs to be addressed. A public gathering is not the most helpful place for this type of confession, however. We are there to celebrate a life that someone else has lived. While we can think about times and places in which we contributed to something negative happening in the deceased's life, those are more personal prayers that can be left for another time like Sunday morning worship or personal devotions. We can also speak with a friend or clergyperson if the need is felt to be that great. There are also more helpful and creative ways of reflecting on and naming things that have happened in relationships. We will deal with some of these ways later.

As we discussed in the previous chapter, there are times when the deceased may not be remembered all that fondly so our wording may have to be changed accordingly. We may not like changing the words of cherished and traditional prayers but it may be the most helpful and pastoral thing to do. In fact many, if not most denominational resources are designed to be changed whenever we feel a need to do so. We can avoid dangerous ground by simply focusing on the notion that the deceased is at peace. We can talk about their race being over and so on. This is yet another place where the airing of dirty laundry is neither acceptable nor welcome.

There are special prayers that are helpful in military situations. In our present time there always seems to be a war going on somewhere. With so much chaos in the world it only seems logical that there will come a time when we will be asked to officiate a funeral for someone killed in one of these situations. It's at these times we can turn to those who have made their way before us. Ernest Black wrote the following prayer while serving in the First World War:

> "That fear and wounds and death may pass me by
> Is not the boon, O Lord, for which I pray,
> For having put the rim within my lips
> I do not ask to put the cup away.
> But grant the heart that Thou hast given me
> May in the hour of peril never fail,
> And that the will to serve and do my part,
> May ever o'er my will to live prevail."

A prayer such as this could be used during the funeral of a veteran or a currently serving member of the armed forces. People in uniform share with the rest of us the challenge of processing emotions and expressing their grief. They too often find themselves shocked and speechless in the face of death.

Perhaps another effective way to address the loss for words is the inclusion of music in the service. Not only are we questioning, storytelling people we are also musical people as well. Regardless of whether or not we're actually good at it, we love singing and we love listening to music. The old silent films, for example, couldn't have existed without music. Ludovic Bource once said, "In a silent movie, music is essential for telling the story and accompanying the emotions."[19] Music invites emotion and helps it "do what it has to do". Music can also be a safe way of helping express our thoughts, beliefs and emotions. An Eton Headmaster once said, "Music is the least dangerous of the arts."[20] Perhaps the main reason for this is its relative safety and flexibility. Perhaps another reason is how it works so well with something like ritual. For the religious person music can, to borrow a term from Phyllis Tickle, "open the soul".[21]

The rituals we have celebrated throughout history have incorporated music as a powerful part of their work. Nicholas Wade writes, "All religions are centred on rituals, and rituals include music." We may be surprised by the types of music used in funerals throughout history. How many of us would appreciate the use of drums, for example? When it comes to things like drumming, Wade writes, "The music that accompanies these (rituals) often includes percussive effects ... widely held to be a way of communicating with the spirit world."[22] There is a good reason why music is included in ritual and that's because it has power. Keith Richards of the Rolling Stones once wrote, "You can build a wall to stop people, but eventually, the music will cross that wall." Richards went on to use the crumbling walls of Jericho as an example of what music can accomplish. All it took were "a few trumpets" to bring down a wall of brick and mortar.[23] Western society seems to have lost this sense that music is a central part of rituals such as funerals and we have lost a lot because of it. George Orwell once described western funerals as being "beastly mummeries."[24] I believe it's the lack of music that helps render them so. Perhaps it's because music is such a deep and intimate part of our everyday lives.

Music permeates every part of our lives, including our health. It establishes a rhythm or beat to which we can live and move. Oliver Sacks once wrote, "Every disease is a musical problem; every cure is a musical solution."[25] Some of his patients couldn't function without a song going through their minds. Sacks speaks of a patient who needed to be humming or singing while eating and getting dressed. If that song were interrupted his activity of the moment would stop. He would be unable to continue.[26] When it comes to grief music helps us keep moving. It helps us think, remember, and share. It helps us join with others and rebuild the lives that have been affected by loss.

Sacks also tells a story about the time he was walking to the Bronx hospital where he worked. He was grieving the loss of close relatives and feeling emotionally numb. He was going through the motions and working like a robot. He couldn't feel much of anything. While he was walking he noticed something interesting happen. It was like his emotions began thawing. He could feel again. He also noticed that while this thaw was taking place there was music playing from a radio sitting on the ledge of a basement window down the street from where he was. He remembers that "suddenly life and the world and joy and memories all flooded back to me, and I wanted to stay by that window …"[27] Sacks told Eric Friesen in a radio interview "music can evoke the deepest emotions and moods and states of mind, which can be absolutely overwhelming and mysterious."[28]

It's for these reasons that music is critical to an effective funeral. Music touches us with an emotional and psychological intensity that is difficult to describe. Perhaps we can put it this way: Music gives us a sense of deep reality. In other words, music goes beyond words and brings mind, body and spirit together in a profound, transformational way. Many believe that music can accomplish so much more. For the Berawan people in Borneo music is believed to reach the deceased and give them directions on how to find the "land of the dead". These "instructions" can last for hours.[29] They are also consistent with the efforts of other cultures to help move ghosts and spirits through the one–way door to the afterlife. Perhaps "shove" is a better word to use than "move" when it comes to describing this effort.

Music can also inspire us by breathing new energy into us so we can continue grieving and rebuilding our lives. When describing the funeral of civil rights leader Martin Luther King Jr., writer James Baldwin called it "the most real church service I've ever sat through in my life, or ever hope to sit through." The one thing that made the service "real" for Baldwin was the music. The solo, especially, "rang out" for him and added to the intensity and meaning of the experience.[30]

Mention of the soloist is important here as we have to state the difference between music in general and singing in particular. While listening to music is important it is extremely difficult to actually sing at a funeral. I officiated at a funeral for a church choir member and his colleagues from the church choir found it extremely difficult to sing, even when it was a cherished and enduring part of their lives. The ancient Israelites faced exile and loss and found it almost impossible to sing as well. The Psalmist tells of the people hanging their harps because they couldn't play or sing "in a strange land".[31] For most of us, funerals are "strange lands". We don't know what to think or how to feel. We don't know what to do with the emotional energy being generated. We don't always know what to say or do. We need guidance and music can help us navigate these struggles. However, it has to be something we listen to and not actually sing.

As I have already mentioned, music has had a central place in the funeral ritual from almost the very beginning. It may have something to do with the drumbeat that projects the thumping of our hearts. It could be that lyric that helps us express our emotions. Kathleen Corley tells of how ancient traditions have recorded the fact that men and women were hired to play instruments such as the flute and harp.[32] Women were also hired to sing but, for some reason, early church leaders put a stop to that practice.[33] Luckily we've undone much of this work and brought music back into the midst of the funeral.

Music is another one of those elements in the funeral that can bring religious and nonreligious people together. However, the different expectations both groups bring to a service may sometimes cause conflict. Many of us simply cannot seem to find a way to understand this attempt at community building. We dismiss a lot of the music we hear at funerals. The Roman Catholic church provides an example of this in the opinion of a recently retired Pope. Joseph Ratzinger, now Pope Benedict XVI dismisses nonreligious music as being "utility music" when it is used in rituals.[34] This is a rather crass opinion that doesn't strike me as being either pastoral or humane. Perhaps Benedict should share his thinking with the cast of the comedy troupe, Monty Python, who sang *Always Look on the Bright Side of Life* at fellow cast member Graham Chapman's funeral.[35] This song was meaningful and it was funny. This is why it has an important place in funerals. Who can argue with John Cleese when he says, "No subject is ever too serious for humour."[36]

What religious people may not realize is that secular music has been a part of worship since about the thirteenth century when a form of renaissance music called the "motet" was introduced into Roman Catholic vesper services.[37] This relationship between secular music and sacred worship continued to evolve and really came alive during the renaissance. Elwyn Wienandt writes, "During the fifteenth and sixteenth centuries polyphonic mass settings were often based on borrowed material — tunes taken from secular or sacred compositions that already had a successful, independent existence."[38] This secular music has affected worship into the present day and the funeral ritual is one place where we see this the most clearly.

Nonreligious people can relate to secular music but they can also find value in more sacred offerings. This may surprise a number of readers. For people without spiritual or religious inclinations, religious music can still trigger associations and memories that are still important and meaningful. There seems to be something in the rhythm of a song or other piece of music that helps us think in ways other activities simply cannot. There may also be a bit of nostalgia. When helping plan a funeral recently a nonreligious member of the family requested a traditional hymn for the service. When I asked why he wanted this particular piece he said that he remembered it from when he was growing up and attending church with his parents.

In saying that, it's important to keep in mind the fact that we cannot expect too much from music. It's not so much what enters our ear — it's how our brains and spirits respond to what's happening around us. Oliver Sacks says that music, itself, doesn't have meaning.[39] Meaning is what we give it. Perhaps this is one of the reasons why it has such a way of bringing people together. Sacks talks about music as being a "communal experience".[40] Whether it's the rhythm of the piece or the message communicated by the lyrics music helps build a sense of community and shared experience. Sacks writes, "Rhythm turns listeners into participants, makes listening active and motoric, and synchronizes the brains and minds … of all who participate."[41] Music, in one way or another, affects our entire being. In many congregations Sunday morning services include music with a beat that gets people moving in their chairs and pews. While some of us may dismiss this movement as something I call "ecclesiastical aerobics" it can work in some situations. Movement can, for example, gives us energy for when we need it the most. A similar thing happens when we tap into the energy and flow of a rock concert or athletic match. Perhaps one of the main reasons for this is music's binding quality.

In a cognitive sense, music is therapeutic when it helps us organize and reorganize our thoughts. In fact, Oliver Sacks suggests, "music therapy, for some patients, can succeed where conventional speech therapy has failed …"[42] Many patients living with brain damage find that singing words can help them communicate when they cannot generate language in more conventional ways. Music therapy is a familiar part of any activity program in hospitals and other health care facilities across North America and for very good reason. Whether it is singing or listening music helps us remember and communicate. This is why music is so important for many patients living with dementia. People living with dementia can become extremely isolated and music helps develop and maintain connections and bonds with family and friends.[43] Autistic children can gain from being exposed to music. Temple Grandin points out in her book *Thinking In Pictures* that studies have shown that "some autistic children can learn to sing before they can talk."[44]

Music can also help us heal physically. During both World Wars doctors noticed that the condition of wounded soldiers quickly improved when they listened to music. Their pain was more easily managed and their vital statistics even displayed marked improvement.[45] Perhaps one of the reasons was that it helped take their minds of the crushing reality around them. They were reminded of previous times in their life when they were whole and hopeful. They were reminded of home. They were reminded of what grounds them and helps them hold out hope for a new and renewed life beyond their current experience.

Music can change our emotional state and get things moving. Sometimes this can happen in an extreme way. Music can touch people experiencing emotional numbness, for example, and bring them to tears almost instantly. William Styron once said that music "pierced my heart like a dagger".[46] To African Americans, "Moving spirituals embrace the joy of reuniting with deceased relatives and finally achieving peace." According to Hooyman and Kramer, music such as this helps promote the public expression of our emotions and can ultimately help "make grieving easier".[47]

One evening I was watching an episode of the television series *House* and heard Josh Ritter's song *Good Man* for the first time. The song instantly reminded me of a friend who had recently died of brain cancer. Doug loved music and he loved being around people. Each word of Ritter's song reminded me of Doug's life and how it ended far too soon. Each word of this song went straight to my soul. Perhaps Oliver Sacks summarizes these thoughts best when he writes, "while such music makes one experience pain and grief more intensely, it brings solace and consolation at the same time."[48] Hearing Ritter's song and remembering Doug was an intense experience and it did bring "solace and consolation". Ludwig Feuerbach offers a good reason for this when he writes, "Music is the language of feeling; melody is audible feeling — feeling communicating itself."[49] Feuerbach later goes on to refer to the music as being a "monologue on emotion."[50] "monologue" is a good word to use here. Grief is a personal journey and it's not unusual to find ourselves working through this process alone. Regardless of who shares our grieving it often comes down to that connection between ourselves and the music. We're the ones who assign meaning and we're the ones who responds to what we're hearing.

The reason for this seems clear enough. Penny Colman writes, "In music that deals with death, the lyrics express disparate feelings — sadness, heartbreak, anger, disbelief, and sometimes relief that a person's pain has ended. So do sounds and rhythms — the wail of the saxophone, the muffled beat of a drum, the swelling chords of an organ, the hard and driving beat of rap, trumpets playing taps, or a band in New Orleans that is cheering up mourners and sending a dead soul on its final journey."[51] People request an incredible variety of music when they plan a service. such as bagpipes, drums, gongs,[52] and guitars. Typically, it is asked that people sing the traditional hymns and listen to the contemporary music. I recently attended a funeral where we were asked to sing along to John Denver's *Sunshine on My Shoulders*. It was eye–opening to hear so many people singing along to the music and it hit me that more people were singing along to the nonreligious music than the religious music. It may have something to do with how we access the music in our lives. When was the last time we tuned into a Christian radio station? When was the last time we searched for Christian music online? Even when we do access these stations how often do they play the more traditional music we once heard at funerals? My hunch is that the response to this question is "not very often".

One of the challenges of creating a list of appropriate music is the constant change in musical tastes. A person cannot keep up with the flow of new songs that could be played prior to, during, or following a service or ceremony. Even as I type this I am listening to Jim Cuddy's new single, *Pull Me Through* on the radio and I find myself wondering if this would be a good choice for a service. Some selections will surprise, and perhaps even disturb us. We have to be careful about letting our thoughts and feelings interfere with the selection of appropriate music for the service. We may not be fans of country and western music, for example, but that doesn't mean we deny requests such as Garth Brooks's *The River* or *The Dance*. There are times when it's even appropriate to hear something like Guns and Roses' *Sweet Child of Mine*.

The key is to find something that is meaningful to the family and friends of the deceased. It doesn't matter if it's opera or heavy metal. Who cares if it's punk or classical rock? Friends and family will want to select something that reflects the personality and outlook of the deceased. We can celebrate the life of a spouse and father by playing a song like Vince Gill's *The Key To Life*. We can choose more classical pieces such as *Kyrie*

Eleison. Songs like *Mr. Tambourine Man* may have inspired someone who came of age in the sixties so it is important to include these as well. For larger occasions such as a military funeral, songs like *Scottish Soldier* may be appropriate, depending on the ethnic background of the deceased.

The possibilities are endless. This can be both a blessing and a curse. Music is a blessing when it is understood as being a gift. People wanting to sing a song in honour of the deceased may approach us. There may be others who have gone the extra step by actually writing a song themselves. This is an important gesture that can easily be included in the service. My only caution is that some of the wording may not be appropriate so it's best to check out the lyrics and help make suggestions if changes are necessary. We encourage the gift being offered and still offer some thoughts and guidance on the musical selection. If we do not offer guidance we run the risk of experiencing the "curse" part of music in a real hurry.

Some families will request and prepare for a video tribute. This is a time when photos are projected onto a screen at the front of the room or chapel. One or two songs that help establish a certain mood and common theme normally accompany these photos. A song such as Alan Jackson's *Remember When* helps achieve this goal. You may want to encourage the choice of a more edgy song like Nickelback's *Photograph*. Again, a lot depends on the deceased and their taste in music. We should also balance the tastes of the deceased with those gathered for the service. As I write this chapter I'm working with a family who has lost a serious Johnny Cash fan. One of the songs they are including in the service is *Jackson*. Family members have freely admitted to me that they aren't too keen on the song but they are honouring the deceased by having it played during the video tribute. In this case one thing we could offer is a compromise. We can play *Jackson* but we could add music to the service that meets the needs of the people gathered for the service.

Sometimes families turn to us to help them with these suggestions and compromises. This could leave us at a bit of a loss so it's often helpful to have information at our fingertips that could help us at the last minute.

Service leaders who are frequently called upon generate a lot of information and make a number of lists. One of the lists we create and maintain deals with music. We are often asked about appropriate music for services and it is appropriate to consult the lists we keep in our files. With technology changing so rapidly we may be able to access these lists from a phone or a tablet.

I remember the moment I began keeping a list of music. I was asked to officiate at the funeral of a friend. During that service we heard Sarah MacLachlan's *I Will Remember You*. The song left such an impression on me that I went home and wrote it down. It continues to be the first entry in the music list I refer to whenever necessary. And I continue adding to this list. As I've been writing *Dead Reckoning* I've added such songs as Karla Bonoff's *Goodbye My Friend* to the list. Singers such as Linda Ronstadt and John Barrowman have sung incredibly powerful versions of this song and I recommend them whenever I have the opportunity. It's not really a religious song but, like many other pieces it speaks to much of our grief experience.

Other service leaders will include different selections in their lists. These will be very personal resources. Many of our personal choices will be songs we've heard at other funerals or they will be drawn from other places in our lives. We can also invite our friends, parishioners and colleagues to let us know when they've heard music at funerals that they feel we can use in our work. They may attend a service and find a piece of music meaningful and that experience may help our efforts. Friends and family may also have a negative experience with music and we can gain from that as well.[53]

As we build our lists and gather our resources it's important to keep them in a safe place so that they are never lost. Regardless of whether or not they're on memory devices or in "hard copy" format, we may also want to keep copies in a separate location from where we normally work. If something happens to either home or office we may be stuck when we need to find a song or other piece of music for a service.

A recent article on funerals names the following songs as being popular requests at funerals:

> *My Way* (Frank Sinatra)
> *Wonderful World* (Louis Armstrong)
> *Time to Say Goodbye* (Andrea Bocelli and Sarah Brightman)
> *Unforgettable* (Nat King Cole)
> *The Wind Beneath My Wings* (Bette Midler)

The same article[54] also names some unusual selections that may be requested:

> *Ding Dong the Witch is Dead* (From the soundtrack of *The Wizard of Oz*)
> *The Show must Go On* (Queen)
> *Stairway to Heaven* (Led Zeppelin)
> *Highway to Hell* (AC/DC)
> *Another One Bites the Dust* (Queen)
> *I'll Sleep When I'm Dead* (Warren Zevon or Bon Jovi)

Some of these songs may be popular but they may not always be meaningful or well received. Take *My Way*, for example. Many find this song self–centered. Catholic theologian Richard Neuhaus referred to *My Way* as "the ballad of Narcissus".[55] Others, however, will consider it a statement of independence and individuality. This is especially true if we listen to Sid Vicious' rendition of the song.

Music is important for more than just words. In some cultures the tune itself is just as important as the lyrics. This is especially true of music played on particular musical instruments. In Scottish Highland culture, for example, bagpipes are important. Historian Robert Morgan writes of Canada's Cape Breton Island culture, "No wedding or funeral was complete without a Piper."[56] I found this out a number of years ago when

I officiated a funeral where we had to cross a body of water in order to reach the burial site. We crossed the water in a fishing boat and as we made our way, a piper played *Amazing Grace*. I found it to be an incredibly powerful moment. Bagpipe music can be heard in many other places as well. A Scottish friend of mine once observed that there seems to be more bagpipes per capita in North America than in all of Scotland itself.

In some cultures marriage songs are selected for funeral rituals.[57] Marriage songs symbolize the reunification of the deceased with previously departed friends and family. While contemporary mourners may not want wedding songs at the funeral they're planning we may want to encourage the selection of music that address themes such as harmony, reunification, and new beginnings. Angela Sumegi cites the Gurung death ritual as an example. She writes, "(These) rites emphasize death as a moment for reconciliation and harmony."[58]

If families have questions about music they can speak with the funeral home staff or the service leader. Most, if not all funeral homes have somebody available to help the family choose music for the different parts of the service. Some religious organizations try to establish guidelines and set limits on what music can be played at their funeral services. Roman Catholic Archbishop Denis Hart, of Melbourne, Australia, for example, once forbade the playing of football anthems and "popular" songs at funeral mass. He claimed that they "are inappropriate and can even make grief worse." I wonder how he knows that. I'm not aware of any studies that support Bishop Hart's claim. I also wonder if he knows that spiritual songs like "Swing Low Sweet Chariot" are sung at soccer and rugby matches. For Hart, the funeral service was to focus on "the solemn nature of death and is not designed as a celebration of the deceased's life."[59] While this may put him at odds with the wider culture, Archbishop Hart is correct about one thing: Religious groups do have the right to name the ground rules for services in their buildings. If families cannot abide by these rules they can go elsewhere to hold their service. Many do just that.

Many mourners personalize the funeral of a loved one in more ways than simply music. Both religious and nonreligious readings bring comfort to people with words and thoughts listeners have found helpful throughout history. Paul Irion writes, "The rich experience of others who have gone through bereavement and undergone the process of mourning can be shared with the mourners at the funeral."[60] Like music, readings can also help mourners begin the process of putting their thoughts and feelings into words.

When selecting a scripture or poetry reading we can ask a few simple questions: How is this going to sound to the grieving person sitting in the chair or pew? How are they going to respond to and interpret the wording and sentiments that are being communicated? What is the message they are going to perceive? How are these words going to renew their energy and spirits?

Finding a helpful reading can be challenging. A section of scripture, for example, may use words like "death" and seem helpful but don't really work when read in their entirety. As we have previously discussed, John 14 is one such reading. It is about Jesus promising his listeners that he will "prepare a place for them" in his "Father's house" where there are many rooms. While these verses may be comforting they don't really talk about death, loss, and grief as we understand them today.

Another reading is 1 Corinthians 15:55 in which Paul writes, "Oh Death Where is thy victory, Oh Death where is thy sting?" This may be a helpful scripture sentence for chapel or graveside services but the wider section doesn't really work out; especially when we talk about the wages of sin being death. Our listeners will not want to hear anything about that during a service. If you want to preach about the wages of sin being death then save that scripture and sermon topic for a regular Sunday morning service. You'll have more time to work with the theme and a better opportunity to explain your ideas during a more extended sermon time. You'll also have an audience that may be more receptive to what you have to say.

For me, the two Bible readings I use most are Psalm 23 and Ecclesiastes 3:1-8. There are many others used in traditional religious services but I find these two to be the most useful in most situations. These are the two that help cross the bridge between nonreligious and religious. There are a variety of translations you can choose from but I prefer the *New Revised Standard Version*. The language is up to date and reflects continuing efforts to improve on the accuracy of the translations. It's also easier to read out loud in public.

Psalms are also effective in both religious and nonreligious services. Psalms are ancient songs and poems that help listeners understand and cope with the problems, issues, challenges, and questions that fill their lives. The Rev. Dr. William McCullough once wrote, "The Psalms ... abound in human despair and unanswered questions."[61] It can be said that the Psalms are both religious and spiritual documents that can be listened to and relied upon by an extremely wide group of listeners. Personally, I like their clarity, intensity and focused way of sending a message. Perhaps this is why they've been so effective in so many pastoral situations throughout the centuries.

As I have already indicated, another helpful and familiar reading is Ecclesiastes 3:1-8. I find the reading from Ecclesiastes helpful in times of extreme conflict and stress. There can be conflict in almost any situation and it's important to be aware of where this occurs in each and every instance. Conflicts can vary in their intensity. Some conflicts are fairly low key and can be sorted out over coffee. Other conflicts can cause rifts between people that will never be repaired. Conflicts can be internal as well. Gardner Murphy once wrote, "We are all at war with ourselves."[62] We can push this thought one step further by suggesting that we are often "at war" with others as well. We can turn to this reading as a way of comforting people with the message that we can all find a place where we can end this way and find peace.

Like the Psalms, Ecclesiastes is one of those in–between readings that is helpful in both religious and non–religious contexts. I've met with families who have been extremely honest about challenges and difficulties they have had with the deceased. There are cases in which few people have anything positive to say about the person. One advantage the Ecclesiastes reading has is that it ends with a simple phrase: "There is a time for peace".

This covers a lot of ground and is an important point for families wondering how they can remember a person for whom they have little, if any positive regard. We can find a way to assure them that their loved one is at peace. We can remind them that the deceased person's work is complete and that their race is done. These are helpful thoughts in situations where there have been strained and difficult connections between people.

Looking beyond the Psalms and Ecclesiastes, another reading that may be helpful is one that is also used in weddings. It's 1 Corinthians 13:1-11. The important line in this reading is the one that says, "Love never ends." God's love never ends for either the deceased or the mourners. God's love is big enough to embrace each and every one of us. The love we have for someone doesn't stop when that person dies. The love we have for others continues long after they're gone. Charles Taylor writes, "Though loved ones move in and out of our lives, the capacity to love remains."[63]

Regardless of how comforting a reading may be, not everybody wants to hear solely from the Bible at the funeral. It's often appropriate to hear from other sources of inspiration and insight. Nonreligious readings can be included in almost every type of funeral. A.E. Harvey writes, "In a typical funeral held in church, a scripture reading may be supplemented, or even replaced, by texts which have caught the popular imagination as more credible and reassuring statements about life after death than anything in the Bible ..."[64] While there may be some "crossover pieces" that can work in different types of services it can be tricky to use scripture where religious content isn't really welcome. This is where poetry and other inspirational readings become important. Philip Levine stresses the importance of poetry when reviewing a person's life when he writes, "The experience of any human being is worthy of poetry."[65]

For me poetry is the language of ritual. Clergy constantly rely on poetry to capture the intensity of an occasion. More traditional preachers often suggest that sermons are built around three points and a poem. Perhaps we can suggest here that each and every service needs to include poetry. Whether it's a piece that's quoted in a Sunday sermon or something read at a time of transition clergy have often written their own material for many occasions. Robert Herrick is one example of a clergyperson who wrote poetry. While much of his work has been described as being "cheery" he did write poems that can be included in funerals. Perhaps the most memorable of his lines is "Gather Ye Rosebuds while ye may,/Old Time is still a flying:/And this same flower that smiles to day,/To morrow will be dying."[66]

Writer Jorge Luis Borges once told an interviewer, "Poetry springs from somewhere deeper; it's beyond intelligence. It may not even be linked with wisdom. It's a thing of its own; it has a nature of its own."[67] Perhaps poetry is effective because it springs from the soul and reflects the intensity of our emotional experience. It may also connect us with the deeper realities of life and our world. This is one of the reasons why Japanese Zen Buddhists experiencing the dying process are encouraged to write poems.[68] These poems capture the thoughts of the dying and leave a record of how they understand what is happening to them. This is part of how poetry works; it expresses something that we cannot put into mere words. There is a power that is beyond words. One poet wrote that the key to poetry is "in the space between the words."[69]

One of these deeper realities is the movement of time and how we change as history unfolds. Writers can sometimes capture what is happening as we pass through the different points on our life cycles. Northrop Frye once wrote, "The sequence of seasons, times of day, periods of life and death, have helped to provide for literature the combination of movement and order, of change and regularity, that is needed in all the arts."[70] This is why poets such as Horace[71] are frequently included in funerals.

There are a number of poems that are appropriate in a situation in which families request little, if any religion. The intensity mentioned earlier can be seen in a poem such as W.H. Auden's *Funeral Blues*. Auden tells us to do things like "stop" and "silence". He orders the dogs to stop barking and concludes by saying that "nothing now can come to any good." Auden says these things in a way we can identify with. Our world stops and changes as we come to grips with loss. We want everything to be silent while we struggle with what's happening in our personal worlds. Why do people go to work when someone we love dies? Why aren't we reading about this death in the newspaper or hearing about it on television? These words and ideas capture some of the intensity we go through when we lose someone close. We can almost feel the intensity coming off the page and this could be something we would like to accomplish when leading a funeral service.

Poems can also capture the need to express our thoughts and feelings and share any emotions we're experiencing. I officiated a service for a young woman whose parents enjoyed reading William Blake's poetry so I read one of his so–called "Notebook Poems".[72] The one I chose began with the words "Never pain to tell thy love" and includes mention of a "traveler" who arrives when the loved one departs. It's a poem that is both easily understood and helpful when preparing a funeral message. Here are a few other possibilities:

> "From too much love of living
> From hope and fear set free
> We thank with brief thanksgiving
> Whatever gods may be
> That no life lives forever;
> That dead men rise up never;
> That even the weariest river
> Winds somewhere safe to sea."
> **Algeron Charles Swinburne, "Collected Works"**

> "For this is wisdom – to love and live,
> To take what fate or the gods may give,
> To ask no question, to make no prayer,
> To kiss the lips and caress the hair,
> Speed passion's ebb as we greet its flow,
> To have and to hold, and, in time — let go."

F. Scott Fitzgerald, quoting Ella Wheeler Wilcox, in "This Side Paradise", p. 194

Achievements
"To have lived well,
Laughed often and loved much;
To have gained the respect of intelligent men
And the love of children;
To have filled a niche
And accomplished a task;
To have left the world better —
Whether by an improved poppy,
A perfect poem or a rescued soul;
To have appreciated earth's beauty
And not failed to express it;
To have looked fro the best in others,
And to have given the best of yourself.
That is achievement."
Robert Louis Stevenson.

Emmerson writes a version of the above poem but I prefer to use Stevenson's wording.

Sunset and evening star,
And one clear call for me!
And may there be no moaning of the bar,
When I put out to sea,
But such a tide as moving seems asleep,
Too full for sound and foam,
When that which drew from out of the boundless deep
Turns again home.

Twilight and evening bell,
And after that the dark!

And may there be no sadness of farewell,

When I embark;

For tho' from out our bourne of Time and Place

The flood may bear me far,

I hope to see my pilot face to face

When I have crossed the bar.

Alfred, Lord Tennyson

Tennyson's poem is helpful as it uses words that reinforce the notion that in death we can pass through the gateway from one reality to another.

Not all literature is created equal, however. There is a difference between what we read in a classic novel and what we encounter online. We have to choose what we read carefully. We can ask the family what was meaningful to the deceased. We can try to find something that responds to their wishes. The storytelling that happens during the preparation time will help with this selection. When it comes to choosing readings for services we can ask ourselves one question while meeting with the family and friends of the deceased: As we heard about the life of the deceased which Bible stories or poems come to mind? So often we find ourselves relying on such a small group of poems and scripture readings that we lose touch with other, perhaps more appropriate portions of the Bible. Regardless of what we select and agree to, in each and every service the poem and its message have to come across as being genuine. They shouldn't be "gushy", or "sappy". A funeral director and I were talking about these poems and how tough they were to read when I told him that I want the following "Haiku" that I wrote to be read at my funeral:

I'm dead.

I'm in the box.

Deal with it.

We cannot use poetry to help deny the reality of loss and death. We cannot help people avoid their feelings. That's not what poetry is for. Literary critic Douglas Bush once wrote, "The poet's business is not to 'rhyme the stars and walk apart' but to grapple with life."[73] Some poets accomplish this more effectively than others. One poem that denies the reality of death is *I Did Not Die*. I dislike using this poem for obvious reasons. We cannot claim that the deceased did not die when evidence to the contrary is all around us, especially when there is a casket or urn sitting at the front of the church or chapel. All that this poem does is help people dwell in their denial and resist reality. Death is real and we should not be reading anything that tries to convince us otherwise. I use the word "should" intentionally here. We may have strong feelings about a poem but families may have even stronger feelings about that same poem. As difficult as it can be, this is one of those times when we should concede the point to the family.

One way we can meet the family halfway is to use any part of the poem they request. It isn't always necessary to read the entire piece. It may be appropriate to simply read three or four lines that get to the point. At Gonzo journalist Hunter Thompson's memorial service the following section was read from Samuel Taylor Coleridge's *Kubla Khan*:

> Weave a circle round him thrice
> And close your eyes with holy dread.
> For he on honey–dew hath fed
> And drunk the milk of paradise.[74]

These older poems can be tough to read publicly. For me it's often difficult to pronounce many of the old words and names. People constantly tell me that I am not alone. One thing to keep in mind when speaking with people asked to read something is pronunciation. Not everybody is familiar with many of the names, words, and place names they encounter in the poems and sacred texts they are being asked to read. I attended a funeral in which the widower was asked to read from the Old Testament. In the stress of the occasion he completely mangled the name of the religious book from which he was reading. That threw him off for the rest of the reading and it took something away from the reading itself.

Always ask readers about names and words they are unfamiliar with. We can also encourage them to simply do their best with those words and carry on as best they are able. One thing I tell people is that if they don't know how to pronounce a name or big word then odds are nobody else does either. It's sometimes best to give it your best shot and just keep going. People rarely challenge the reader on words they may have mispronounced during the service. I've never had anybody stand up in the middle of a reading and say to a speaker: "You said that wrong!" It's not a competition in which people keep score. The important thing is that the reader did their best with what they were asked to read.

Every once in a while someone who has written a poem for the funeral will approach us. When we hear these requests to read an original poem, we should remember the words of Oscar Wilde, who once wrote, "All bad poetry springs from genuine feeling."[75] The contents of the poem may be from the heart but it doesn't always sound good when read in public. It's almost impossible to say "no" to a gift like this. We can suggest alternatives, however. People can be encouraged to either place their poetry in the casket or have it cremated with the deceased.

Prayers, music and literature often capture the inner workings of our minds and spirits. This is often the material that helps us relate to the divine around us. This is also what gives our ritual depth and power and beauty. It may also help us prepare to hear the story of the deceased and understand their contribution in a new way.

Phase Four: Education — Eulogies and Tributes

When I was serving as a congregational minister I always entered the names of the deceased in a church register. This is a book of both legal and historic value. It not only contains the names of the deceased, it also captures any other information church officials or vital statistics people find helpful. This information is also critical to historians researching the history of a particular region or time period, but regardless of the peripheral information, these individuals remain simply a name. They're letters on a page and that's about it. We don't know what they looked or sounded like. We don't know what they enjoyed or what others thought of them. What have no idea what angered them. Joyce Youings notes this reality in her historical survey of sixteenth–century England. She writes, "(I)n parish registers people simply have a name: they are neither rich nor poor, neither master nor servant, neither saint nor sinner ..."[1]

When I would record these names I would think of each individual and try to remember the stories and memories I heard at their funeral. I would also remember the photographs I'd seen and the laughter and tears that were offered. The sad thing is that there isn't any room in these registers for stories and other special thoughts and words. There's no room for the kind of history our society needs to build strong roots. I've always wondered what it would be like to attach a copy of a person's eulogy to each entry in the church register. It would probably take up too much space but it would help record the three dimensions of a person's life for future generations. Perhaps the most important way of capturing these three dimensions is the eulogy.

For me, one of the most creative and powerful eulogies I've ever heard of was delivered centuries ago. Attila the Hun died in the year 453 C.E. He was one of those larger than life historical figures who dominated a large area of the known world in his time. When it came time for his funeral a very interesting thing happened. Prior to the secret burial of his body, horsemen from his tribe entered the ritual space, rode in circles around his body, and told stories of his exploits. These memories and stories reflected the varied emotions they were feeling. They captured and celebrated what he had accomplished. They told stories reflecting how Attila touched each and every one of their lives.[2] This was an extremely creative and highly intense way of delivering a eulogy. William Shakespeare once wrote, "For God's sake, let us sit upon the ground and tell sad stories of the death of kings."[3] This is exactly what Attila's followers did.

While I am not recommending the horse riding thing for contemporary funerals it is storytelling like this that keeps a person's memory alive, if only for a short while. Shakespeare stated, "There's hope a great man's memory may outlive his life half a year." It seems a natural part of our being to want our memory to live on well after we've gone. We want to be remembered and not disappear completely. Warren Zevon captured this notion well in his song entitled *Keep Me In Your Heart for A While*. We want people to remember us beyond the point of our deaths and find some example and inspiration in our lives. Eulogies are perhaps the best way to begin this work of remembering a person whose "deeds exceed all speech", to quote yet another term from Shakespeare.[4] This chapter is about putting deeds into words. Perhaps this is one of the best ways for any one of us to be remembered. Oliver Sacks writes, "If we wish to know about a man (sic), we ask 'what is his story — his real, inmost story?' — for each of us is a biography, a story."[5] It's because of our individual stories we can be considered "unique".[6] Attila was certainly unique and was remembered in what his followers considered the appropriate way.

We are a storytelling people and brief narratives about an individual and their contributions to the lives of people around them can help make a funeral meaningful. There are many reasons for this. Since the earliest campfires, stories have helped us learn more about the world and people around us. Stories have entertained and educated people of many generations. They have told us about the universe that enfolds our tiny planet. They've helped us keep up with the news and gossip of what's going on in our families and communities. Stories have offered history and insight that help give listeners a sense of place and identity. Carmine Gallo, a public–speaking consultant I mentioned earlier, tells us that "Researchers have discovered that our brains are more active when we hear stories."[7] When we hear stories we ask questions and search for answers and meaning. We also learn about our place in both family and wider community. Christian Smith writes, "… we not only continue to be animals who make stories but also animals who are made by our stories."[8] Smith also writes, "(Stories) convey significant points. They are designed to draw the audience to an explanation, a revelation, and understanding or an insight about life and the world."[9]

Sometimes we don't realize the effect a person has had on their family and community until someone speaks about their time among us. We can't all be one of the "big personalities" historians write about. We're not generals and politicians. We're not scientists who win Nobel Prizes and cure diseases. But so what? Sometimes it's the small gestures that make the biggest differences. A small bug can cause a serious itch and significant movement. But we don't always know when these small events in our lives make a difference. Karl Marx once wrote, "Men (sic) make their own history, but they do not know they are making it."[10]

Whether it's big moves or small contributions eulogies explain and share this important history. They also enlighten and inspire and move us. Vladimir Lenin's widow Krupskaya offered three sentences in her eulogy at his funeral that summarizes how eulogies work. Her first sentence was, "I have been in my mind over the whole of his life, and this is what I want to say to you." Here she refers to a process through which she reviewed their time together and developed a series of things she wanted to talk about. She then said, "He loved with a deep love all of the workers, all of the oppressed." In other words, she identified the people he cared for and in doing so identified some of his deepest commitments and priorities. Finally she said, "I should probably never have spoken about it at any less solemn moment."[11] This is what a eulogy is: a gathering of information about the deceased, a statement of what they believed in and who they cared for and a brief note about the need to say these important things during a ritual such as a funeral. This chapter will take each of these three elements and examine them further. I will also discuss the overall importance of having eulogies and tributes in the first place.

While some religious traditions may frown upon the inclusion of eulogies and storytelling in funeral services, I will argue that they deserve a continuing place within the ritual itself. Check out some of the five million hits you get when Googling "Eulogy" and you'll quickly find out how true this is. Stories help us validate the life of the deceased and acknowledge the pain felt by the grieving survivors. These are pastoral realities the church cannot ignore or push to the sidelines. Life is a gift from God and we should talk about how each and every person uses that gift. How a person uses their gift can give us some insight into the potential we have. We're offered a chance to figure out what we can do and where we can go. Stories offer us a lot to think about.

Jesus, himself, preached by telling open–ended stories that challenged his listeners to think for themselves. He turned their thinking and belief systems upside down and helped them relate to their world in a new way. He spoke at their level of understanding so that they would understand the point he was trying to make. "Understanding" is an important word here. Talking about the deceased and sharing episodes from his or her life helps us understand their values, commitments and priorities. They help us understand why they approached life the way they did. Smith writes, "In order to construct a narrative, the storyteller selects specific events from the past that serve as the vehicles of commentary and meaning making."[12]

Stories and eulogies are something we can all offer. The people in our lives are more than mere names so everyone deserves a tribute of some sort at their funeral service. As we said at the beginning of the book, offering words of remembrance and appreciation are not just for professionals. The Huns described near the beginning of this chapter were neither trained writers nor professional orators. They knew their deceased friend in a direct and intimate way. They spoke from both memory and the heart. In other cultures the storytelling moves beyond words and includes music and dance. While we can all tell stories, however, it becomes increasingly difficult to do it in a public context. The experience of death and the anxiety about public speaking can be an intense combination. Not everyone can find their way around and through these extremes.

Perhaps it's for this reason that many of these cultures seem leery of allowing friends and family members to speak at a funeral. Historically, early eulogists were often paid professionals.[13] A story is told of a south sea island that was visited by a very important person. To celebrate this visit a huge banquet was held in honour of the visitor. At one point in the feasting a professional orator stepped forward and began praising the guest. He was filled with praise of how the visitor had graced their presence and brought many blessings upon them. When the speaker had finished the guest stood to respond. The chief held him back saying, "You will have an orator speak for you as well. On this island we have professionals speak on formal occasions. Speaking like this is not for amateurs."[14] This thinking has certainly changed in our present day. While extremely intense and potentially quite difficult, eulogies are for everyone who feels able and that's what gives them authority and power.

Most of us can experience a lot of things and meet some extremely interesting people in the years we've been given. It doesn't really matter how many years of life we accumulate, however. While too many lives are cut short there is still time to affect the lives of people around us. Infants fill their parent's lives with love, affection, hope, and promise. Young people and adults experience love and growing independence and accomplishment. Each and every happening and encounter has a story. As difficult as it may seem, finding the most important story is the key to a meaningful eulogy. And finding the most helpful words with which to tell this story is equally meaningful.

Writers such as Malcolm Gladwell constantly remind us of this when they suggest that each and every individual has a story.[15] One thing they tell us is that it's sometimes the most short and simple stories that are the most informing and meaningful. In fact, Gladwell has developed a career out of finding neat and underrated stories and sharing them with his wide circle of readers. The challenge with writing a eulogy or tribute is that the person at the centre of the story is no longer with us. They're not around to tell us what to say. They're not here to tell us which of their experiences were the most important for them. So the eulogist faces an uphill battle when trying to capture the life of a friend, colleague, or loved one. This can be tricky. Who is going to tell the story of the deceased now that the deceased has gone? Who is going to review the life of a friend, colleague and loved one? Who is going to tell us that the deceased was important and meant something in the grand scheme of things?

To be perfectly blunt, somebody has to do it. Somebody has to speak for the deceased. We all have a right to have our story told. Without this story being told the silence descends all too quickly on what we have done to contribute to our world. The eulogist has to find a way to reach into the past and bring out the essence of the person being remembered. We do not always know how to do this. We live in a society that obsesses about the present and future. Nathaniel Hawthorne once wrote, "The present is burthened too much with the past."[16] While this represents the thinking of many people it's not quite true here. We know precious little about history and what has happened in the past and that has harmed our life and work here in the present. History gives us roots and provides perspective.

Funerals remind us that the past is important. They help us make the shift from obsessing about the present and future to offering some respect for those who have preceded us. We're looking back and remembering someone's time among us. Once again, Shakespeare wrote something that is applicable to our work here. He said, "There is a history in all men's lives."[17] Genealogists have been putting this on t-shirts for years and it's also an important statement supporting our work of leading funeral services. When we turn our attention to the past we get some sense of how a person lived and how they related to the people around them. We're able to see their life from a new angle. We are able to draw conclusions about a person's life based on what they said and did and how they lived their lives. An ancient Greek philosopher was once quoted as saying, "Until he is dead, no man (sic) can be called happy — only lucky."[18] Funerals and eulogies give us that chance to confirm a person's happiness and so much more.

While the likes of Woody Allen may dismiss a lack of attention to the past as being "denial"[19] there are times when it offers inspiration and hope. A review of someone's life and contribution is one of the things that give the funeral depth. I once asked a funeral director the most important quality they look for in a funeral celebrant. She thought for a moment and said that she valued someone who could meet with the family and prepare a highly personalized service that could incorporate as many of the family's wishes as possible. The development of a highly personalized service is an important consideration when reflecting on the importance of the funeral. It's also a critical dimension of any eulogy or tribute. We are telling the story of a person's life among us. We're helping people confront a variety of questions about the story and life of the deceased. How did they contribute? How were they unique?

Perhaps we can also add a couple of other questions. What have we learned from the deceased? What else can we hear about them? In 2009 a so–called spiritual medium by the name of James Van Praagh wrote a book entitled *Unfinished Business*.[20] The subtitle of this book is "What the Dead Can Teach Us About Life". In this book, Van Praagh talks about reaching through the wall between worlds and pulling lessons through from the other side.[21] Eulogies help us reach through the wall. Some traditions call this a thin space between heaven and earth.[22] We do this when we examine the life of the deceased and build a story around their time among us. Through our words we try and share the deceased's final message and legacy to our listeners.

We don't need psychics or mediums to do our work, however. When I learn lessons from people's lives I do so by hearing about their lives on this side of the curtain. This is enough information for our work. While our methods will differ from Van Praagh's we are asking the same question each and every time we prepare for and lead a service. What can the life experiences of the deceased tell us about our own lives? Through observation we can learn what to do and what not to do in our own lives.

Learning what not to do is an important point here. James Baldwin once attended a funeral and came to the conclusion that "Every man in the chapel hoped that when his hour came he, too, would be eulogized, which is to say forgiven, and that all his lapses, greeds (sic), errors, strayings from the truth would be invested with coherence and looked upon with charity."[23] Perhaps stories are the most important when they help us change the course of our own lives.

In talking about a person's past, especially of someone who has died, we essentially speak for them. They no longer have a voice. We are asked to become advocates. A number of years ago I read a science fiction novel entitled *Speaker for the Dead*. Written by Orson Scott Card, *Speaker* is about a young man wandering the known universe speaking at people's funerals. His speaking was different than anything we offer or hear in most of today's services. The book came about as the result of Card's experiences with funerals and how they edit and change the life stories of the deceased. Card writes, "we erase (the deceased), we edit them, we make them into a person much easier to live with than the person who actually lived."[24] Card goes on to say, "I thought that a more appropriate funeral would be to say, honestly, what a person was and what that person did."[25]

At one point in *Speaker*, Card writes, "... serving as a priest to people who acknowledge no god and yet believed in the value of the lives of human beings. Speakers whose business it was to discover the true causes and motives of the things that people did, and declare the truth of their lives after they were dead."[26] This is not a new concept as Voltaire once said, perhaps a little harshly, "One owes respect to the living: To the Dead one owes only the truth."[27] Lives have value and it's critical we speak about them as honestly as we can.

When we prepare a eulogy or message we have a responsibility to be as accurate about the life of the deceased as possible. To borrow from the terminology of Orson Scott Card, we have to "get it right."[28] One example stands out for me where people offering eulogies at one particular funeral did not "get it right". Pat Tillman was a professional football player who was at the top of his game prior to the earth shattering events of September 11th, 2001. As a result of 9/11 Tillman turned his back on a lucrative athletic career and joined the United States Army and was eventually deployed to Afghanistan where he was killed by friendly fire. At his funeral dignitaries such as John McCain and Maria Shriver offered their tributes to Tillman's sacrifice. They made religious references and referred to Tillman's reunion with loved ones who had previously died. They talked about Tillman being in a "better place". In response to these statements Tillman's brother countered these sentiments by saying things like "He wasn't religious and is not with God." Richard Tillman summed up his thoughts by saying, "He's (Expletive) dead."[29] This is a blunt and necessary repudiation of what was said at the funeral. It's also about a "blunt and necessary" lesson to those of us leading and speaking in services. We have to clear away the BS.

One of the things we have to clear away is this notion that when people die they go to a "better place". When we say that a person has "gone to a better place" we call into question their lives on earth. We tell their surviving friends and family that the deceased is somehow better off without them. Survivors may be left wondering what's wrong with them. Instead of claiming that the deceased is now better off without the people they left behind I say that they are with God and waiting for us to join them. Or better yet, we can simply say once again that "They are now at peace".

Given the importance of speaking about a person's life I continue to be surprised that many religious organizations frown upon the use of eulogies in their services. The Roman Catholic Church, for example, says that "there is never to be a eulogy" in the funeral mass.[30] Eulogies are often relegated to the times when friends and family "visit" or "view" the body prior to the funeral.[31] I've also seen eulogies offered at the conclusion of the funeral mass.

There are many other Christian communities that would agree with this thinking. Those of us who live in Canada witnessed an example of this at the state funeral for the Honourable Jim Flaherty on April 16th, 2014.[32] It was a service based on the liturgy of the Anglican Church of Canada. The tributes were offered prior to the beginning of the religious service. Thomas Long summarizes these religious reasoning behind this separation of tribute and worship when he writes, "preach the gospel, and don't preach the life of the deceased."[33] This may sound principled but it is more than a little harsh and may not be helpful for families seeking a more personalized service. Fragmented rituals are rarely if ever effective. At the very least they're pastorally problematic. We cannot separate the life and faith of the deceased. They have to be brought together and celebrated as a whole. Why not talk about the life of the deceased at their funeral? According to the Christian tradition we are all creations of God and should therefore be shown that respect when we're remembered after we die. Perhaps this is why so many people are turning away from the church during critical transition moments.

In this vein, Edward Searl has created a personal and unique type of "human–centered services"[34] where "The eulogy is the focal point of a funeral or memorial service."[35] The church can both learn and relearn from this approach. Given a choice between the two positions I always err on the side of telling the story of the deceased. I will always choose to celebrate a life within the act of worship itself. To me, this is what forms the core of effective worship and storytelling. This is one of the main reasons why people show up at the funeral in the first place and why I usually introduce the eulogy with the following words:

> "William Shakespeare once told us to "Give sorrow words, the grief that does not speak knits the overwrought heart and bids it break". We are here to give sorrow words. We are here to tell stories and offer some testimony to the life that —— has shared with us.

With this in mind I would like to invite —— to come forward and share with us some words about their Grandfather's life. "

This Shakespeare quote may make us sound pretentious but there is a valid reason why we can include this line in our service materials. While Shakespeare's writing may sound strange to our contemporary ears he is a grounded and sensible writer with a decent insight into human nature. This Shakespeare quote in particular helps establish what we are trying to accomplish during the tribute time. Christian Riegel writes, "For grieving to be effective, the emotions of loss must be translated into words and must be articulated."[36] So we give sorrow words and pray that they touch people in a new and profound way.

While words and wording are important there are a few more things we can keep in mind when moving into the educational phase of the funeral. They may seem like mere loose ends but they are still important. On a practical note, I would urge you to use both names when inviting the eulogist to come forward. I was officiating a service with a large number of listeners gathered to honour the deceased and support his surviving friends, colleagues, and family members. When I invited the eulogist to come forward I only used her first name. Judging by the look on a number of faces I could tell that there was more than one person sharing that particular name. To minimize confusion, we should probably use the full name of the person offering the eulogy or tribute. We should also meet them face–to–face prior to the service so that we are able recognize them in the congregation and make eye contact with them when we reach the time for their contribution to the service.

When we meet the eulogists we can take the opportunity to invite them to word things in a way that is both genuine and caring. They should talk the way they would in everyday conversations. They can also quote the deceased whenever possible. As most literary critics will tell us, there are many different ways of telling a story. Writers have used many different styles over the years and perhaps the two most common styles are novels and short stories. V.S. Pritchett describes the difference between the two styles by writing, "The novel tends to tell us everything whereas the short story tells us only one thing, and that, intensely."[37] We cannot tell the entire story of the deceased within the time limits of the service. This would take too long. We have to find a way to focus on the important things we want people to know about the person whom we have lost. We cannot lose our main point among the huge number of details in a person's life. This takes a lot of work but it's ultimately worth it.

People may find the act of gathering information for the eulogy difficult. Historian John Lukacs once wrote, "The past is very large, and it gets larger every minute: We do not and cannot know all of it."[38] It doesn't have to be that difficult and intimidating, however. The person asked to write and offer a eulogy becomes, almost by default, an amateur historian. They also assume the role of storyteller or bard. David Finch once wrote, "Great stories help us understand our world and expose us to different points of view."[39] In her book, *Kitchen Table Wisdom*, Rachel Remen writes, "Stories allow us to see the familiar through new eyes."[40] This is an important goal whenever we prepare a service and help someone write a eulogy. The eulogist has the opportunity to give us some idea of the deceased's point of view and also some perspective on their life among family and friends.

Historically, addresses such as eulogies served a couple of different functions. In the early church Saints were remembered with works that listed their virtues and miracles. Stories were told of how their holy lives contributed to the life and growth of the church. Some of these tales got a little far–fetched but the speakers and church leaders were trying to make a fairly large point with these speeches. They were trying to communicate God's power and ability to reach into people's lives to affect great things. Some of these addresses were a little extreme and have come to be called "sacred fictions".[41] This extreme approach to recounting a life has evolved.

One of the things people tell me is that they want to stress the humanity of the deceased. They don't want them turned into a "saint". This is based on the above notion that sainthood is something that sets us apart from the average person. We've come to think of saints as being perfect people or those who have everything figured out. This certainly isn't the case. Perhaps we've misunderstood the meaning of the word "saint". For me one of the most realistic definitions of the word "saint" is offered by human rights activist Aung San Suu Kyi. She writes, "Saints ... are the sinners who keep on trying."[42] To call someone a saint is to say that they're a human being who has cared, responded and served. This is probably how most of us would like to be remembered.

Today a eulogy is to leave friends and family with a better sense of who the person was and what they meant to the people around them. Again, this is not something that we're used to doing. We do not always know where to begin. When I meet with families I'm usually asked what a person says in a eulogy. Robert Gerwarth suggests that telling a person's story consists of information described as being both "autopsy" and "portrait".[43] When it comes to funerals I prefer obituary and narrative. We can include information that is normally included in the obituary announcement that can be published in newspapers or on the Internet. This is what I call the "nuts and bolts" of a person's life. This obituary–type contribution includes things like where the person was born, had lived and worked, any appropriate family details, etc.. This is the best place to name names and offer thank significant people.

The second type of information is narrative. This is where we can revisit the image of horses riding in circles while their riders speak of the deceased. The eulogist can tell a story drawn from the deceased's life. This story can give listeners more insight into the person's life. The stories don't need to be original. Many stories are timeless. In services like this people can hear the same stories over and over again and listeners who knew the deceased rarely grow tired of them. The American author, bell hooks, once wrote, "Hearing the same story makes it impossible to forget".[44] We would like to ensure that the deceased is "impossible to forget".

So how do we write something that is "unforgettable"? How do we draw that picture in a person's mind that will remain for an extended period of time? When writing a eulogy we can borrow an idea from Elizabethan era scholars teaching their students how to develop an argument. They taught their students to begin by drawing a line and placing pieces of their argument along that line. As they assembled and sorted these pieces a final shape would come together and they could proceed from there.[45] When we assemble the story of a person's life we can do the same thing. We can draw this line and place any collected stories and pieces of information along it. We do not always have to organize our stories chronologically along this line. We can organize our stories according to theme, relationship, geographical location or almost any other pattern we feel is appropriate.

As we collect and organize the stories from a person's life there are some things we should be careful about. Perhaps one of the things that should remain private in some cases is the actual cause of death. While it may be helpful information for the preparation phase of the funeral it is not necessarily public information to be dealt with during the service itself. While ancient eulogies frequently contained this information it may not be something listeners are comfortable with today.[46] In a recent service I was asked whether or not mention should be made of the deceased's alcoholism. After discussing the matter with the family it was decided that it would be best to remain silent on the topic. While there is no right or wrong answer to this dilemma, granting surviving family and friends some control in this instance can be comforting. A public ceremony is no place to air dirty laundry or settle scores. It's not a place to tell people what they should do with their lives. People can draw their own conclusions from what's been said.

The eulogy may also be a time to refrain from inside jokes that few beyond the deceased's inner circle would understand. Humour only works when people make the necessary connections and understand our references. I dealt with one family in which the deceased's son–in–law had a nickname for her. He called her the "L'il Bitch". She knew he called her that and it was a shared nickname within a small, more intimate group of family and friends. They told me that I could mention this nickname in the service and I told them that I wasn't sure it would be appropriate as many of the people attending the service didn't know about the nickname and probably wouldn't see the humour or meaning in it. Looking back, I'm not sure that was the appropriate advice but it made sense at the time. It's important to remember that what makes sense at a given point in time could be remembered as a tremendous mistake when seen in hindsight. Perhaps it's always best to err on the side of discretion and silence.

In trying to communicate the most humane and compassionate eulogy we have to keep in mind that it's both a written and spoken piece of work. The actual writing of the eulogy should take a lot of care and attention. We have to be careful how it sounds when read aloud. We may want to invite a second set of eyes and ears to review our material and make suggestions whenever necessary. When describing the process of writing the eulogy for his aunt's funeral, Endre Farkas recalled, "I crafted sentiments, choosing words for their meaning, their sounds, their rhythms." He goes on to add, "I aimed for a striking opening image, good transitions, a moment of levity and a tearjerker ending."[47] In order to do this effectively the eulogist may want to go through several rewrites and rehearsals.

A eulogist may be wondering what type of style they should use when writing the eulogy. We can write it as a series of episodes and stories. We can also write it in the form of a letter. I've made this suggestion numerous times to families having difficulties finding things to say about their deceased loved ones. One way to help people think about what should be in the letter is to ask what people would want to say to the deceased if they were present and standing in front of everybody. Dorothy Lander and John Graham–Pole have coined the term "Love Letters to the Dead".[48]

Letters aren't the only way to address our words to the deceased. In Japanese funerals the tribute is called a "Chouji" and is directed at the deceased in the presence of the mourners. The family of the deceased can arrange for someone to make this address and they can allow people from the congregation to offer their more personal goodbyes. These farewells can be both spoken and sung. They may take a variety of forms. People take this opportunity to say things that have previously been left unsaid.

They can also express feelings and emotions that may or may not be known to the deceased. They take this opportunity to deal with unfinished business.[49]

Tributes don't always have to be in spoken words either. Betty Jane Wylie tells the story of one funeral she attended where people offered a dance in tribute of their departed friend.[50] Historically music and dance have been inseparable when it comes to rituals like funerals. It can be one of the key elements to a deep and meaningful celebration of someone's life. Margaret Laurence once wrote, "Life is for rejoicing — for dancing."[51] We can celebrate someone's life by dancing in a way that captures part of a person's gift and legacy. Nicholas Wade writes, "Because music and dance are inseparable in primitive cultures, it seems likely they coevolved, soon being joined by the first forms of religious behavior."[52] When it comes to music and dance Nicholas Wade observes that many languages use the same word for both.[53] Creative dance is an interesting and visual way of expressing emotions that cannot be put into words. Almost any type of music or costumes can accompany a dance tribute. It can be an extremely personal moment.

Another form of eulogy or tribute is the so–called "open mic". This is an unplanned time when people come forward and share thoughts and memories about the deceased. It's random and often unscripted. On rare occasions "open mics" can be appropriate in situations where there are small groups of people expected at the funeral. They can also be appropriate in those situations where there is some confidence that there will be no disclosures that will shock or embarrass the family.

There are some real challenges with open mic opportunities, however. For one thing, there are times when stories are told in which the content shocks or embarrasses the family. Speakers will also arrive at the front of the service space and promptly forget what they would like to say. In moments of panic they can spit out almost anything. They could accomplish the same thing if they were angry at something the deceased had either said or done to them while they were alive. This can lead to some intense moments — especially if the person in question is inebriated. While

I was writing this chapter I led a service in which the family said they were OK with an open mic segment. When I invited people to come up and say a few words, the first one was an individual who staggered towards the front demanding a chance to speak. When he stood behind the mic he leaned in and promptly froze. After a few tense moments he stood up straight and started beating himself on the chest repeating, "I love you guys" over and over. Finally he stopped and shook his head. "That's all I got," he said and plunked himself down among the immediate family in the front row. I was glad he stepped down voluntarily. While potentially therapeutic for the service leader, pummeling a drunken eulogist at the front of the church or chapel often adds little value to the funeral itself.

As we have been discussing, funerals are incredibly intense times and this pressure may affect a person's memory when it comes time for them to speak. There's nothing more uncomfortable than that silence when people realize that the speaker has forgotten what he or she had intended on saying. The finally challenge has to do with names. The service leader simply cannot know each and every person attending the funeral. What usually winds up happening is the service leader points to a person and says something like, "You're next." This may not be the most dignified way to proceed at this particular point of the funeral.

Based on the above information I make the following three suggestions whenever I discuss a possible open mic segment with the family:

1. Speakers should write down what they have to say. This ensures that they share only what they want and it reduces the risk of the person forgetting what they want to say. As I mentioned earlier, there is nothing more uncomfortable then that awkward silence that develops when a speaker forgets what he or she hoped to say. There are ways to minimize this awkward moment. One pastor lets people know that the open mic is coming up at a later part of the

143

service and that people who may want to say
something should be ready to step up and share
whatever it is they feel called to say. It's important
not to wait around. If people aren't moving forward
then we have to move on to the next part of the
service.

2. Close friends and family should have some idea of
what a speaker is going to say. It's not that they
should have a chance to censor the tribute but they
have a right to some peace of mind that they will not
be surprised or embarrassed by what is said. The
eulogist needs to be reminded, for example, that
stories told in personal conversations are not always
the same type of stories that can be shared at a larger
and more public gathering.

3. As I have indicated above, we are going to need the
full name of each speaker to the service leader prior
to the service.

If there are going to be any shocks and surprises during the service
the most likely spot will be during the eulogies and other tributes. How do
we respond to these surprises? How do we deal with a tribute that is clearly
inappropriate for a public service? How do we refuse someone who has
invested a lot of work into a letter or tribute? These are tricky questions.
When surprises do happen it's important to know what to do. This one
crisis point can make or break the funeral. It's that one moment when many
of us want a large hook with which we can pull the offending speaker away
from the podium. But all too often we don't have a hook so we're left to
figure things out for ourselves. It's important to know how to respond to
comments, disclosures, and surprises that threaten to throw the service
we've prepared off track. I asked one experienced pastor about this very
situation. Perhaps the best way to respond to surprises, according to this
pastor, is to be honest. We can be honest about the complexities of life and

the fact that none of us is perfect. We all have loose ends in our lives and we cannot ensure that everything has been properly dealt with before we die. These are some of the things we can tell a shocked and perhaps traumatized gathering. We really aren't focusing on behaviour. One pastor told me that he thinks it's OK to hear about people's weaknesses. Another pastor suggested that we try and stress the complications in each of our lives and talk about the different experiences and memories of a person. Many of us have made decisions and offered suggestions that have sent people raging out the door. Denominational offices have received angry letters from families and individuals who have experienced a service leader establishing and enforcing boundaries. A lot of care and compassion have to go into the act of refusing the request of a good friend or family member.

Another consideration when writing a eulogy is that people can only absorb so much information in one sitting so it's important to prioritize what we have gathered. I've had to sit through fifty minute eulogies and they're no fun at all. Considering our time constraints what are the important things we can say about a person? What do people need to hear and learn?

Regardless of whether or not we're focusing on our strengths or weaknesses, spoken eulogies are one form of tribute. We've also discussed the gift of music and dance. Still another form of tribute is the slideshow that combines photos of the deceased with some of their favourite music. Slideshow tributes are becoming increasingly popular. The right mix of image and song can be powerful, especially when it comes to things like memory and recall. People watch the photos and remember the events and experiences from where and when these photos were taken. The old phrase says that a picture is worth a thousand words. Photos combined with music can be worth far more than a thousand words. Carmine Gallo argues that we remember photographs a lot more frequently and easily than spoken words.[54]

For good or not–so–good, slide show tributes have become an increasingly common component to funeral services. Families and gather photos and using the latest computer software assemble a tribute that combines visual aids and music that is meaningful to the mourners and the deceased. Sometimes one of these photos can be used as one of the opening steps in our message.

As I have said earlier in *Dead Reckoning*, the best place for these slideshows is immediately following the spoken tributes. They can complement each other and have a lasting effect on listeners and survivors.

Regardless of the form this tribute takes it's sometimes difficult to learn anything about the life of the deceased. This is especially true in the case of what's called a "trustee service." It's depressing how many people die alone in North America. Statistics indicate that the number of single–person households is increasing[55] so this is a major issue. With nobody to plan their funeral the responsibility is often assumed by a public official who is sometimes labeled the "public trustee". In some cases both the trustee and the funeral directors will not have access to friends or next of kin. They may not even be certain that anybody is going to attend the service. In these situations it's still important to offer a dignified service for the deceased. But how can we prepare a service when we have no information about the person's? How can we tell a story when all that we have is silence?

Trustee services present a unique challenge to service leaders. We will be asked to officiate services arranged by people other than surviving family and friends. Unfortunately when funeral directors contact us there's often precious little contact information they can offer. While there are no family members available there may be an opportunity to contact friends, colleagues, and neighbours of the deceased. It's often helpful to initiate contact with them and find out whatever information we can use in the service. In cases where there is no family available to help plan the service we have to look for other ways to gather some history. Sometimes this involves reaching out to friends and acquaintances of the deceased. Kevin Little discusses the importance of meeting with these friends of the deceased when preparing a trustee service. He talks about one situation where he was asked to officiate at the service for a homeless man. The only people he could meet with were other homeless people so he joined some of them in a coffee shop and found the ensuing conversation "rich and heartfelt".[56]

When people do attend these services I make the point of asking about the life of the deceased. In the brief period of time available I ask about the birthplace and early years of deceased. I also ask about the career he or she had and also whether or not they had any family I could mention. I try and incorporate as much of this information as possible into my notes. When I read these notes I then have a time of silence so that people can collect and focus their thoughts and memories. I usually invite people to speak from where they are sitting and share what they know with the rest of the gathered congregation. It's one of those rare moments when an open mic can actually work out well. This is an extremely helpful way of personalizing the service and celebrating the life of the person who has just died. Pulling a lot of information together at the last minute and using it in a funeral is something I call "liturgical improv".

Regardless of whether or not we're able to meet with friends and family of the deceased, knowing little about a person's history means that we have to approach the service and tributes in a different way. I usually prepare an extended version of a simple graveside service so that if people do attend the service they will not go away feeling ignored or short–changed. Some examples of the things I would add to extend the service: a two to three minute meditation, the Lord's prayer, Psalm 23, etc..

We may have to prepare these services without any contact with family or friends. In this case it's important to rely simply on what the funeral director has told us. This may not lead to an extensive tribute or eulogy but it can show that we have done our best. Sometimes even the smallest personalized statement is greatly appreciated.

Under more conventional circumstances perhaps the deceased can be our biggest help when writing a eulogy. Dying individuals may have written and recorded presentations to be read or played at their funerals. This is something Sandra Martin calls "the living obit".[57] People who know they are dying can record in their own words a piece that can be played as a tribute. These tributes can also be saved on disks so that friends and loved ones can replay them whenever necessary. These "living obits" can also find their way onto the Internet. In some situations, depending on what is being said, they can go "viral". There are websites that allow people to record a piece to be available for downloading. One example of this is entitled *The Last Word* and is provided by *The New York Times*.[58] Just about anything can be recorded including stories and memories of the person's life, or things the person has learned through the years. Some have even included favourite jokes and sayings. Perhaps the most poignant "living obit" is called *The Last Lecture*. Before his death scholar Randy Pausch created a talk about his experience with pancreatic cancer. It's a piece about his life and things he had learned along the way. It was originally aimed at his children but found a large audience on the net.

Depending on what is happening in the world around the family and friends of the deceased funerals can often become political events. In 1975 African students in Soweto rose up against their nation's apartheid regime. Students were being killed for standing up to the government and their funerals became events where church and community gathered to make a statement.[59] The eulogy is one of those places where we can speak of the beliefs, convictions, and politics of the deceased. If we do this, however, we have to be aware of how the listeners will respond. There may be some fallout from what we say. But this doesn't mean we have to be silent and afraid of people — we simply have to be aware.

Political statements and poignant memories aside, sometimes a eulogy simply boils down to a list of a person's interests and hobbies. These, alone, can speak volumes about a person's life. Jokinen writes, "For the modern undertaker in the arrangement room, a man (sic) is defined not by his faith but his hobbies and quirks."[60] Therese Rando writes, "Tributes paid to your lost loved one emphasize the worth of that person and establish that he is worthy of the pain you currently feel."[61] She goes on to add, "You may hear stories about the deceased that you never knew before and learn many things about the person that you can cherish for the rest of your life."[62]

When it comes to creative gestures it's important to offer whatever introductions and instructions people need in order to fully appreciate, understand, and value what is happening. I was told a story about something one minister did at the beginning of each service. As people were entering the chapel they were handed a small stone. One guest received the small, polished stone and promptly popped it in her mouth. The director witnessed this and quickly informed her that she had just consumed a small stone. She spit out the stone and entered the chapel as if nothing had happened. At the conclusion of the service everyone was invited to take the stone with them so that they would have something by which to remember the deceased. It would have been helpful to have given everyone these instructions as the stones were being handed out. The lesson for us when trying something new and creative in a service is to ensure that we avoid confusion and misunderstanding by being upfront as soon as possible with any necessary explanations and instructions.

There are many ways to tell stories. We can speak and dance. We can move in circles and project photos on a screen. But one thing remains above each and every creative possibility and that's telling a story and building an enduring legacy. When building a eulogy we do this by reviewing the life of the deceased, naming the important things and people in their lives, and stating how important it is to say these things in the funeral service. This is one of the ways we show our love for the departed. This is also one of the ways we prepare to carry the spirit and legacy of the deceased while we move on with our lives.

Phase Five: Transition — The Message

Throughout history Christians from a variety of traditions and denominations have come to value an educated ministry. This is why many denominations have built and developed many highly regarded colleges and seminaries. The explanation for this commitment to an educated clergy and leadership is captured by Canadian historian Duff Crerar when he writes, "The seminary had always played a decisive role in equipping clergymen (sic) for Christian service."[1] "Equipping" is the key word in this quote. Seminaries help students develop the skills and body of knowledge necessary for their work and service. This education is not always as comprehensive as it needs to be, however. When I speak with preachers about their seminary educations one of the things I'm consistently told is that they didn't receive a lot of training when it comes to funerals. How many times did we reach the end of a preaching class, for example, and find ourselves asking, "What about funerals? What do we say? What can we say?" Some professors tried to answer these questions in what little time the schedule allowed but it usually didn't add up to a lot. A friend of mine suggests that a major reason for this lack of time and instruction has to do with the fact that seminary professors tend to be scholars and not pastors. While there is a lot of truth to this theory there is still the reality that funerals don't always have a major place in seminary curricula.

What we have learned through the years has been largely self–taught and that is not always a good thing. This is especially true when it comes to sermons and homilies. In this chapter I address what can be said during the transitional phase or message part of the funeral. For me it's this phase of the funeral that provides the hinge on which the funeral turns. In other words, we make the transition from remembering the past to naming the reality of the present and addressing some of the questions and issues faced by survivors. The best way to mark this transition is through the message we offer following the eulogies and tributes.

When addressing these issues and questions we pursue what seems to be a timeless quest. This quest is to put our experience of death into words. Denis Diderot is one example of a historic figure confronting the reality of death. He once wrote, "Everything comes to nothing, everything perishes everything passes, only the world remains, only time endures."[2] This may seem like a defeatist way of stating a foundational reality but it is clear, effective and honest. It's also one of those brief statements that covers a lot of ground in a very limited space and I envy that kind of economy, especially when it comes to marking transitions in the midst of the funeral service.

Within the funeral service we've taken the opportunity to state the reality of death within the family and community. We've heard something of the life that has been lived among us and we've also been granted some insight into the impact the deceased had on people's lives. What we need to do at this stage of the funeral is to change direction from the life that has been lived to the journey before us. That is not an easy shift to put into words.

I cannot sugar–coat this challenge. It can be an uphill struggle. I've been personally trying to find these words for decades. Many years ago, when I officiated at my first funeral, the funeral director tried to be helpful and offered some free advice. I remember his words to this day. As we were waiting for family and friends to arrive he said "Talk to them about the meaning of life and death". I gave him the thumbs–up sign but really had no idea what he was talking about. I didn't know that his words capture that central notion of what a funeral has come to be about. I didn't know that many ancients considered the main purpose of the funeral to be to "make clear the meaning of death and life."[3] What did I know about the meaning of life and death? I certainly didn't know how I was going to pull off that kind of talk with such a narrow window of time. I knew he meant well but his advice left me speechless which isn't a healthy space to be in when you're about to lead a service. What was I going to say about the meaning of life and death? I can't remember what I said to the grieving listeners that day but I hope it was helpful and came close to saying something meaningful about life and death. At the very least I hope I didn't make their experience any worse.

Looking back at this suggestion, advice and response I'm mindful of something Woody Allen once said. He quipped, "I wish I had some kind of affirmative message to leave you with. I don't. Would you take two negative messages?"[4] While I understand what Allen was trying to say I'm not sure our listeners would accept any negative messages. But this statement does reinforce the difficulty of choosing words to describe our reality. Instead of trying to put our experience into words perhaps we should just quote Temple Grandin and say, "unless there is death, we could not appreciate life."[5]

Those of us who are asked to lead funeral services are normally expected to take some time and offer our own thoughts on such topics as the meaning of life, death and the loss of someone close to us. We're also asked to speak about realities like fear and uncertainty. In more traditional religious circles these opportunities are called sermons or homilies. Perhaps a more helpful and contemporary term is message.[6] Many hear the word "sermon" and think about previous experiences of clergy droning on and on about boring or useless topics. Or they remember a stereotypical "hell and brimstone" sermon where the preacher tried to "singe the pews". This is why we need to use different terminology. Different words help us shift our thinking. We no longer have to remember negative experiences. We can think of something new instead and proceed from there. "Message" is perhaps the word that is closest to sermon or homily. Another possibility is "revaluation".[7] This is simply the examination of a person's life and a reconsideration of how it affects us.

Regardless of what we call them, messages do not have to be like the sermons we hear during Sunday morning services. According to Augustine the preacher's "job" is to accomplish three things: "to teach, delight and persuade".[8] Of these three things "teaching" is the only one that works in the funeral setting. It would be better if the Sunday morning and funeral sermons were treated as being quite different from one another. We'll explore the different reasons as we make our way through this chapter. For one thing, Sunday sermons don't have to dwell on death, the state of a person's soul, or teachings about the afterlife. Sunday sermons can explore topics and situations that are wider ranging than what we address at funerals.

Given people's rather high expectations and complex problems presented by funeral messages, we may feel overwhelmed and tempted to leave these messages out of our service altogether so that we can focus on the tributes and other contributions. There are services in which the tributes have run overtime and listeners are running out of steam. In these cases it may be helpful to simply omit the message and try to end the service as efficiently as possible. While this may seem like the easy way out and help our time management it may not be helpful for the family. Many come to a funeral service looking for something that helps them deal with their loss. They're looking for something that helps them confront the reality of death and what this loss will mean to them. Words of comfort and hope from the service leader can help survivors respond to many of the troubling things they've heard or experienced in the time leading up to the service. The eulogy tells them about the past but it's the message that helps them deal with the present and make their way into the future.

Perhaps the first challenge in creating a meaningful message is anticipating, hearing and responding to listeners' expectations. As I've already stated, this is difficult. Messages are challenging and we don't always get them right. Some of the things we have to say will not always be received well and could lead to serious consequences. In his book on the Hell's Angels motorcycle gang Hunter Thompson introduces us to a rather gutsy preacher who throws hellfire and brimstone at the captive audience of bikers before him. He claimed that "the wages of sin are death". He kept using terms like "sin" and "justification". Instead of converting listeners to his way of thinking he lost most, if not all of the gathered congregation. Many of them walked out on him. This was obviously a preacher who was clearly out of touch with the people attending the service. While his words may have been technically correct in a religious setting they were inappropriate and out of place in a funeral.[9]

There is often that tension between the content of a religious proclamation and a more finessed promise of hope and comfort. Too often preachers err on the side of religious proclamation and this often alienates us from many of our listeners. So we can ask once again, what do we say? What's that formula that will grant us a powerful and effective message each and every time we step into the pulpit? Unfortunately, the answers to the questions begin in the negative. Service leaders are constantly being told what not to say when leading a funeral. We hear people's stories about funerals they have previously attended. Many are clear about what has helpful and what was not helpful. We've heard about the clergy who has either been too religious or not religious enough. We've heard about clergy who talk more about themselves than the deceased. We've heard the complaints about clergy who have missed the names of family members or read a boring obituary. As one pastor said to me, "There are millions of things I can't say — tell me what I can say."

Here's what we can say: we can begin by naming the reality before us. We can address what the survivors are saying and asking. People are wondering why their loved one has died. They're thinking about where the person's soul might have gone. They are asking questions about God, the afterlife, and life itself. Many of their questions revolve around one word: "Why?" They also ask, "What now?" Kent Richmond is a pastor who has personally experienced pain and suffering and assures us that these questions are completely normal.[10] Mourners may be confronting spiritual issues and crises. Richmond writes, "When … suffering comes to those we have loved and whom we know have spent their lives giving themselves for others, it is natural for us to raise questions about our faith."[11]

Many of these questions arise out of things that have been said to survivors. Unfortunately, well–meaning people can say the dumbest, most harmful things when someone dies. There are many examples of what people say that can cause harm and pain. One in particular stands out for me. When the offshore oil–drilling platform, *Ocean Ranger,* went down in a storm off the coast of Newfoundland and all aboard were lost, surviving family and friends were confronted by a shocking lack of answers to their deep and powerful questions. Well–meaning individuals talked at length about how the rig's sinking was the will of God. They heard all kinds of other things as well. One young widow asked, "How could the loss of eighty–four men be God's will?"[12] The message part of the service gives us a chance to address harmful ideas like these and the conversations that help bring them about. We can also find a way of saying, "I don't know why these things happen — let's search for some answers together."

It's for this reason that the most important part of any message is the beginning. We've said this about the funeral itself and we can repeat the notion here. Like any good book that first sentence is what makes or breaks the overall work. It's that first sentence that hooks us in and shoves us into the argument or story. It's from that first sentence we begin the work of addressing key issues and questions. For the funeral of a young person, for example, we can begin the message with the words found on a sign over the office door of an Oxford professor, "Death in old age is inevitable, but death before old age is not."[13]

When we move beyond the message's opening words we can focus on other things. Messages can contain many different types of ideas and information. For one thing, messages can include metaphors and illustrations to help people understand what is happening. These metaphors are word pictures that help us understand something that is almost impossible to clearly explain or define. A box of chocolates, for example, can be a metaphor for the rich and complicated love we may feel for another. We can talk about motorcycles symbolizing a person's love of the outdoors and life on the open road. I've led services where I've begun the message by mentioning a person's obsession with their "Harley" and how this helps us remember and understand her life journey. We can use words and ideas in the same way that a painter uses paint and color. The Very Reverend Michael Standcliffe, Dean of Winchester once said that "Words are to the preacher what pigment is to the painter and stone is to the sculpture."[14]

For me one personal example of "word painting" stands out. I recently officiated at a funeral for a young child where I pointed to the teddy bear on the table by the child's urn and used that stuffed animal as a way of talking about how survivors could relate to one another as they grieved their loss. I told them about the teddy bear I had as a child and how it was a source of comfort, warmth and security for me. I talked about how it seemed to listen as I poured out my young heart to it. I told the people in the congregation that as the days and weeks unfolded they had to be teddy bears for one another. In other words, they could be a source of comfort and warmth for the people around them. They could also listen to one another as they struggled with the questions and challenges they were facing. I also invited them to be present in those difficult moments when all that was needed was to be nearby for others as we muddle our way through the questions and challenges these times of loss can bring. To reinforce the power behind this metaphor teddy bears were handed out to the children attending the service. This type of gesture is nothing new. Anthropologist Lucy Mair once wrote about a Pacific islander who saved up a lot of money during his life. His intention wasn't to spend it and impress people. He had the money handed out at his funeral.[15]

Gestures and metaphors like this are important in those times when words fail us. It's for this reason that metaphors can also have an important place in religious services. In the New Testament Paul talks about running a race.[16] A race is something that people from a variety of spiritual positions can understand. We can compare the start and finish of a race to the earthly life of a human being. Not all races are alike, either. I know a couple of people who race cars as a hobby. One person races cars in the Mojave desert while the other prefers a more conventional racetrack. We can keep these different contexts in mind when we focus our thoughts and comments on the unique race of each and every person whose life we celebrate. For one thing we can talk about beginnings and endings. We can talk about a person's navigation through life and their decision–making along the way. We can give listeners a sense of what "fueled" the deceased. We can even talk about pit stops and problems along the way.

We may also include a story as part of the message and many readers may find this surprising. We've already discussed storytelling in some detail but we can address another aspect of the topic here. By the time phase five of the funeral has been reached we've hopefully heard numerous stories and memories of the deceased. We'll have heard about the effect they had in people's lives. We'll have heard stories about their efforts and accomplishments. We will also have heard stories about those human times when efforts and plans didn't work out as expected. Including a story in the message can help connect what we have to say with larger themes, especially as they address the transition we've been talking about. Preaching scholar Paul Scott Wilson observes, "Sometimes I learn more about the faith from the stories than from the sermon's well–crafted points."[17]

When it comes to the story we've been talking about, we can include some mention of what the deceased believed in. We can build on this story and talk about how we may learn from and find inspiration in the words and actions of the deceased. In some religious traditions this broader story will include whichever deity the person worshipped. We can talk about the deceased being in God's presence. This story will also convey whatever concept of the after world is a part of their religion's teaching.

Service leaders can take some time and offer some hope for the survivors. But speaking about hope in a time of loss and grief can be risky. We have to be careful in how we communicate this notion. When it's done well the words we offer about hope can make a significant difference in the experience of listeners. Adam Gopnik once wrote, "… the hardest weather makes the nicest wine."[18] Perhaps the best way to tell people that there is hope is to suggest some vision of how the person lives on. We can talk about how the harsh storms of death can lead to new beginnings in our lives. Storms are intense and potentially dangerous events. Storms also ease up and move as time passes and the energy shifts. The rain and clouds move away and the blue sky returns. We can reassure people that we have every confidence that the deceased is both with God and at peace.

Even though many of us are preachers serving in a congregational or institutional setting the content of the message does not always have to be religious. It doesn't have to focus exclusively on a small group of insiders while the rest of our listeners sit and wait on the sidelines. We can include material from many different sources and speak to many different people. Vincent Van Gogh once said: "It must be good to die, conscious of having performed some real good and knowing that one will live through this work, at least in the memory of some, and will leave a good example to those who come after."[19] These are similar sentiments to a folk song entitled *Rise Again*. *Rise Again* is about living on in the words and actions of those we have left behind. It's an old theme but the words in this song are powerful and give it new life. We can talk about a person's works and gifts, and how those works and gifts touched the lives of those around them. We can introduce concepts such as legacy and memory. We can help people remember things they had learned from the deceased and think of ways they were inspired by them.

As we make our way through the message we can be checking to see if our listeners are "with us". Sometimes we'll know by a person's body language whether or not they're hearing, listening to and understanding what we have to say. One "blurry" sentence or idea could derail our entire effort. Sometimes we make mistakes without actually making a mistake. There are occasions where people have remembered us saying something without those words really being uttered. We humans have been known to "hear things". Peter Urs Bender writes, "Listeners judge you by what *they* think you said, rather than what was intended."[20] The words we do say may have consequences we did not intend. People will hear what we have to say and choose their personal response accordingly. While we cannot control the reactions to everything we say we do have to be cautious and minimize the risk wherever possible. This can be a real challenge, especially in a service where we focus on the person and not religious content. Historically we have not been so successful when trying to be clear. Thomas Long uses the word "vague" to describe services such as celebrations of life.[21] We can say the same about many religious funerals as well. This observation is both accurate and unfortunate. Celebrations and funerals cannot be "vague" and be effective at the same time. The message itself is that one point where we work the hardest to be clear. Messages can be planned and delivered in a way that brings a tremendous amount of comfort to the bereaved.

Clarity, meaning and sensibility can be achieved in many different ways. Perhaps one of the most interesting ways is in simply being blunt. Psychologist Robert Kavanaugh once recalled a funeral sermon given while he was an altar boy. At the appointed time in the funeral mass the officiating priest approached the casket of the deceased, pointed to it, and said, "If the top of that casket suddenly popped open and old John sat up, he wouldn't know where he was. He was never inside this church a day in his life. Pray for him".[22] Being blunt is extremely risky and not something I would suggest people "try at home" but it is an option and one that may come in handy once or twice in our careers. It's something we can do when we've worked hard to find the right words and tone.

Perhaps our first attempt at clarity can be made when we're preparing the service. One of the pieces of advice I remember from my seminary days it that we should be able to summarize our sermons in one sentence. Carmine Gallo takes this one step farther by suggesting that we summarize our thoughts in the form of a 140–character Tweet.[23] Once we have our thoughts and materials focused to that extent we can continue with our work. This isn't as easy as it sounds but it is a critical step in helping our message make sense to listeners. How can we summarize our funeral message in one sentence? How can we summarize the entire life story, vision, hopes and dreams of the deceased into one relatively brief string of words? This second question may seem tricky but it's not impossible to answer. An artist by the name of Rachel Berman once wrote in a letter to a friend: "All I ask of life these days is a body that will get me from place to place and a mind that works well enough to compose my 'stories'."[24] While this may not be the summary we would hope for it is one sentence we can use with some effectiveness.

Perhaps this is one of the primary differences between Sunday and funeral sermons. While we may not always find concise answers to these questions while preparing the funeral they can help us identify not only the important pieces of a person's life to raise during the service. We are also given the opportunity to talk about how the deceased has touched the lives of the people who shared his or her life. Sunday mornings, on the other hand, give us a chance explore more general subjects. We have more time to discuss the big questions people are asking and go into detail we simply do not have time for during a funeral.

We have to be careful within the context of the funeral when trying to deal with many of the questions people may be asking themselves. Some questions can be introduced and dealt with in the funeral while others will require more time and attention. H.L. Mencken once wrote, "For every complex question there is a simple answer and it is wrong."[25] Many of the deeper questions cannot be answered in the brief amount of time we have available for the message or the entire service itself for that matter. Bertrand Russell suggests that these questions are best left to philosophers and he probably has a point.[26] The basic funeral is usually about 30 minutes. That means the service leader is left with about five minutes for the message. When we reflect on all of the questions being asked and issues being dealt with by the mourners we quickly realize those five minutes simply aren't enough. Perhaps the one thing we can accomplish in such brief a time is simply point to where we need to begin the grief journey. And with the time remaining we can then encourage them to move beyond the starting line.

In helping people begin their grief journey we can encourage them to find a direction in which they can move. We can also gently push them in that direction. This isn't easy. We don't always want to do this work. The most helpful response to this challenge is to simply use the word "focus" in our pastoral and public work. The second most important word is "prioritize". What's the most pressing question being asked? How can we answer that and still have time for other questions? We don't have all the answers and there is nothing wrong with this. While it may be helpful to say, "I don't know" it is also helpful to assure people that we should continue to pursue our questions. Just because we don't have an answer doesn't mean there isn't something out there that can't point us in a helpful direction.

When I was young I enjoyed throwing stones into water. One of the reasons for this was the effect the impact of the stone had on the surface of the pond. It was neat how the energy would push circles of water out from the place where the stone hit the water. This is something called "rippling" and it's a metaphor used in psychology. Eminent psychiatrist Irvin Yalom talks about the importance of "rippling". The concept is built around the effect a stone or object have when they fall into a still pool of water. The energy created by the impact circles out and affects the water around the point where the rock strikes the surface. Yalom teaches that we affect the people and world around us. It can be something big or small. Something we say, for example, can touch a person's life so that they turn around and do something positive and helpful for somebody else. Rippling includes both the positive and negative things we say and do. Yalom writes, "Rippling refers to the fact that each of us creates — often without our conscious intent or knowledge — concentric circles of influence that may affect others for years, even for generations." He goes on say, "… the effect we have on other people is in turn passed on to others, much as the ripples in a pond go on and on until they're no longer visible but continuing at the nano level." This is what rippling is all about.[27]

In speaking about how a death or situation has affected listeners it's often tempting to explain how God or some other deity is working in a situation. This is important because it addresses issues such as cause and blame. Again, this is something that can get us into some serious and unnecessary hot water. Our message cannot be defensive. Our messages cannot be judgmental either. God doesn't need to be defended. In saying this we can help change the channel on what listeners may be thinking, saying and asking. There is no need for us to defend a deity or an ideology. We are not there to judge people's lives or how the survivors go about their days. At no point during the message, or the entire funeral for that matter, are we to sit in judgment of the deceased or those who grieve them. When we do something like this we run the risk of shutting down the listening process completely and that could affect mourners in the long term.

Religious leaders have a responsibility to tread with caution when developing their message for a funeral. But we also have a responsibility to take reasonable risks when we can. This is important when it comes to mentioning God's love, presence, and compassion. Pastor Rob Bell rightly observes, "The Christian faith is big enough, wide enough, and generous enough to handle that vast a range of perspectives."[28] And there is a "vast range of perspectives" in almost every gathering of listeners we encounter and address.

Instead of defending a deity or trying to convert people to a certain religion we need to be reaching out and trying to help mourners acknowledge the presence and reality of death. Richmond writes, "Though everyone knows that death is a part of life, it is not something we readily discuss or consider."[29] So we, as preachers, as in a position to name reality and also grant permission to discuss this reality with the people around us. The ancient teacher tells us that there is "a time to be born and a time to die."[30] He or she also says that there is a time to speak. Funerals are our time to speak. They also help others to speak as well. We can build on this thinking about death by trying to help people live every moment to the fullest. Richmond writes, "A memorial sermon that lifts up the satisfying memories can help."[31] We can cherish the memories we have of the deceased and we can commit ourselves to making new ones with remaining those who remain.

In sharing the memories, however, clergy should refrain from sharing personal experiences. I remember a funeral director was telling me about one preacher who spent most of one service talking about his children, vacation, and family. Very little of his service was focusing on the deceased. I heard a similar sermon not very long afterwards. This sermon was about thirty minutes long and in that extended time only five of those minutes focused on the deceased. I found this eye opening and it helped me reflect on my own work. Unless it involves the deceased we have to keep our personal material to a minimum. It's important to use personal information, stories, memories, etc. exclusively in cases where there is a real connection with the life and experience of the deceased. Without this tie–in there's no way our anecdotes will be helpful or even understood. When we attempt to weave our personal experience into a message we must ensure that it genuinely connects with the life of the deceased and the overall point we're trying to make.

One of the dangers of storytelling in the message is duplication. One thing that often happens in a funeral is that the eulogist and service leader are often working from the same body of information. In order to avoid duplication it is best to say that the eulogist has already covered certain ground and that you found it important and meaningful. We can say things like, "The eulogist has told us about X, Y, and Z and I found this important and meaningful." In some cases we may want to simply work around the duplication the best that we can. This effort to reduce duplication helps free some time and energy for more important thoughts and words such as the change that one particular death brings to our lives.

In trying to be comforting and hopeful, one sentence I always include in a funeral message is a clear statement that the person has left us physically and that they will be missed. This is probably the one point in the message where we're being the most explicit about the transition mourners are experiencing. This is the point around which everything turns. Siddhartha Mukherjee writes, "In the end, every biography must also confront the death of its subject."[32] The biography of the deceased may end with their death but that doesn't mean the rest of our stories end with it. People's memories of us do not go completely silent when we die. Our stories continue so it becomes our challenge to explain and describe how the deceased lives on in others. This reflects the honesty and realism we've been discussing throughout this book. Dead is dead but life goes on in a number of different ways.

One thing we can talk about in our message is the importance of ongoing contact with the grieving survivors most directly affected by the death. We can encourage phone calls and coffee appointments. We can talk about the importance of observing the anniversary of a person's passing. We can help people focus on the bonds that remain. Like the song *Rise Again* says, through these things we find new and continuing life. I usually begin this part of the message by saying something like, "our time here together may be brief but the road ahead is a long one." We're telling people here that they've turned a corner and are now heading in a new direction. This also reinforces the earlier notion that the funeral is a beginning. It's something we have to move beyond if we are to deal with our grief.

Even if we're confident that all of our bases are covered, it's often helpful to have extra material available for when the eulogist comes up short with only a brief tribute or someone isn't able to speak at all. Some people, especially those with little public speaking experience, will speak more quickly when they are nervous and this will affect the amount of time it takes them to read the eulogy. Have some history and stories of the person ready to fill in some time and stretch the length of the service to where the family needs it. The extra material also comes in handy if we have to eliminate part of our message because of duplication.

This is why the message has to be printed out in hard copy. We can make last minute changes depending on what happens both before and during a service. This is why we should always have a pen or pencil with us whenever we lead a service. There was one funeral service where I found myself pacing out in front of the funeral home. As I was going back and forth I heard the piper warming up around the corner of the building so I went to find her and touch base. One of the things we discussed was the music. She told me that one of the pieces was a traditional piece simply named *MacCrimmon*. When I told her that I had never heard of it she told me the story behind the music. The Chief of the Clan MacCrimmon died and his friends and family went into a deep grief. The music expressing this grief is quite slow and plodding. As the survivors tell stories about the chief's life the music picks up and the becomes more upbeat as the clan gains strength from these memories and stories. As the piper told the story it occurred to me that I could use that in the message I had prepared. When the time came to offer a message I told the story behind the music and proceeded accordingly.

Throughout history public speakers have been urged to avoid notes. Pueblo storyteller Leslie Marmon Silko once wrote, "Where I come from, the words that are most highly valued are those which are spoken from the heart, unpremeditated and unrehearsed." She goes on to say, "Among the Pueblo people, a written speech or statement is highly suspect because the true feelings of the speaker remain hidden as he reads words that are detached from the occasion and the audience."[33] Druid priests also insisted on avoiding the printed page when going about their duties.[34] The challenge here is that we do not live in a society that trains us to think and speak on our feet without notes. Our memories seem to work a lot differently than in those days when speakers had to rely on the oral tradition in order to establish and perpetuate a literary and educational legacy. While some of us have mastered the art of preaching without notes it's not something I'd recommend to everyone. While there are times when we can go "off script" and not use notes this is a difficult expectation for a funeral. Emotional stress, alone, can force mistakes that can be potentially quite embarrassing for both speakers and listeners.

One good reason why we should put everything in writing is that some brief passages are quite risky, however, and should be "premiered" before a couple of people prior to the service. I was preparing for the funeral of an older gentleman who had been a hippy in the sixties. The details of his life brought to mind something the late Hunter Thompson wrote a long time ago. Thompson wrote, "Who is the happier man, he who has braved the storm of life and lived or he who has stayed securely on shore and merely existed."[35] I checked with some family members, received their approval, and used the quote with some effect. In an earlier chapter I mentioned the need to rehearse. Ensuring that the message is helpful, effective and meaningful is one of the reasons why practicing is important. I have done this on a couple of occasions and the results have been quite positive.

As with the above Thompson quotation, a lot of our material may come from the things we read. Professional and leisure reading can inspire our ideas. Every once in a while something is written that triggers a thought I can use. I was reading through an interview with the poet Elizabeth Bishop, for example, and ran across the word "Anjinhos". It means "Little Angels" and Brazilians used it when referring to babies and young children who had died.[36] Many of us will be asked to officiate at funerals for both stillborn babies and babies who lived only a short time. Largely due to the ages of the deceased these are extremely difficult and intense services. Many of us may want to avoid these types of services but we can't and shouldn't; certainly from a pastoral perspective. As Elaine Ramshaw writes, "the parents need others to recognize the reality of both the baby's existence and the parents' grief." Ramshaw goes on to add, "there is a ritual need to say good–bye, to acknowledge an irrevocable loss and to begin to let go off all the hopes and dreams that were bound up in the anticipation of the infant's birth."[37] Religious people will want to commend their child to God. For this reason words like "anjinhos" can be filed away for future use.

The information we squirrel away can help us when it comes time to delve into the more complex questions people are asking. They want to know that we've been struggling with these questions and concerns as well. Jan Linn writes, "The minister who admits to honest struggle in matters of faith and refuses to pretend that difficult questions yield easy answers is a person to whom laity who struggle and question in the same ways can relate. This is a good thing because the nature of our vocation is to raise questions and avoid simple answers."[38]

This level of honesty should be apparent from the beginning of our message. As I have already mentioned, that first sentence says it all about what we are trying to communicate to people. Perhaps the clearest introduction to a funeral message I have come across is from the pens of William R. Baird, Sr. and John E. Baird, and they write, "None of us likes to think about death. We are concerned with life, with our dreams and hopes for the future, with our plans for the days ahead, and with the goals we seek to attain. The end of life seems far away, and death is something that happens to someone else."[39] For someone having a pleasant and positive disposition throughout life, we can begin a message by quoting a line of poetry by someone like Matthew Arnold. Arnold once wrote, "Well hath he done who hath seiz'd happiness."[40]

From the first sentence to the concluding words of our message people need hope and comfort, and if we accomplish anything in what we say let it be these two things: that death is real and that even in the face of death we try and "seize happiness". These words help mark the transition between death and new life. Through these words we're reminded that with the loss of someone close we have to pursue new challenges and opportunities. This gives life perspective and depth. It also motivates us to use our time wisely. These are what creates memories and this is what our messages have to point toward.

Sample Sermon for a Young Person

The following is a sermon I offered for a young person killed in an automobile accident. While I have changed the name I have left everything else intact. It's not really religious but it does speak to some of the realities and issues faced when a young person dies well before their time.

A number of years ago a movie came out called the Lion King. On this movie's sound track there is a song entitled "The Circle of Life".

As the song says, the circle of life is that journey we begin at the moment of birth. It's a journey that proceeds from that moment of birth and continues as we make our way through infancy, childhood, adult years, and mid–life.

In most cases this circle is completed in its own natural time. Too many times, however, this circle ends all too quickly and tragically and we are left in shock and silence.

John's life ended all too quickly and we are left with questions that seem impossible to answer. Most of these questions will never be answered.

As we struggle with what has happened and where we go from here I would offer one simple thought:

We can be assured that as we continue into the days and weeks to come we will not be making our way alone. John will be with us in a new way. John will be with us whenever we share stories and memories. He will be with us when we look at photos and gather as family and friends. And this is an important thing to remember as we consider the future.

We can know that John is with us in our minds and in our hearts. He lives on in our words and in our actions. He lives on in our hopes and in our dreams. He lives on in the everyday happenings, goals and plans of our day–to–day routines.

For this we can be thankful. Amen.

Phase Six: Closing Moves

A friend of mine once asked me about my funeral wishes. How did I want things to go? What did I want to have happen? What did I want people to say? I thought a moment and told him I wanted to be taken out into the middle of a lake and burned in a dory. It seemed like a perfectly reasonable thought at the time. If it made sense for some of the higher ranking Viking leaders then why not me? Upon hearing my "last request" my friend shook his head and said, "That would be a waste of a perfectly good boat." He had a point so I let the matter drop. Regardless of where it leads, however, any conversation about endings is important.

In this chapter we're going to close the circle and discuss the completion or ending of the funeral service. This will help make a transition back from ritual–time to real–time. At the beginning of the funeral we acknowledged the loss of an individual and the break this loss renders in our lives and community. As we make our way through to the closing steps of the funeral we prepare to come full circle and return to our everyday lives. When we do this we face the task of mending that break and living through our loss. Sometimes "living through" means releasing the person we've lost and moving on with their abiding voice and presence in our lives.

The closing moves of a funeral are those moments when we acknowledge the reality of having to let go, set the deceased free, and begin the process of moving on. Sometimes the "setting free" may sound magical or formulaic and there's nothing wrong with that. It's a natural part of the overall transition process. Throughout history people have set the deceased free in a variety of ways. We've sung songs and recited poetry. We've read letters and carried bodies from one place to another. Paul Radin recounts, "Among the Maori, as among the vast majority of primitive peoples, a charm is recited over the corpse of a child in order to dispatch the soul to the spiritland."[1] According to Radin, the Maori sent the soul on with the following words:

> "Farewell, O My child! Do not grieve; do not weep; do not love; do not yearn for your parents left by you in the world. Go thou forever. Farewell forever."[2]

This quotation is an excellent summary of what we are called to do in the final phase of the funeral. In other words, we "send" the deceased to the next phase of their journey. Some ancient cultures would perhaps prefer the word "push" to "send". Based on my research to this point I would be tempted to use the word "shove" but I leave the exact wording choice to the reader. Some communities have been so desperate to move spirits onward they've hired so–called "sin–eaters" to assume the worldly sins of the deceased so that their transition to the afterlife would be more smooth.[3] Regardless of the wording or reasoning it's helpful to have this "moving" statement late in the service. Ideally, we place it prior to the dismissal. The technical word we use for this statement is "committal". This is one way in which we bring the service to a close by saying several things about the shift that happens next.

In terms of the exact wording of a contemporary committal, I've always found the following helpful:

> "Just as these flowers have grown from the earth and the dust we commend —— to the elements: earth to earth; ashes to ashes, and dust to dust. We commend him to the loving care of God, and to the community of family and friends who have gone before. We commend him to that place where there is neither pain nor suffering; but a warmth and peace that is beyond our understanding. A warmth and a peace that unites us all."

I will often repeat the committal at graveside. Whenever I do this I change the wording slightly so that it doesn't sound like I'm repeating myself. Regardless of our location, I use wording that reflects the context. Here is what it can look like once we add this simple quote:

> A great writer (Oscar Wilde) once said that where there is sorrow there is holy ground. Just as these flowers have grown from the earth, the dust, and the ground we commend —— to the elements: earth to earth; ashes to ashes, and dust to dust. We commend him to the loving care of God, and to the community of family and friends who have gone before. We commend him to that place where there is neither pain nor suffering; but a warmth and peace that is beyond our understanding. A warmth and a peace that unites us all.

The service leader could also quote an Ancient Hebrew term. The ancient Hebrews once referred to Human beings as being "creatures of clay".[4] Using this term the committal would look like this:

> The ancient Hebrews once referred to Human beings as "Creatures of Clay". Just as we have grown from the clay and the dust and the ground, we commend Jane to the elements: earth to earth, ashes to ashes and dust to dust. We commend her to the loving care of God and to the community of family and friends who have gone before. We commend her to that place where there is neither pain nor suffering but a warmth and a peace that is beyond our understanding; a warmth and a peace that unites us all.

Once we have made our way through the committal we can move on to other statements and gestures that help us bring the service to a close.

One way we can move from the committal to the closing blessing is to place items either on top of the casket or beside the urn. One or two people can approach the front and place letters and poems written for the occasion. After the service the funeral directors can place the flowers and poems inside the casket if that is what people have requested. This can be a helpful gesture for some of the people at the service. One of the ways we deal with and ritualize grief, for example is to write stuff down. In his biography of Francis Walsingham, John Cooper notes the fact that a scholar by the name of Thomas Gardiner "wrote verses" when grieving the death of a friend.[5] When Walsingham died poet Thomas Watson wrote a poem to mark his loss.[6] I know a lot of people who respond to the death of someone close by either writing letters, poetry, and even in some cases, songs. There are several symbolic ways by which we can try to send these messages on to the deceased person. We can bury our letters with other mementos in the person's casket. The letters can be burned with the deceased if they are cremated.

We may also set our letters, poems and thoughts afire by using the candle that had been lit early in the service and drop the flaming paper into a metal bowl that has been set up at the front of the chapel for this very occasion.[7] This may take time depending on the size of the gathering so keep in mind that it may not be well received when a service has already taken up a fair amount of time. We can either burn the letters ourselves as the second part of the committal or invite family members to come forward and burn the letters themselves.

Committals can also be followed by the presentation of flowers. Flowers can be placed at any time during the service. The family can place them on a table near the urn or casket as they enter the chapel to begin the service. The flowers can also be placed on the casket itself. The advantage to having the flowers placed on the casket is that they can remain in place throughout the trip to the place of burial or cremation. Friends and family can place them as they light the candle. I'd like to offer one caution, however. If too many people step forward to present flowers a roadblock of sorts could be created and this would add a significant amount of time to the service. In some cases it may be appropriate to place flowers as we depart the chapel. We can place the flowers on the casket as it remains at the front. We can also place flowers on the casket as it waits in the lobby while final preparations are made prior to placing it in the coach.

Committals help us send the deceased on their way but that, in and of itself, does not bring the service to a close. Those of us who remain need to be sent on our way as well. People attending the service need permission to depart and return to their altered lives. The closing blessing is an important way to return people to their normal lives. They have stepped away from their lives on order to attend this funeral. They have remembered and honoured the life of a friend, colleague, and loved one. They have offered their condolences and shared in a chapel service and begun grieving the loss of someone close. It is now time to send them back into their lives in light of the hard reality that someone close to them is missing. This is why we have to ensure that our wording is precise, pastoral and moving. With this in mind, we can say something like the following:

> "At the beginning of our service today we lit a candle. As we bring our time to a close and make our way into the days and weeks to come may we carry a spark of this light with us on our way. May we carry —— in our minds and in our hearts and may we leave this place in peace. Amen"

If the candle lighting is not included in this service you can bring the service to a close with the following:

> It is said that the closest bonds we will ever experience are bonds of grief. As we bring our time here to a close and make our way into the days and weeks to come may we carry John's memory with us and hold it close. May we nurture the bonds that remain and honour John in everything we say and do. May we carry John on our

minds, our hearts, and our spirits this day and every day.
Amen.

A more conventional dismissal can also be used. Many of these can be found in either written or online resources. Our respective denominations and religious traditions may prescribe or even dictate the use of a particular blessing. A lot depends on our requirements, tastes and whatever sense of the family's needs we have derived from the preparation meeting as discussed in the earlier chapter on preparation. A religious dismissal can go something like this:

> God once told the people of Israel: "My presence will go
> with you and I will give you rest." May God's presence
> be with us as we go from this place and make our way
> into the days and weeks to come.

And the following is an even more traditional blessing from Numbers 6:24-25. It can be used at the end of a service.

> May God bless us and keep us;
> May God's face upon us and be gracious to us;
> May God's love go with us this day and every day,
> And grant us peace now and always — amen.

The above blessing can be done while we are actually facing the casket so that we can address the deceased. We can recite the above blessing but change words like "us" to "you". We can also add the name of the deceased at the beginning of this prayer. So the prayer becomes:

> ———, May God bless you and keep you;
> May God's face upon you and be gracious to you;
> May God's love go with you this day and every day,
> And grant you peace now and always — amen.

In the state funeral for the Honourable Jack Layton, The Rev. Dr. Brent Hawkes used the metaphor of passing a torch from one person to another.[8] It's a metaphor that can also be found on the wall of the dressing room of the National Hockey League's Montreal Canadiens. This is also something we can use. I led a service for a young teacher and one of the things we mentioned was the need to carry on with her work and community involvement. Someone would have to step into her classroom, for example, and teach her class. Someone would have to take her place around the community association board table. Still, others would need to grab a softball glove or hockey stick and take their place on the bench, on the ice, or on the field. When we die things have to be done to keep our community moving.

Some of our clients will have some ideas of what we can say and will make requests to help ensure that the service closes on a personalized note. Whenever someone requests something above and beyond what we normally offer in a funeral we always have to ask for clarification to make sure we are clear on what they're asking. A number of years ago I was asked by a family to conclude a service with the *Irish Blessing*. I agreed with the request claiming that I knew exactly what they wanted. When the service in question drew to a close I offered the following closing blessing: "May you be half an hour in heaven before the devil knows you're dead." It had never occurred to me that there was more than one Irish blessing. The family of the deceased was quick to teach me a new one.

Before bringing this part of our chapter to a close I would like to make one final and practical comment about what happens when we have completed the service and are in the process of helping people make their way from the worship space. If funeral directors are present at the service then it is important to wait for them to help usher people from the service space especially if unfamiliar with the venue. A funeral director told me of this one occasion when a relatively new minister was officiating at a service and for some reason didn't wait for the directors to enter the chapel when he had completed the service. He led the family down a side aisle in the chapel and approached a door he thought was an exit. He brought everyone to the door and swung it open. It was a closet!

When we offer the dismissal sometimes our work has yet to be completed. Many people belong to organizations such as lodges and the Royal Canadian Legion (a military organization). Representatives from these organizations sometimes want to share in the funerals of their departed members and offer an ordered farewell when the "regular" or "religious" funeral has been completed. What I have done is bring my part of the ritual to a close and then invite representatives from an organization to come forward and offer this goodbye. Many of these goodbyes are spoken while others are more physically expressive. Here in Canada, the Legion, for example, includes what's called a "Poppy Ceremony" as part of their farewell ritual. Members, family and clergy attending and leading the service take poppies and pin them to a Styrofoam cross at the front of the service space. There's no need for service leaders to know the farewell gestures of each and every organization. We can clarify the details of these farewells prior to the service. Representatives from these organizations are usually more than willing to brief us on what they have planned. It's a rare occasion when we have to say "no". I've never had to decline a request to have an organization say goodbye at the close of a funeral and I hope I never will.

Announcements following the closing dismissal also tell people where to go next. Are we going to take the body of the deceased to the place of burial? Are we invited to a reception? Where do we go and what do we do? This is why I leave the announcements to the end. Many of us forget what's said at the beginning of the funeral. Announcements are an opportunity to let people know if there's a reception time where they may meet the family and offer a personal word of condolence with individuals they may know. It was once said that a "jolly glasse and right Company" could cure almost all ills.[9] We can stress the importance of such fellowship and community when we let people know about the reception. Another announcement we can make concerns the burial service that may follow the chapel funeral. For those who are able this is an opportunity to share one final step with the deceased. They will be going is graveside so it's to that part of our closing phase we make our way to now.

If we are going to a graveside service following our time in the chapel we should put some thought into that part of the overall ritual as well. Graveside services demand our ongoing attention because they are both powerful and meaningful. A number of years ago I officiated at a graveside service with a small group of people attending. We were at that point in the service where our heads were bowed and offering some silent words for the deceased. We didn't notice that a member of our group was looking around and up in the sky. Roughly halfway through the prayer he said in a loud and excited voice "Holy shit!" Startled out of our silence we looked at the person who said it. He was looking and pointing towards the sky and had the most amazed look on his face. Flying slowly high above our location was a pair of bald eagles. Our service came to a sudden halt and nobody said a word. This was an extremely powerful moment and spoken words would have really messed it up. People from many ancient cultures would have completely understood our response. To them, birds climbing in the air like that would often mean that the souls of the deceased are ascending to heaven.[10]

Regardless of whether they're a part of a wider funeral ritual including a chapel service or stand–alone events, graveside services can be powerful experiences. It's because of this power that graveside services accomplish many things. They tell us what we believe about life, death, and the afterlife. They help people take that next step into a new reality. In this section I will address both realities and suggest some ways we can enact them through what we say and do at the graveside. Paul Irion writes, "It is an extremely difficult time for mourners because it represents the time when they leave the body of their loved one in the grave."[11]

There are several ways we can experience reality before, during, and following a graveside service. The first way is simply distance. Physically moving from the chapel to the graveside is an active break that signals the end of one ritual and the beginning of something new. Catherine Bell tells us that movement from one place to another is important in ritual.

It helps reinforce the reality that a serious transition has happened.[12] We can also say that we're marking a change in the deceased's work status and just about every other status we can think of. In the case of a funeral, at the very least a person is making their way from the inside of a building to the outside and the natural elements.

The second way we experience reality at graveside is through the visual field experienced by the survivors. Whether the deceased is being buried in the traditional sense or "niched"[13] people are looking at a hole of some kind. They are confronting reality in a way that cannot really be captured in a chapel, church, or community hall. They are experiencing and staring down fears that have terrified people for centuries. In some cultures people would spend time praying and meditating in cemeteries as a way of facing and resolving these fears.[14] Sometimes the intensity of this moment pushes us to do some risky things. Former Soviet Union leader Joseph Stalin, for example, was so overwhelmed by the death of his wife Kato he literally jumped into her open grave. His fellow mourners had to remove him before they could proceed with the service.[15]

For many the reality and finality of the graveside experience forces fears and anxieties about death to the surface. It's the one moment where we face the future and our own mortality, limitations, and death. This is not always something we anticipate when we attend a graveside service. Irvin D. Yalom writes, "… a common but often unappreciated part of mourning is the survivor's personal confrontation with his or her own death"[16] This realization of our own mortality cannot be underestimated. Staring into a hole in either the ground or a wall helps ensure that we cannot avoid even a cursory reflection on our personal mortality.

As we have previously discussed, one of the religious phrases that helps us address this fear and anxiety is "fear not".[17] This is a powerful statement for a reason. These words give us some reassurance that something else happens that moment following our death. Tradition has tried to describe that "something" but we'll have to see for ourselves when that moment arrives. Reassurance doesn't resolve or cancel our fear, however. Another word that helps us address the fear and anxiety people may be experiencing is love. Theologian Helmut Thielicke describes love as being "The positive power that conquers anxiety".[18] One expression of love that is most effective here is that which is shared among family, friends and community. While it is not always possible to love people with whom we have had a troubled and troubling relationship we are invited and called to find love where we can find it. It's this shared love that makes it important to get together and share that final moment at graveside.

Before we move too far into our consideration of how we manage contemporary graveside services we need to lay some groundwork. We have to address the fundamental question: Why do we have a graveside service, especially when we've just experienced a chapel or chapel–type service? Why do we need to watch the casket descend into the ground or the urn placed in a niche? Why do we need to hear someone say words of comfort? For many of us it brings closure to the funeral ritual. For others it's a sign of respect to accompany the deceased to their final resting place. We can't seem to rest and move on until the grave is "closed" or the niche sealed. In the paragraphs that follow we'll discuss the importance of the graveside service and how it works. We'll talk about why it's important. In military circles, for example, burial is seen as being a "fundamental religious duty".[19] Even for nonreligious people burials are powerful "spiritual" moments. This can be factored into the materials we bring to graveside.

Burial practice began at the very beginning of human history. Wade Davis claims that Neanderthals were burying their dead almost 70,000 years ago.[20] These dead were treated with an amazing amount of respect and dignity. The Neanderthal people took pains to protect and provide for their dead. They surrounded the dead with stones to protect them. They left tools, weapons, and food in their graves to provide for their needs.[21] Scholars refer to these items as being "grave goods"[22] and they tell a story about what the Neanderthals believed and how they valued their departed. Catherine Cottreau–Robins defines archaeology as being "the study of past peoples based on the objects they left behind and the ways they left their imprint on the world".[23] We can study what the Neanderthals left behind and we can also study the items left behind by so many other peoples and cultures.

Why did people leave these "grave goods" behind? What were they trying to say about their lives and beliefs? Why did they put so much effort into "staging" their burial places? Was it to meet a need or fulfill a perceived duty? There may be a simple reason for of this attention to detail at burial sites. Burial practices often reflect a fundamental human fear of the dead themselves. Or to be more precise, we tend to fear the spirit of the departed. In many non–literate societies people believed that the spirit of the deceased returned following death. This is called "reanimation".[24] Burial practices often reflect that tension between wanting to hold the spirit of the deceased close and also wanting to appease and control that same spirit.[25] We also want this same spirit to "go away" and settle into whatever new reality awaits on the other side. For many communities and cultures, people have wanted to lock the dead away so that once they've reached their new lives in the next world they have no way of coming back.[26] Perhaps this is why we have tied up the dead and locked them into boxes and caskets. Perhaps this is also why we bury people as deeply as possible or practical. My personal favourite way of holding someone down so that they can't return is the Viking method of rolling a huge stone onto the deceased. This seemed to ensure that they weren't going anywhere or returning to the community any time soon.[27]

Still, other communities have left religious items with the dead in order to assist in their move to their new reality. These items were often connected to a community's worship life and made some statement about what members thought about what happened when we die. In one Palaeolithic gravesite in France, for example, archeologists found cowrie shells placed neatly around the corpse. These particular shells were believed to symbolize the way we pass through on our way to new lives. Placing them with the deceased was a means of helping the deceased on their way. Riane Eisler also suggests that they help the deceased return to the world of the living through physical rebirth.[28] Some depictions of this new journey were more dramatic than others. The Vikings used to bury more important people in boats and ships as a way of speeding them towards the afterlife.[29]

Attempts to deal with fear and tension have affected burial practices for centuries. While some of these ways sound quite conventional to our ears, others may be unsettling or perhaps even offensive. It doesn't really matter what we think. When it comes to academic subjects such as history and archeology context is everything. A particular practice made perfect sense at the time and that's what counts. The Aztecs of Mexico, for example, practiced both burial and cremation. They reserved burial for those dying under certain circumstances. They would bury people, for example, who would die as a result of drowning or childbirth. It was seen as a kind of respect and reward.[30] Everyone else was cremated. Aboriginal people here in North America have practiced everything from mummification to cremation.[31] They have also buried people in the ground or suspended them in trees.[32]

Some cultures have even included cannibalism in their burial rituals.[33] As troubling as we may find this idea it made deep and profound sense to the communities and individuals who practiced it. Angela Sumegi describes these rituals as being "very formal, solemn and sad". They were a way of connecting the deceased with their community in a new and spiritual way.[34] They were a way for survivors to incorporate, internalize and embody the qualities and accomplishments of the deceased. By consuming parts of a warrior, for example, the survivors believed they would be adding the bravery of the deceased warrior to their own lives. If the warrior was brave it was believed those consuming him would become brave.

When not practicing cannibalism communities have buried their dead in more public places such as tribal longhouses or religious chapels.[35] It's not until recently that religious individuals have been buried in consecrated cemeteries.[36] Some forms of burial are quite intriguing. Archaeologists in Greece once discovered the body of an infant at the bottom of a container of honey.[37] The Ancient Babylonians did the same thing with their dead.[38] Prior to burial, the Persians once covered their dead in wax.[39]

Regardless of how we respond to past burial practices, burial sites offer a tremendous amount of information about how individuals, families, and communities lived and died.[40] We can learn a lot from the items we find and even the skeletal remains of the deceased themselves. We can find out what they did for a living and the strength of the economy when they died. We can assess their social status. We can even discover what the person ate and how healthy they were when they died.[41]

We can also discover what they believed. Some scholars believe that burial sites reflect what people thought of the afterlife.[42] Many believe, for example, that the spirit leaves the body at death but at some future time will return to visit, borrow, or even reclaim it. Many Christians believe that there will be a future resurrection and that our bodies should be kept for that occurrence. Leslie Stevenson argues that this is "another of the essential doctrines of Christianity".[43] This explains why the early Christian church in Europe frowned upon the practice of cremation. They dismissed it as being "pagan".[44] Many of us are rethinking this. When the time arrives for this resurrection to happen I'm not sure we're going to want what's buried in the ground. If Christians could see what the body looks like when it decomposes they would probably take a pass on the retrieval part of this process and request a new body from their maker. That would be the smart and less "icky" move.

Concern for the environment is another reason why we may consider cremation over a more traditional burial. When we discuss things like public health we can debate the benefits of the different ways we can be buried or niched. Should we be embalmed and buried in caskets? Embalming is the removal of vital organs of the deceased and the replacement of the blood with a pinkish fluid. It's a practice that became popular during the American Civil war and continues to be popular today, although some, like writer Sarah Murray, may consider the whole concept "weird".[45] In many ways it seems little different than the ancient Cheyenne practice of covering the bodies of the deceased with red coloured paint.[46] N.J. Berrill refers to the embalming process as "pickling".[47]

One of the most recent conflicts I've had to deal with concerned the question of whether or not the deceased should be cremated. These debates and discussions can become extremely emotional. They can include theological considerations and environmental implications. Conflicts this intense can affect the outcome of the funeral service itself. In terms of the environment, cremation requires the burning of a lot of fuel while burying embalmed bodies takes up a lot of space. This contributes to an expanding "environmental footprint". Perhaps the answer lies in some "green alternative" we have yet to discover. Perhaps we can return to a time when bodies were left to be dealt with by more natural elements.

Social philosopher Jeremy Bentham chose a rather unique location for his funeral. He had been afraid of graveyards since childhood and found them a literal waste of good land.[48] Instead of being buried in the conventional way of his time he donated his body to science and had his funeral in the same operating theatre in which his body was dissected. Following this dissection his remains were placed on permanent display for people to see.[49] For Bentham perhaps this is what the afterlife looked like.

Regardless of whether we're pickled, dissected, dipped in honey, burned, eaten or wrapped in burlap, many of the artifacts found in early graves reflect this belief in the immortality of the spirit and the returning to visit or completely reclaim the body. As we have already mentioned, artifacts are also included in graves to help spirits move into the afterlife. These artifacts also tell us something of what people believed to be the afterlife activities of the deceased. Ancient Chinese royalty, for example, were buried with goods, tools, food, drink, and even entire groups of servants or knights so that their efforts will live on in another plane of existence.[50] The ancient Chinese were not the only ones to include family, friends, and servants of the deceased. Cultures like the Aztecs buried the ashes and bodies of people who sacrificed themselves in an effort to provide companionship for the deceased as he or she made their way into the next world.[51] A nomadic and adventurous European people called the Avars included dead horses, horse riding equipment, clothing, accessories and weapons in their graves as these things reflected their lifestyle.[52] At a place called Sutton Hoo archaeologists found a large boat that had been buried with someone.[53] Women and men from a variety of cultures were buried with pottery.[54] Sometimes items left in the graves were souvenirs of the travels of the deceased.[55]

Once again, many ancient practices continue to this day. People will place stuffed animals and letters into the caskets of people being buried. We also place food and even the "cremains" of previously departed pets. Sometimes these same objects are placed in the containers of those being cremated. Including these items helps the living with their grieving and can be something we encourage when we meet with the family.

Modern practices now involve technology. There is one Swedish company that even installs sound systems and internet access in caskets in case the deceased has a need to use them. These systems are powered by connections leading to solar panels atop the tombstones.[56] Of course, not everybody can afford a solar powered tombstone with all of the bells and whistles.

Even a lack of belief can affect our burial practices. Historically, the deceased were buried near a holy place like a church. As many people moved away from a religious orientation cemeteries moved away from the churches. Eire writes, "Partly for reasons of public health, but also partly because of secularizing pressures, burials began a gradual migration from the vaults beneath churches or churchyards to lots no longer adjacent to churches, and eventually to much larger areas outside cities and towns."[57] Today these cemeteries resemble parks and offer space for a variety of religious and nonreligious rituals.

Perhaps Penny Colman summarizes this changing history best when she writes, "Regardless of what happens to corpses — from inhumation and cremation to cryonic suspension — most of them get put into things. And people have found a variety of ways to contain corpses and cremated remains."[58] In many cases, the "things" Colman refers to are placed either in the ground or some other place as a part of the wider funeral ritual. I've seen cremains buried in homemade wooden boxes and even in baked bean tins.

For the graveside service we're being asked to lead in the present day the ritual that accompanies these placements can take many different shapes and sizes. Most of the time the service leader reads their way through the graveside ritual. The ancient druids used to sing the words of the graveside service.[59] This common experience and variety of ritual possibilities may have something to do with the finality of what we are doing. This is another one of those times when a death becomes real and individuals begin to understand the significance of what has taken place.[60] When we begin to experience this reality unfolding in our lives some strange things may begin to happen. When George Bowering lost his father, for example, he wrote, "I was shocked to observe myself rushing from my Protestant family formation to kiss his coffin."[61]

J.K. Morrison suggests that the graveside may actually be more important than the actual chapel service itself.[62] Perhaps the most important reason why this moment is so powerful is because, as we have previously discussed, the mourner sees the open grave or hole in which the urn will be placed and that is a powerful image to confront. The death becomes real and we cannot escape its effect on our lives. This can be one of the healthiest times of the overall grief process. John Calvin would be a historic figure that would agree with this. Herman Selderhuis writes, "He thought it best to go directly to the cemetery and deliver the funeral message there, so that people heard the message right at the grave."[63] In an effort to simplify funeral rituals it came to pass that the entire Sixteenth Century funeral happened at the graveside.[64]

This timelessness can be reflected in any resource we borrow or create. Perhaps the best way to accomplish this is by beginning the graveside service with something like the following:

"From the beginning of human history we have brought our family and friends to places where we offer our continuing thoughts, prayers, and goodbyes".

We can follow these words with a brief prayer where we can say something like:

"We have done all that loving hands can do. We commit this mortal body to the ground, but we rest in the assurance that our friend is in thy hands."[65]

We cannot avoid or change reality so we as service leaders may as well use our words to address it.

As we make our way through the graveside service and help listeners confront the changes loss brings, different seasons of the year can be incorporated into your service materials. A local funeral director was telling me that he has heard clergy focus on seasonal themes when leading graveside services. We can make reference to the weather conditions and changing seasons. We can talk about the changes that nature brings to the world around us. We can talk about the change that turns winter into spring. We can use these references as a way of discussing how people live on with friends and family. Perhaps the best time of year for this is autumn. The leaves are changing colour and falling from the tree. It's the perfect time to name the cycle of life in which we all find ourselves.

One way we can include seasonal themes is in how we introduce certain elements of the service. It can something as simple as adding a sentence to the beginning of a prayer or the introduction to a poem or Bible reading. In one autumn graveside service I began the act of committal by saying:

"Just as the leaves from the trees have their time and fall to the ground in autumn, we acknowledge —— as one who has walked among us. We commend him to the elements ..."

The word "elements" can describe a variety of place as graveside services do not always have to happen on solid ground. On rare, yet equally important occasions, burials also happen at sea. This happens quite frequently in combat situations. In the heat of a conflict there may be no opportunity to transport the dead back to dry land so they have to be "dropped" into the water. Burial at sea may also be necessary in peacetime. There may be reasons why ships cannot make it to port where they can leave a body to be buried or cremated. This type of burial is both practical and powerful. It's also extremely symbolic and meaningful. It's for this reason that the "landed" deceased may also request a sea burial. Funeral industry critic, Jessica Mitford, had her ashes spread at sea.[66]

I will mention here that a burial during wartime is the one time when we can make an exception to the rule that we cannot read a funeral out of book and simply drop a name into the text whenever we run across a blank on a page. As military chaplains have discovered the hard way there simply isn't time to either learn about the life of the deceased or make contact the family when preparing a funeral. Chaplains may also be faced with the task of burying more than one soldier at a time. This is the one occasion when it is both practical and recommended to read a funeral out of a book.[67] There will be a chance for a more conventional memorial service back on the home–front once the surviving family and friends of the deceased absorb the news and review their options.

When it comes to peacetime in the present day a more detailed graveside service may be requested for those times when there is no chapel service. For these occasions here is a simple order of service you can use:

1. Procession to Graveside
2. Welcome and Introduction
3. Prayer
4. Reading

5. Eulogy / Tribute (Optional)
6. Time of Silent Prayer and Reflection
7. Committal
8. Blessing or Dismissal

While there may be some similarities between chapel and graveside services let's review some of these elements and briefly discuss them.

As in the chapel service it's helpful to begin the graveside service with a welcome and introduction. We can use this as a way of recognizing the shift in location and outline the reason why we're doing so. Why have we moved and why are we here? Those are the questions we can deal with right from the start. In doing so we can say something like:

> "We offer our continuing thoughts, prayers, and goodbyes today we as we bring John to this place of burial. We consider his place among family and friends and the gifts he offered while among us. We ask God's blessing on his continuing journey even as we ask God to help us say those goodbyes."

A service leader can omit the last sentence and make other wording changes for non–religious services. It may be helpful, however, to include a statement that the departed has made some transition and is continuing the journey in a new way. Here's a non–religious variation of the above welcome and introduction:

> "We offer our continuing thoughts and goodbyes today we as we bring John to this place of burial. We reflect on his place among family and friends and the gifts he has offered so many."

This opening may sound brief but there can be advantages to brevity, precision and simplicity. If you do feel that this opening is a little too brief there are a couple of things you could try.

One thing that can be added to this introduction is a brief list of the positive gifts the departed has offered the people who shared his life. We can talk about where they've lived and what they have done. The celebrant can mention qualities, priorities, commitments and interests not already mentioned in the previous funeral service. The celebrant can mention important relationships that were life giving and meaningful. There is a wide range of possible things a person can include here. We can say things like, "We offer thanks for his compassion and understanding." We can add, "We celebrate his commitment to his spouse and children." These statements can certainly be altered to reflect the individual's life situation. The finished product may look something like this:

"We offer our continuing thoughts and goodbyes today we as we bring John to this place of burial. We reflect on his place among family and friends and the gifts he has offered so many. We offer thanks for his compassion and understanding. We celebrate his commitment to his spouse and children."

As I've stated earlier in the chapter a religious prayer can follow the Welcome and Introduction. Most, if not all denominational resources include prayers for these occasions. Wherever possible, we can either adapt these prayers to be consistent with how we would usual word things or write our own "from scratch". These materials can be saved for future use. As our thoughts about funerals and burials grow and develop our resources will evolve as well.

Instead of offering a prayer, if the family has requested a non–religious service then one or more poems can be included here. You can choose from any number of appropriate poems. There are extensive lists of examples that can be found in both published and online resources. We can also include a poem or two on those occasions when families do not feel comfortable with scripture readings in the service. Funeral homes will have a list of poems we can borrow from. The poems they have available are often those that appear on service folders that are often handed out prior to the chapel service. If the poem on the service folder is appropriate for the graveside service we can read that and invite people to follow along.

For those who do prefer the inclusion of scripture there are two main readings I rely on and these are also mentioned in previous chapters. They are Psalm 23 and Ecclesiastes 3:1-8. Families may request other possibilities and we can add those wherever and whenever possible. The two key words to keep in mind here are "context" and "practicality". We can choose readings that are both concise and appropriate to the outdoor setting.

We can follow the reading with a time of silence in which we can reflect on what we're seeing and feeling. We can think about the finality of this shared moment with the deceased. Perhaps we can even contemplate that hopefully far off moment when we are brought to a similar place by the people dealing with our death.

Following this silent time we can also use a variation of the closing dismissal I use when closing services that have included a candle lighting ritual. We can offer the following:

> "As we bring our time to a close and make our way into
> the days and weeks to come let us carry John with us in
> hearts, minds and spirits. May their memory live in
> everything we say and do. May their spirit live on in each
> of our lives this day and every day. Amen."

It is appropriate to follow the closing blessing by inviting final farewell gestures such as the placing of flowers or the filling in of the grave. Earlier in this book I mentioned a graveside service in which people were asked to place stones in the ground with the urn of the deceased. Some families prefer to throw dirt into the grave of their loved one. In some communities and cultures it is not unusual for friends and family to actually fill in the grave. I spoke with one woman whose family lived in Canada's north and they regularly dug and filled in the graves of family and friends. This may not always be possible so it is important for someone to ask cemetery management what is permissible when it comes to tailoring the graveside service to meet people's needs.

The closing phase of the funeral continues the process of making the loss real. This helps groups and individuals make their way through their grief. Regardless of how we bring the funeral ritual to a close we can help survivors encounter reality and process the experience in a way that helps them grieve and move forward.

Evaluation

Whenever I meet with clients in the days leading up to a funeral I'm typically quite casually dressed. I'm usually wearing things like collared plaid shirts and cargo pants or shorts. This is why people seem surprised when I arrive at the funeral location just prior to the actual service. I make a point of dressing quite differently for that moment in time. People look me up and down and say things like, "You clean up well." I wish I had a nickel for every time someone said that. When it comes to feedback everything about our work is up for examination. In the internet age the phrase "everyone's a critic" is all too true. We all want to comment on the people and events around us. We all want to evaluate, critique, grade and offer our two–cents worth. Everything is fair game, including our work of leading funerals.

Perhaps we're the biggest critics of our own work and there's nothing wrong with that. Professionals in many different disciplines consider it a part of their work commitment to look back and examine things they have said and done. Retired astronaut Colonel Chris Hadfield is an example of a highly trained professional whose priority was to constantly evaluate and rethink what he did in both his training and actual time spent on both the space shuttle and the International Space Station. Constant evaluation was a matter of life and death for Colonel Hadfield and his colleagues. He claims that astronauts are "perpetual students" who are always preparing for the tests and projects ahead. For every day in space Hadfield estimates that months are spent in training and retraining.[1] Sometimes we may dismiss this commitment as being unique to a small group of professions but this commitment to continuing education, however, also applies to our work of leading funerals.

All too often we may dismiss education is being something that ends when we reach a certain age. It's something that we experience when we're growing up and preparing ourselves for life in the "real world". When we graduate from high school or university we "move on" to get a job and settle into some adult routine. What we don't always realize is that we never stop learning and this is why many organizations talk about "continuing education". This may not be something we enjoy thinking about but it is a critical part of our ongoing lives and work. Joan Chittister writes, "We love the learning period of early adulthood but ignore the experience that comes with maturity."[2] As the world changes around us we constantly experience the need to reflect on our work and learn new skills and ways of doing things. Technology, alone forces us to adapt and move in ways we may find challenging and overwhelming. But this constant training and retraining is a must if we are to grow and mature in our work.

Constant evaluation is a critical part of our effectiveness and success. Evaluation is how we review and learn from what we have done and what has happened around us. But for evaluation to work it has to be done every time the work of leading the funeral is complete. We cannot avoid it or put it off, regardless of how stressed we become as a result of our work. Herodotus once wrote, "The beginning and end of a matter are not always seen at once."[3] When we're preparing a service we don't always know how something is going to develop in real time. Sometimes the end or conclusion of something can be just as important as the beginning. Whenever we try something that does or doesn't work we grow and increase our chances of being more effective the next time we're asked to lead a service.

What I am referring to is the evaluation of the funeral service we have just concluded. Change is a constant we all experience and evaluations help us understand how we can bring about change and enhance our own work. The ancient Greeks once said that we couldn't step into the same river twice and this piece of wisdom is still valid today. The water our feet initially touch will be long gone by the time we remove our foot and place it once again in the same location. We can also say that we cannot do the same funeral twice. Each and every one is unique. In being unique, however, they can still grant us an opportunity to improve our overall "game" and help us maintain our readiness for future efforts.

Healthy amounts of critical self–awareness help prevent momentum from blinding us and carrying us into dangerous waters. W. Edwards Deming warns that leaders can head into dangerous situations when we "rely on momentum of past performance".[4] This self–awareness is important because it can sometimes identify problems that affect more than one area of our work. The Bible warns us about the dangers of filling old wine skins with new wine. New questions and challenges require new ways and approaches. It's not that "old" is necessarily bad or harmful it's just that we are constantly working with new people and situations and the expectations, alone, can push us in new directions with how we approach our work. A Zen master was once asked to share something of his life's history with his students. He thought for a moment and then simply told them that his life was "just one mistake after another".[5] That is the ultimate in self–awareness. It's also the ultimate act of evaluation.

Evaluating our work is never easy. It often seems as if our lives are, as the master says, "just one mistake after another". This is a reality that seems universal. In their book entitled *Thanks for the Feedback,* Douglas Stone and Sheila Heen write, "When we ask people to list their most difficult conversations, feedback *always* comes up."[6] When it comes to feedback it's important to remember that the key person in this entire process is us.[7] We're the ones who led a particular service and we're the ones who have to find a way to keep improving our efforts so that we can continue serving people in a helpful way. Stone and Heen write, "Broadly, feedback comes in three forms: appreciation (thanks), coaching (here's a better way to do it), and evaluation (here's where you stand)."[8] We will be discussing each of these forms in this chapter.

There's really no definitive way of knowing whether or not a particular funeral service "worked" and was effective. There are no checklists, tests or grades to help bring the experience to a close. Unfortunately, there's no set of criteria by which we can measure the effect of what was said and done unfortunately. There are no referees or umpires trained to know what to look for. It's not like a figure skating competition in which judges watch an event and then score what they saw by holding up large cards with numbers boldly displayed for everyone to see. There isn't a lunatic chef screaming at us and telling the world that our food is crap.

Mind you, sometimes I wish there was someone out there telling me how to do things and reviewing my work when it was complete. I know that when I led my first funeral I wanted a how–to book or instructor to help me through it. I wanted a how–to book I could open so that everything would be organized into easy to use steps. I needed something that was so foolproof even a beginner such as myself could use it. When I was finished with that book I wanted someone to evaluate my work and give me a list of things I needed to do in order to improve. Unfortunately such a combination of how–to book and coach didn't exist so I had to muddle through on my own with whatever help I could find.

Whether or not a service was effective ultimately depends on the opinions and needs of the people in attendance. They're the ones who hear, interpret and ultimately respond to what we say and do. Each and every individual will evaluate a service based on a personal set of criteria. Many of us want words of comfort and assurance. Still others may want to learn more about the life of the deceased. Perhaps something was indeed said that offered someone hope and comfort. Something may have been said or done that helped initiate a healthy grieving process. A musical selection or poem may have brought peace to a chaotic situation. The eulogist may have been silent on contentious issues in a person's life and that could bring relief to listeners. Regardless of whether or not something worked we still need to evaluate. We have to review the service and make choices about our work. People will try and help us with this process but the responsibility for choices and future directions remains with ourselves. We cannot allow the personal opinions and judgements to put us off our game. We still have to find a way to evaluate our work.

But this does not mean we ignore the input of others completely. Ignoring feedback is one thing that can and will lead to the kind of arrogance I mentioned at the beginning of this chapter. Even though we make the decisions we still require input wherever possible and necessary. Irvin Yalom once told therapists to "Take advantage of opportunities to learn from patients."[9] The same is true of the family members we deal with for each and every funeral. We have to learn from our clients, our colleagues in the funeral industry and even ourselves.

One overriding problem here is that something may be remembered that wasn't actually said or done during the service. Evaluation relies on a decent memory and that's not always possible when we're under a lot of stress. It's one of those disconnects that can occur between speaker and listener. Part of our work is to sift through what has been said and done, find the gaps and things we should have done differently and make changes where necessary. To borrow from a Biblical image some of what we will sort through will be wheat and some will be chaff. The trick is to know the difference. I had an encounter following one service where a family member cornered me at the reception following the service. He offered me the following words: "The service was good but you were awfully serious and somber up front there. You didn't smile once and you should smile more when you speak like that." I'm not sure if that was wheat or chaff but I did want to ask the person if they realized we had just been through a funeral. But even with this unusual feedback we still have to find those things we can use in the future.

We are left to sift through all of the different pieces of information we've been given and think about ways in which we can makes changes and improve our performance and resources for the next time we are called upon. But we cannot use this information to create universal rules, however. This sorting can lead to some anxious moments. What are we going to hear and read? How are we going to have to change in order to improve and make things better? Perhaps we can begin by learning from our more obvious teachers. Sometimes stress and anxiety force things to the surface for us to examine. Rollo May, for one, suggests that stress and anxiety can be a wonderful teacher and that certainly applies here. He writes, "Anxiety illuminates experiences that we would otherwise run away from."[10]

It's important to keep in mind that just because something works in one situation does not necessarily mean that it is going to be effective in another. I remember Canadian sports personality Ron MacLean telling the story of a field goal kick he made during an important high school football game. It was a critical kick and everything went perfectly. The snap, hold, and kick all went perfectly. He did everything he was trained to do. He had worked hard to reach that point. The kick should have been easy. Previous kicks had gone straight through the uprights. It was ruled a wild kick, however, and an opposing player ran the ball back for the game winning touchdown.[11] Everything can work according to plan and yet we can still be accused of making a mistake. Sometimes even the smallest mistake can lead to huge results. To quote musician Jimmy Buffett, "Remember, it can all go to hell at any minute."[12] In all too many situations "minute" is far too generous. "Instant" would be a more appropriate word. Hopefully I don't sound too flippant and dismissive when I say this but "that's life".

But even when things "go to hell" and are at their worst we have to find a way to carry on. We have to carry on by examining our performance with openness and honesty. Former G.E. CEO Jack Welch once said, "Face reality as it is, not as it was or as you wish it were."[13] Wishful thinking may feel good but it doesn't help us improve and grow. Reality changes us so Welch also said, "Change before you have to."[14] If something didn't work then so be it. Make the necessary changes so that the next family is helped in a more positive and effective way.

It's not easy to predict how a funeral will go. Evaluating a service when it is complete can be equally problematic. This is unfortunate in a way because by the time the service is complete the damage may already be done. But even though one situation ends badly doesn't mean we allow history to repeat itself. Even the most negative experiences can be spun into gold. A retired U.S. Navy pilot once wrote, "Experience is something you simply cannot buy."[15] This wisdom also applies to the task of leading funerals. The more services we lead the more experience we collect and this is one of the ways we become more effective. To Carl Rogers, experience is something we can trust.[16] Experience teaches us many things. Morton Hunt writes, "... experts have their knowledge organized and arranged in schemas that are full of special shortcuts based on experience."[17]

Even though we may be at a point in our work lives where we think we're prepared for anything evaluation can still keep us humble. I use words like "humble" and "humility" carefully. Humility is something we do not always understand. Being humble does not mean that we have to turn ourselves into doormats. For me, Kevin Seasoltz offers the most effective definition of humility when he writes that the humble person "quietly acknowledges both his strengths and his weaknesses."[18] The only change I would make would be to add "clearly" either before or after "quietly". So humility is quietly and clearly acknowledging our strengths and weaknesses. And when we know our strengths and weaknesses we know, to borrow Ben Witherington III's terminology, "one's place in things."[19]

Our challenge is to identify our strengths and use them whenever we can. We have to name our weaknesses and try to improve them.[20] Hooyman and Kramer write, "Self–awareness should be an ongoing process of monitoring one's personal reactions to one's bereaved clients' losses and grief responses ..."[21] As painful and distasteful as it may seem we cannot be afraid of addressing our weaknesses. Arlene Dickinson writes, "The more mindful you are of your weaknesses, the more likely it is that you'll be able to overcome them or compensate for them in the future."[22] Some of our mistakes can be extremely public and embarrassing. Public speaking expert Peter Bender writes, "The best speakers all become good the hard way: they have spoken to many, often hundreds, of audiences on the same topic. In the process, they probably made many embarrassing mistakes. Their ability to conquer fear and failure helped them learn from these mistakes."[23]

Because it can be so difficult, evaluation requires initiative. While it's great to know what went well we don't always want to know when something doesn't work. It's often difficult to place our work under the microscope. It's not always easy to check in with people and ask how they experienced the funeral. It's something we have to do, however. At the very least, this can help us avoid being blindsided by complaints and concerns. How many times have we found ourselves in a situation where we were the last to hear about a problem or crisis? How many times have we asked people why we were never told and they responded by saying, "You never asked"? We have to get used to asking questions and it is especially important to do so following each and every funeral we lead.

In case we're at a loss for words or ideas Paul Irion once provided some questions that can be of value in our present day. He once asked: What did the mourners need and what happened in the service to meet these needs?[24] How did the service help them begin the grieving and transition process? Did the funeral deal realistically with death?[25] We can also ask more pragmatic questions like, "Were there any technical glitches during the service?" or "Did things go smoothly between myself, the funeral directors and other participants?" Perhaps a related question can be, "Was the funeral comforting?" I've previously mentioned how people can come to a funeral service anxious about what they will experience. Have we put them at ease? Did we burden them or bore them? Did the funeral help people learn more about the deceased? Did it help them remember? Did it help them with their grieving? Did they understand you?

This last question is of particular importance in our increasingly multi-cultural world. For many of our clients and listeners English is a second or third language. While their vocabulary and grammar may be functional they may not understand some of the more subtle and nuanced things we say. Some of the expressions we use, for example, don't translate well into other languages and cultures. Some listeners may approach us with questions about word choice and usage when the funeral is complete. This is another opportunity when we can remember the difference between producer and product. Once we say something it's impossible to reel it back in like a fish. If a listener hears something we say and responds negatively to it our thoughts and intentions are irrelevant. This is why some parts of the evaluation process may resemble a conversation more than an investigation.

If you would like to speak with the family about their experience you could reach out, phone them and touch base. You could ask if they would like a visit and schedule one if they respond positively to the offer. Please keep in mind that they may simply thank you and end the conversation there. Don't take it personally. Survivors may want to be left alone or find support in other places. They may not know what to say. They may find it difficult to put their experience into words. It's important to respect their wishes but you can also leave the door open for future contact if that is what they want. Sometimes one member will contact us at a later date and we can arrange a time to speak with them. We have to leave the door open for this possibility.

When we do reach out to survivors we may not receive the information we need. Lots of people will offer general compliments like "good job padre" but it doesn't help us make necessary improvements to how we do things. Jack Welch once said, "The worst sins are committed in boom times, when everybody feels satisfied."[26] People do not always know how to offer feedback in difficult times. We don't always know how to offer negative feedback. We are not trained for it for one thing. How many of us can say that our training included a period of time in which we dealt with our response to the work of others? If we did receive this training how many of us practice it often enough in our day to day lives to be competent?

Contrary to what we may think or have been told negative feedback is not always a bad thing. This sometimes runs contrary to conventional thinking and human nature. How many times have we wanted to stomp away from people who disagree with us or don't like something we've said or done. Even though it's harder work it's often best to respond to negativity with patience and maturity. We can't all be like the old poet Robert Herrick and throw our preaching notes at people who don't agree with us or tune us out completely.[27] We can turn things around to the positive. We can learn a lot from mistakes and disasters. This is an important point on the road to improvement and increasing the quality and value of our work. James Pike once wrote, "We are what we are because of our mistakes — even tragic ones — as much as because of our successes and joys."[28] Even the business world is beginning to appreciate the value of failure and learning from decisions that don't always go according to plan. Based on what I have heard from families and funeral directors, most of the negative feedback we receive can be useful. It's a rare piece of feedback that cannot be resolved or acted upon. While we do receive feedback that is so "out there" that it really isn't helpful we can be assured that most of our mistakes can be fixed.

But one thing we cannot do, however, is get so focused on our mistakes that our performance is negatively affected. We can "freeze up" if we're too hard on ourselves. There has to be a more balanced middle ground where we can learn from our mistakes and move on. We have to find a way to continue functioning when we fail. Gail Vaz–Oxlade writes, "Our mistakes should not define us." She suggests, "If you try something one way and it doesn't work, change how you're doing it."[29] She makes it sound simple and it is. Too many of us invest so much energy in fretting over our mistakes that we miss key opportunities to focus on other areas of our work and that is extremely counterproductive. Learning when to let go is a part of our evaluation work.

Regardless of whether the feedback is positive or negative it may be helpful to write out some notes in response to what we hear and read. These notes can be a reference for future use. This is one way we can address both positive and negative and keep our perspective at the same time. One pastor told me that he was going to start a journal and as I've said before, this is a good idea for both ourselves and those with whom we work. It's helpful to gather our thoughts and questions together and get them on paper or disk. Barbara Ehrenreich concludes that "writing makes things easier"[30] and this certainly applies to the keeping of a journal.

This journal can record the feelings and experiences we have in response to each service we lead. For those of us experiencing a loss journals can help us heal.[31] Journaling can help us discern our strengths and weaknesses.[32] Journaling can also help us make changes to the style and content of the services we offer. We can also turn to our journals when we're struggling with more practical questions like, "Why do I feel so tired after a funeral?" We can periodically review our journal and spot any trends requiring our attention. Joan Didion calls this "keeping in touch" and writes, "It is a good idea ... to keep in touch, and I suppose that keeping in touch is what notebooks are all about."[33]

People will have their own thoughts on how this journal will be assembled. Forms can be created in which thoughts and reflections can be recorded, organized and kept in a file or binder. Journals can be kept in book form. The bottom line is that regardless of what we write or gather or how we store that information journals are for our personal use. Our methods and systems have to work for us. We do not have to and probably shouldn't share them. The information they contain is extremely personal and potentially dangerous to both personal and working relationships. Perhaps the main reason for this is that external readers may not have the education or experience to understand what we've written. This lack of understanding could lead to trouble. It's often best to destroy these journals at the appropriate time. We may want to leave written instructions to this effect in our wills on what to do with our journals in case we pass away before we're able to dispose of them ourselves. While burning them may be the best way to dispose of them there may be situations in which they're transferred to the possession of a seminary or some other archival institution. If and when this happens certain guarantees need to be negotiated so that the information contained within will be used with the appropriate amount of caution and confidentiality.

The information in our journals is, for the most part, based on an incredibly intense experience so we cannot ignore the emotional dimension of what we're reviewing. In some cases we need to be honest with ourselves and acknowledge that we may be grieving along with the surviving family. I've lost friends and family members and have participated in services in which I was experiencing many of the same emotions as the rest of the gathered people. When I find myself in a situation in which I'm sharing many of the same emotions as others I normally share that fact with family and friends. I also try and explain how this emotional connection works. Did I grow up with the person? Did I know them from a previous community in which I lived and worked?

Being honest about our experience of grief helps us care for ourselves and manage our resources so that we can be a help to others. Grief can be a taxing experience and we may find ourselves running low on energy and that can affect our thinking, our drive and our overall job performance. It can also affect our overall "life performance" as well.[34]

When we evaluate a funeral and respond to the results of our searching we're examining some intense and powerful experiences and interpretations. Two people will not interpret an experience the same way. What we say and what listeners hear can often be very different. Perhaps there is something in our tone of voice that rubs someone the wrong way. There may someone in the congregation who doesn't like a figure of speech we've chosen. We can say all the right things and still be wrong in the eyes of our clients. As former Boston Bruin and hockey great Bobby Orr says, "Sometimes you do everything right and the puck bounces the wrong way."[35] I once received a card thanking me for what they had thought was a "good funeral". The person who sent the card included a wonderful note thanking me for some of the things I had said during the service. When I went back and consulted my notes I suddenly realized that I hadn't actually said those things for which I was being thanked. At least I don't recall saying them. People seemed to be experiencing gaps in their memories and filling in the blanks themselves. But at least the puck didn't "bounce the wrong way".

People may also complain about things that we didn't say and they may be concerned about how things happened. Some of these complaints may be legitimate but some of them may be groundless. I remember a colleague showing me an e–mail in which she was called to task for something she said in the service. My colleague showed me her notes and it was obvious that the words mentioned in the message were not there. I'm certain she would have remembered if she had gone "off script" for even a small part of the service. Differences such as these often require clarification if the feedback is going to be helpful to anyone. The key word here is conversation. If people are open to the idea we can suggest a meeting to discuss concerns and problems. It may help the family to open up and release emotional energy. It would also help us learn and improve our work.

In saying this we often need to begin a conversation about concerns families have regarding our work. I would offer one caution at this point. There are potential problems with meeting an angry family and we have to begin by setting some ground rules. We have to be clear about boundaries and have a personal zero–tolerance policy around abuse. Being angry does not give anyone license to abuse another person. What we can try to do is help people focus their anger on an issue or problem that can be discussed and dealt with.

Regardless of whether or not a complaint is groundless we may still find ourselves in a situation where we have to apologize for something we said or did. When we find ourselves in these situations it is important to offer three simple words: "I am sorry." Jan Linn writes, "Many things contribute to strong personal relationships, but none more than saying 'I'm sorry' when an apology is warranted."[36] Apologies are helpful when it is warranted and "warranted" is the key word here. We live in a world in which apologies are thrown around too cheaply and easily. We see this in our church lives and we see it in the world around us. Many of these apologies have little if any value. So if we have to apologize for something we should ensure it's actually going to help us resolve an issue or problem. It is always important to admit mistakes and try to repair any damage done by making them. Irvin Yalom offers the same advice to therapists when he writes, "If you make a mistake, admit it. Any attempt to cover up will backfire."[37] A few words of apology in the heat of the moment can help calm things down so that we can lick our wounds and move on.

A number of years ago an experienced minister was called upon to officiate at a funeral held in a village's community hall. People came from all around to attend and the hall was packed. The service began and proceeded to the moment when the minister read from Ecclesiastes. He reached the point in this reading when the ancient teacher writes, "There's a time to plant, and a time to pluck up what is planted."[38] Instead of saying this exact sentence, he proclaimed in his loudest preaching voice, "There's a time to plant, and a time to f**k up what is planted!" This was apparently one of those moments when the minister in question learned the hard way what not to do in a funeral service. He also learned how important it was to apologize, repair whatever damage he could and try to move on.

One way of evaluating and learning from the funeral experience is to form a group of colleagues whose sole purpose is to meet periodically and discuss recent experiences, questions, and insights. Back in the 1960s a writer by the name of Adam Smith suggested that one of the best things a successful investor does is to "find smart people".[39] This is also true of ministry. I have found that many of us learn as much from conversations with colleagues as from even the most effective courses. Members of this group could swap stories, experiences, and information. They could talk about books and articles they have read and services they have attended. This group could either meet in person or create an online forum. Their questions and stories, alone, would make this effort worthwhile. Machiavelli once commented on the importance of asking questions. He suggested that without questions we cannot inform ourselves or search for important answers.[40]

From this circle of colleagues we can learn from their previous experience. We can also attend the funerals they officiate. Sometimes the best way to learn is by sitting in the congregation watching and listening to others "do their thing". The reverse is true as well. In some situations it may be appropriate to invite a colleague to sit in on a funeral and offer critical feedback on what we are doing. I will invite a colleague to a funeral and meet them later to discuss their observations, questions and suggestions. Peter Bender writes, "The best and simplest way to improve is to pay attention to other presenters and analyze what they do."[41] I should say that I invite people to observe and critique "whenever possible".

Funerals are normally public gatherings where permission is not necessary. We couldn't do this in private services, however. When it comes to private services individuals and families want some control over who attends. Public services are fair game, however. I introduced the brief candle lighting ceremony mentioned earlier, for example, after seeing a colleague include it in one of her services. It's now a standard part of each of my services. While I have changed the wording the essential spirit of the act is the same. We can learn new things when we attend services that others lead.

One activity we can do either as a group or individuals is record our funerals. When I was in seminary we used to videotape sermons. Yes, it was that long ago. It was tough seeing and listening to ourselves preach. It was important to tough it out, however. This is why it may be helpful to use this practice in our working lives today. When Douglas Stone and Sheila Heen discuss the importance of recording ourselves they name things like "tone" and "actions" as things for which we should be watching out.[42] These are things we can't always see and hear and it's both helpful and eye opening to see ourselves in action.

The actions, in particular are something to focus on. Carmine Gallo recommends that whenever we watch ourselves on video we keep a record of distracting and useless gestures. How many times have we watched a speech or presentation and paid more attention to the nose picking or foot tapping than what the speaker actually had to say? The opposite can be true as well. The absence of movement and gestures can also be counterproductive. Gallo writes, "Standing absolutely still makes you appear rigid, boring, and disengaged."[43] Once we figure out what isn't working we can begin the process of refining our approach so that people are listen to what we have to say.

One of the advantages of recording our work in the present day is sheer simplicity. Smartphones often have "apps" that help us record in clear and efficient ways. Playing the service back is easy as we no longer need those huge, clunky machines that constantly eat the old tapes.[44]

It is helpful to ask the family's permission if we are going to record the service for our own use. Funeral homes are now recording services on CD or DVD and may be in a position to make us a copy if we request. This happened at a regimental service I officiated. The regiment made arrangements for a videographer to make a DVD of the service for the family and I was able to secure a copy for myself. A lot depends on the technology they have available and the workload directors are facing the particular day we're there.

We can listen to our voice and the way we say certain words. We can watch how we use our notes or make eye contact with family members and other guests. Professional and amateur athletes do this all the time. They spend endless hours reviewing game recordings and analyzing their performance. Many teams even have coaches to help players with these reviews and that has helped improve performance as well. We are professionals as well and have a responsibility to use every tool at our disposal in an effort to improve our skills.

Our evaluation process should include every aspect of our work, including the collection of materials we've gathered through the years. This includes the prayers and poems we've used in previous funerals. It includes the list of songs and hymns we may have been building. The resources we use are tools and they have to be changed and replaced whenever necessary so we cannot afford to build up too much of an attachment to them. We may find one particular poem helpful but wind up using it so much it becomes boring and odds are that many have heard us use it too many times. We have to be constantly on the lookout for new material. We have to be reading poems and listening to music. Our prayers and other written materials will need constant revision. Some of these revisions will be extensive while others will simply need some "tweaking".

Because there is so much work to do and information to sort through it is important not to rush the evaluation and development process. Growth and improvement take time. Professional development is a gradual process. Linn writes, "The wise path in ministry is to know your limitations and pay attention to them."[45] This attention will take time and energy. It will also require patience. We cannot expect too much too soon. If you're new to officiating funerals you have plenty of time to improve and develop. The important thing is to begin by focusing on fundamentals. Whether it's checking out new music or tweaking the wording of a prayer, when we improve and master the basic skills we can then build on our experience and build a body of work that really helps people through an extremely difficult time.

Evaluating a service is not a one–time experience, either. We have to be constantly reviewing what we do and how we can do it. Athletes repeat motions and movements countless times. Baseball pitchers are constantly throwing in order to learn new pitches and keep their arms strong. Runners keep going around the same courses in an effort to improve their fitness and skills. We have a responsibility to work in the same way. John Gray writes, "The heart of all religions is practice — ritual and meditation."[46] So that means we have to be constantly reading, preaching and leading services whenever possible. We have to be running or swimming our professional laps so that we remain effective and at the top of our game.

We have to be on the prowl for practices and material that help us serve the people with whom we are called to work. There will be several times when we remember a service and think about what we have learned from it. We may read something that helps us understand a word, action, or response. "In order to perfect oneself, one must renew oneself day by day."[47] It's important to remember here that "perfect" is a verb and not a final state of being. We will never be perfect. There will be elements of our work requiring attention and revision. This is a reality we cannot escape. As a Japanese manager once said to a worker: "No problem to report is a problem."[48] None of us is perfect. If we evaluate a funeral and find nothing to change or redevelop we need to go back and start from square one. There's no such thing as a perfect funeral. There has to be something good, bad or different about each and every funeral we officiate. Our future work will benefit from the exercise of evaluating each and every one.

Conclusion

A number of years ago I was arriving home from an extended vacation when the telephone rang. The funeral director on the other end of the line was in a panic. Half an hour before the funeral was to begin the minister they had originally lined up said something the family found inappropriate and was sent away by them. Both the family and funeral director suddenly found themselves in a real bind and were asking me to drop everything, grab some notes and head to the funeral home. I barely had time to change, print something off and drive to the funeral home. Luckily I was able to take a few minutes with the funeral director who was running the service and the family. I discovered as much as I could about the deceased and what the family wanted included in the service and proceed from there.

One of the realities of our work is that every funeral has its surprises. As I have said throughout *Dead Reckoning* no two funerals are alike and there's no way to write a book that addresses each situation. What I've tried to do here, however, is offer some structure and thoughts that provide us with a base of information from which we can work. A South African writer and civil servant by the name of George McCall Theal once described the ideal school as being one where "the teacher could only lay a foundation (and) the pupil must build upon it."[1]

In *Dead Reckoning* I have hopefully constructed a foundation upon which readers can build houses filled with their own skills, ideas and body of experience. It's from these elements that we build a funeral. It's also from these elements that we deal with any sudden storms that break over us. This is where Paul Tillich is correct in suggesting that theory has to match up with practice.[2] When this balance is achieved any journey, especially those over open water, can end with some amount of comfort and satisfaction. We can never plan for every challenge along the way but we can think for ourselves and recognize signs and opportunities when we have to. This not only helps ourselves make our way through the preparation and presentation of the funeral but it also helps us serve the people who have experienced this loss. Helping people through the death of a loved one in an ordered and thoughtful way is what this book is all about.

An anthropologist by the name of E.E. Evans–Pritchard once told a lecture audience that "Faced with life's crises, and especially that of death, men (sic) in their fear and anxiety release their tensions and overcome their despair by the performance of religious rites."[3] Of these religious rites perhaps the most important has been the funeral. When I began writing *Dead Reckoning* my goal was to provide a collection of resources clergy could use when planning and writing a funeral. I wanted to offer that how–to book I mentioned in the previous chapter. I wanted to tell people what they needed to say. I wanted to help them confront the fears and emotions that can be generated as the result of someone dying. I wanted to reduce or eliminate the messiness of planning and preparing a funeral. As I proceeded, however, I was caught off guard by the number of people asking how to use the prayers and other materials. They had no problem finding prayers and other materials. They could piece together their own how–to books. Service leaders wanted to know how to use their materials in a meaningful way. They were looking for explanations and commentary. They were looking for insight and advice. So this is what I've tried to offer here. In *Dead Reckoning* we broke the funeral down into six phases in order to help us organize our work.

In *Dead Reckoning* I've also tried to offer some practical advice on what to do in certain situations. As a variation of an old saying goes: "stuff happens". That "stuff" happens in each of our lives. Things can happen in funerals, for example that will leave us feeling helpless and speechless. Eulogists may show up at the funeral drunk or worse. We may have grabbed the wrong set of notes as we ran out the door on our way to the funeral. The music chosen for the service may wind up being wildly inappropriate for the service we're leading. We may say and do something we later come to regret. A eulogist or someone during "open mic" may "go rogue" and start sharing things no human being should hear. We may be asked questions we have no idea how to answer. One family told me about a time when they were leaving the chapel after a funeral only to find a dead body lying on the steps leading down to the waiting funeral coach. How do we respond to that surprise?

While it is impossible to have dealt with every possibility we can use the six phases outlined in *Dead Reckoning* to build on both personal experience and the experience and insights of colleagues and friends. These situations are becoming increasingly diverse, especially as we are moving into a time when people are doing things like requesting that surviving family and friends not hold a funeral when they die. How do we help survivors reach a compromise with the departed? How do we contribute to the discussion and debate about finding some compromise and middle ground? And this is only one example of how the funeral ritual is changing in our lives and in our time. I'm sure that each and every one of us can come up with our own examples of how the ground is changing beneath our feet.

In saying all of this, however, *Dead Reckoning* is important because there is one consistent thing in our ministry lives and it happens all the time — the phone rings, some bad news is delivered and we have to jump. All of a sudden the sermon preparation is thrown to the side and appointments and errands are rescheduled, reassigned or completely forgotten altogether. Events begin to take on a life of their own. It seems all too easy to get lost in the swirl of activity and carried away by the currents of what's happening around us. In the heat of the moment we jump into a phone booth (They still exist — I've seen them!), put on our imaginary superhero costumes and head to wherever it is we have to be going. Without a map or compass to help us navigate, however, all we do is hit the rocks and when that happens we can't help anybody.

Dead Reckoning is designed to help keep us away from the rocks and with the grieving survivors where we belong. The six phases introduced here aren't designed to be the final word but are meant to be a way of organizing our work with families, workplaces, social circles and communities. They're meant to offer suggestions, ask important questions and introduce topics for discussion that may be new to us. While we will not be able to bring the deceased back to life[4] or, to borrow Phyllis Kosminsky's words, "take the pain away",[5] we can help survivors "muddle through" and find their way through the strange, frightening and stormy seas around them.

When we head into Hamlet's "undiscovered country" we won't be making our way through these waters without markers and signs to point the way. They're like the buoys and markers we see when boating down a river or near a coastal beach. What you're reading now is a roadmap or chart you can use when planning and officiating a funeral. Charts cannot tell us everything about a place where we're going but they can give us a general sense of direction and warn us of potential problems along the way. They can tell us where the larger and more dangerous rocks are located.

Dead Reckoning has hopefully offered some direction and more than enough warnings about possible hazards when it comes to funerals. It's also offered some possibilities for when we have to improvise because each and every situation has its own random element. There are many times when we'll have to figure things out for ourselves. Theory is important but it only takes us so far. There are random elements in our work that cannot be predicted or avoided. A given service may unfold a little differently than I have outlined here but that's OK. Every situation and service are unique.

Every service is important too and deserves our best effort. It's never easy to say "goodbye" to someone but we have to try and give it all of the hard work, compassion, and empathy we can. We also have to get our own house in order when it comes to our own limitations and mortality. Sarah Murray writes, "the ways in which we leave this world speak volumes about the uneasy relationship we have with our own transience."[6] The way we remember also "speaks volumes". Regardless of what happens in our lives our connection to the deceased endures and continues. This bond deserves and needs our best effort and my hope and prayer is that

Dead Reckoning helps us honour how this bond evolves throughout the death and grief experience.

End Notes

Introduction

1. Gail Vaz–Oxlade, *Never Too Late*. (2011) Toronto: Harper Collins, p. 1.

2. Cited in John S. Donne's *The City of the Gods: A Study in Myth and Mortality*. (1965, 1974) London: Sheldon Press, p. vii.

3. Richard A. McCormick, "To Save or Let Die: The Dilemma of Modern Medicine" in *Ethical Issues in Death and Dying*. Edited by Robert F. Weir. (1977) New York: Columbia University Press, p. 183.

4. Edwidge Danticat, "Introduction" in *The Best American Essays 2011*. Introduced and Edited by Edwidge Danticat, (2011) Boston and New York: Mariner Books, p. xvii.

5. Cited in Henry Cloud, *Necessary Endings*. (2010) New York: Harper Business, N.P.

6. Cited in Tom Jokinen, *Curtains: Adventures of an Undertaker in Training*. (2010) Toronto: Random House Canada, p. 93.

7. Matthew 8:21/22.

8. Arnold Van Gennep, *The Rites of Passage*. (1960) Chicago: University of Chicago Press, p. vii.

9. Van Gennep, p. 2.

10. Cited in Lucy Mair's *An Introduction to Social Anthropology (Second Edition)*. (1972) New York and London: Oxford University Press, p. 233.

11. Angela Sumegi, *Understanding Death: An Introduction to the Ideas of Self and the Afterlife in World Religions*. (2014) Chichester: Wiley Blackwell, p. 13.

12. Hunter S. Thompson, *The Great Shark Hunt: Gonzo Papers, Volume 1*. (1979, 2003) New York and London: Simon and Schuster, p. 526.

13. Paul Radin, *Primitive Religion.* (1957 Edition) New York: Dover Publications, p. 283.

14. Bronislaw Malinowski, "Magic, Science, and Religion" in *Magic, Science and Religion: And Other Essays.* (1954 Edition) Garden City: Anchor Books, p. 47.

15. Paul Irion names and outlines this transition in his book entitled *The Funeral and the Mourners: Pastoral Care of the Bereaved.* (1954) Nashville: Abingdon Press.

16. Madeleine L'Engle, *Two Part Intervention.* (1988) New York: Farrar, Strauss and Giroux, p. 228.

17. Allan Kellehear, *A Social History of Dying.* (2007) Melbourne: Cambridge University Press, p. 27.

18. Jay Dolan, *The American Catholic Experience: A History from Colonial Times to the Present.* (1992) Notre Dame: University of Notre Dame Press, p. 62.

19. John Casey offers an excellent survey of various beliefs in the afterlife in his book entitled *After Lives: A Guide to Heaven, Hell, and Purgatory.* I've included this book in the bibliography.

20. Leslie Stevenson, *Seven Theories of Human Nature (Second Edition).* (1987) New York and Oxford: Oxford University Press, p. 30.

21. Robert Fossier, *The Axe and the Oath. (*2010) Princeton: Princeton University Press, p. 136.

22. Douglas E. Cowan and Gary G. Bromley, *Cults and New Religions: A Brief History.* (2008) Malden: Blackwell Publishing, p. 207.

23. Paul Radin, *Primitive Religion*, p. 28.

24. Hugh Kenner, *The Elsewhere Community.* (1998) Concord: Anansi, p. 93.

25. Cited in Adam Leith Gollner's *The Book of Immortality: The Science, Belief, and Magic Behind Living Forever.* (2013) Montreal: Doubleday Canada, p. 19.

26. Cited in Victor J. *Stegner's God: The Failed Hypothesis.* (2007) Amherst: Prometheus Books, p. 79.

27. Stegner, p. 103.

28. Curtiss Hoffman, *The Seven Story Tower: A Mythic Journey Through Space and Time.* (1999) Cambridge: Perseus Publishing, p. 148.

29. Dolan, *The American Catholic Experience*, p. 63.

30. Wade Davis, *The Wayfinders: Why Ancient Wisdom Matters in the Modern World*. (2009) Scarborough: Anansi Press, p. 31.

31. Andre Comte–Sponville, *The Little Book of Atheist Spirituality*. Translated by Nancy Huston. (2007) New York: Viking, p. 8.

32. Comte–Sponville, p. 8.

33. Barbara Silverstone and Helen Kandel Hyman, *You and Your Aging Parent: A Family Guide to Emotional, Social, Health, and Financial Problems* (Fourth Edition). (2008) Oxford and New York: Oxford University Press, p. 123.

34. Paul Irion, *The Funeral and the Mourners*, p. 17.

35. Joyce Youings, *Sixteenth–Century England*. (1984) Middlesex and New York: Penguin Books, p. 178.

36. Nicholas Wade, *The Faith Instinct: How Religion Evolved and Why it Endures*. (2009) New York and London: Penguin Books, p. 277.

37. Philip Jenkins, *The Next Christendom: The Coming of Global Christianity*. (2002) New York: Oxford University Press, p. 3.

38. Herbert C. Northcott and Donna M. Wilson, *Dying and Death in Canada (Second Edition)*. (2008) Buffalo: Broadview Press, p. 102.

39. John Shelby Spong, *Eternal Life: A New Vision*. (2009) New York: HarperOne, p. 4.

40. Spong, p. 134.

41. Erin Moure, "A Year Later, I Am In Lilac Now" in *The Heart Does Break: Canadian Writers on Grief and Mourning*. Edited by George Bowering and Jean Baird. (2009) Toronto: Random House Canada, p. 250.

42. Starhawk, "Virgo" in *Exit Laughing: How Humor Takes the Sting out of Death*. (2012) Berkeley: North Atlantic Books, p. 252.

43. Irion, *The Funeral and Mourners*, p. 35.

44. Irion, p. 84.

45. Irion, p. 85.

46. Alla Bozarth–Campbell, Ph. D., *Life is Goodbye, Life is Hello: Grieving Well Through All Kinds of Loss*. (1982, 1986) Minneapolis: CompCare Publishers, p. 5.

47. Kellehear, p. 24.

48. Aristotle, *Basic Works*. Edited by McKeon. (1941) New York: Random House, p. 689.

49. Carlos Eire, *A Very Brief History of Eternity*.(2010) Princeton and Oxford: Princeton University Press, p. 101.

50. Ronald J. Grimes, *Deeply Into the Bone: Re–Inventing Rites of Passage*. (2000, 2002) Berkeley: University of California Press, p. 3.

51. According to Gerald Hodge, these are individuals born between 1946 and 1965. Gerald Hodge, *The Geology of Aging: Preparing Communities for the Surge in Seniors*. (2008) Montreal and Kingston: McGill–Queen's University Press, p. 11.

52. Hodge, p. 3.

53. Hodge, p. 33.

54. Grimes, p. 60.

55. Ibid., p. 230.

56. Paul Irion, "Ritual Responses to Death" in *Living With Grief*, p. 160.

57. Arnold Van Gennep, *The Rites of Passage*. (1960) Chicago: The University of Chicago Press, p. 146.

58. Van Gennep, p. 147.

59. Jerry Amstutz, "Life Before Winter" in *Leadership*. Winter (2008).

60. Sheila Rule, "At the Secular Funeral A Tango May be Tasteful", *New York Times*, January 10, 1990.

61. Irion, *Living With Grief*, p. 163. Emphasis is Irion's.

62. Millard Fuller, *The Theology of the Hammer*. (1994) Macon: Smyth and Helwys.

63. James Morrison, for example, has used these words to describe funerals. He does so in his article entitled "The Clinical Use of Imagery to Induce Psychotherapeutic Grieving" in *Death Imagery: Confronting Death Brings us to the Threshold of Life*. Edited by A.A. Shiekh and K.S. Sheikh, (1991) Milwaukee: American Imagery Institute, p. 79.

64. Cited in Geoffrey Wall. *Flaubert: A Life*. (2001) London: Faber and Faber, p. 300.

65. Cited in David Hempton, *Evangelical Disenchantment: 9 Portraits of Faith and Doubt*. (2008) New Haven and London: Yale University Press, p. 102.

66. Cited in Christian Riegel, *Writing Grief: Margaret Laurence and the Work of Mourning*. (2003) Winnipeg: University of Manitoba Press, p. 106.

67. A.R. Radcliffe–Brown, *Structure and Function In Primitive Society: Essays and Addresses*. (1952, 1965 Editions) New York: Free Press, p. 146.

68. Edward Myers, *When Parents Die: A Guide For Adults*. (1986) New York: Penguin Books, p. 108.

69. I.M. Lewis, *Social Anthropology in Perspective: The Relevance of Social Anthropology*. (1976) Middlesex: Penguin Books, p. 113.

70. Cited in Lama Surya Das' *Awakening the Buddha Within: Tibetan Wisdom for the Western World*. (1997) New York: Broadway Books, p. 304.

71. Betty Jane Wylie, Beginnings: *A Book For Widows (Fourth Revised Edition)*. (1997) Toronto: McClelland and Stewart, p. 145.

72. Wylie, p. 14.

73. James Turner, *Without God, Without Creed: The Origins of Unbelief in America*. (1985, 1987 Edition) Baltimore and London: Johns Hopkins University Press, p. 166.

74. Steven E. Ozment, *The Reformation in the Cities: The Appeal of Protestantism to Sixteenth–Century Germany and Switzerland*. (1975) New Haven and London: Yale University Press, p. 101.

75. Irvin D. Yalom, *The Gift of Therapy: An Open Letter to a New Generation of Therapists and Their Patients*. (2002, 2009 Edition) New York: Harper Perennial, p. 8.

76. John Shaw (Tr. and Ed.), *The Blue Mountains: And Other Gaelic Stories from Cape Breton*. (2007) Montreal and Kingston: McGill–Queen's University Press, p. xi.

77. Gunter Grass, "To Be Continued …" in *The Gunter Grass Reader*. (1993, 2004 Edition) New York: Harcourt, p. 263.

78. V.S. Pritchett, *The Oxford Book of Short Stories*. (1981) New York: Oxford University Press, p. xi.

79. Cited in Jim Clemmer's *Firing On All Cylinders*. (1992 Edition) Toronto: Macmillan Canada, p. 230.

80. Peter Urs Bender, *Secrets of Power Presentations*. (1991) Toronto: The Achievement Group, p. 30.

81. Thomas G. Long, *Accompany Them with Singing; The Christian Funeral*. (2009) Louisville: Westminster John Knox Press, p. xv.

82. Cited in William B. Ober, *Bottoms Up! A Pathologist's Essays on Medicine and the Humanities*. (1988 edition) New York: Harper and Row, p. xi.

Funeral Ritual

1. Evan Imber–Black, "Rituals and the Healing Process" in *Living Beyond Loss: Death in the Family*. Walsh and McGoldrick eds. (1991) London and New York: W.W. Norton and Company, p. 207.

2. This is something based on a definition offered by Rollo May in his book *The Cry for Myth*. (1991) New York and London: W.W. Norton, p. 290.

3. Kingsley Davis, *Human Society*. (1948) New York: MacMillan, p. 511.

4. Davis, p. 512.

5. John Casey, *After Lives: A Guide to Heaven, Hell, and Purgatory*. (2009) Oxford and New York: Oxford University Press, p. 18.

6. Jean Meslier, *Testament: Memoir of the Thoughts and Sentiments of Jean Meslier*. Translated by Michael Shreve. (2009) Amherst: Prometheus Books, p. 45.

7. Robert Fossier, *The Axe and the Oath: Ordinary Life in the Middle Ages*. (2010) Princeton and Oxford: Princeton University Press, p. 131.

8. Clifford Geertz, *The Interpretation of Cultures*. (1973) New York: Basic Books, p. 140.

9. Cited in Phyllis Kosminksy's *Getting Back to Life When Grief Won't Heal*. (2007) New York: McGraw–Hill, p. 57.

10. Herodotus, *Histories*. Wordsworth Classics (Hertfordshire, England), 1996, p. 150.

11. Kosminsky, p. 57.

12. Geertz, p. 168.

13. Jokinen, *Curtains: Adventures of an Undertaker–In–Training*, p. 145.

14. Albert Camus, *Algerian Chronicles*. Edited and Introduced by Alice Kaplan. Translated by Arthur Goldhammer. (2013) Cambridge and London: Harvard University Press, p. 70.

15. Cited in Rodney Stark's *Discovering God*, (2007) New York: Harper Collins, p. 14.

16. Radin, *Primitive Religion*, p. 289.

17. Long, *Accompany them with Singing*, p. 77.

18. John Stubbs, *Reprobates: The Cavaliers of the English Civil War*. (2011) New York: W.W. Norton and Company, p. 13.

19. Bonnie Effros, "Death and Burial" in *Medieval Christianity*. Edited by Daniel E. Bornstein. (2009) Minneapolis: Fortress Press, p. 53.

20. Effros, p. 64.

21. Joan Marshall, (2009) *Tides of Change on Grand Manan Island*. Montreal and Kingston: McGill–Queen's University Press, p. 279.

22. Kathleen E. Corley, *Maranatha: Women's Funerary Rituals and Christian Origins*. (2010) Minneapolis: Fortress Press, p. 2.

23. Corley, p. 18.

24. Corley, p. 79.

25. Corley, p. 90.

26. Corley, p. 17.

27. Corley, p. 18.

28. Ibid., p. 18.

29. Corley, p. 19.

30. Arnold Van Gennep, p. 50.

31. Christian Riegel, *Writing Grief: Margaret Laurence and the Work of Mourning*. (2003) Winnipeg: University of Manitoba Press, p. 13.

32. Radin, *Primitive Religion*, p. 82.

33. Mircea Eliade, *Rites and Symbols of Initiation: Mysteries of Birth and Rebirth*. Translated by Willard Trask. (1958) New York: Harper Torchbooks, p. 4.

34. Froma Walsh and Monica McGoldrick, "Loss and the Family: A Systematic Perspective" in *Living Beyond Loss: Death in the Family*. (1991) New York: W.W. Norton and Company, p. 9.

35. Northcott and Wilson, p. 87.

36. Beverley Raphael, *The Anatomy of Bereavement*. (1983) New York: Basic Books, p. 37.

37. Adam Leith Gollner, *The Book of Immortality: The Science, Belief, and Magic Behind Living Forever*. (2013) Montreal: Doubleday Canada, p. 27.

38. bell hooks, *Belonging: A Culture of Place*. (2009) New York and London: Routledge, p. 5.

39. Cited in Nora Foster Stovel, *Divining Margaret Laurence: A Study of Her Complete Writings.* (2008) Montreal and Kingston: McGill–Queen's University Press, p. 83.

40. Elaine Ramshaw, *Ritual and Pastoral Care.* (1987) Minneapolis: Fortress Press, p. 26.

41. For the religious leader Elaine Ramshaw deals with this topic in her book entitled *Ritual and Pastoral Care*, p. 14.

42. Barry Broadfoot, *The Pioneer Years*, 1895-1914. (1976) Toronto and Garden City: Doubleday, p. 82.

43. Ramshaw, p. 71.

44. Malinowski, p. 52.

45. Malinowski, p. 53.

46. Paul E. Johnson, *Psychology of Pastoral Care.* (1953) Nashville: Abingdon Press, p. 258.

47. Malinowski, p. 48.

48. Malinowski, p. 51.

49. G. Campbell Morgan, *The Westminster Pulpit: The Preaching of G. Campbell Morgan (Volume One).* (1954) Westwood and Los Angeles: Fleming H. Revell Company, p. 29.

50. Robert L. Millet, *Grace Works.* (2003) Salt Lake City: Deseret Books, p. 111.

51. Viktor Frankl, *Man's Search for Meaning (Revised and Updated).* (1984) New York: Pocket Books, p. 117.

52. Neuhaus, *American Babylon*, p. 213.

53. Neuhaus, p. 215.

54. Bozarth–Campbell, p. 11.

55. Joan Chittister, *For Everything A Season. (2013 Edition)* Maryknoll: Orbis Books, p. 119.

56. Chittister, p. 122.

57. According to Stephen Reid, prisoners who are caught crying are described as "bitching up." Stephen Reid. "The Art of Dying In Prison" in *The Heart Does Break: Canadian Writers on Grief and Mourning*. Edited by George Bowering and Jean Baird. Random House Canada (Toronto, Ontario), 2009, p. 286.

58. A.C. Grayling, "Funerals" in The Form of Things: Essays on Life, Ideas, and Liberty in the 21st Century. (2007 Edition) London: Phoenix, p. 21.

59. Grayling, p. 21.

60. Nancy R. Hooyman and Betty J. Kramer, *Living Through Loss: Interventions Across the Life Span*. (2006) New York: Columbia University Press, p. 15.

61. Anthony Swofford, *Jarhead: A Marine's Chronicle of the Gulf War and Other Battles*. (2003) New York: Pocket Books, p. 105.

62. Effros, p. 54.

63. Peter Berresford Ellis, *A Brief History of the Druids*. (1994, 2002) London: Constable and Robinson, p. 137.

64. Chittister, *For Everything A Season*, p. 122.

65. Susan J. White, *Christian Worship and Technological Change*. (1994) Nashville: Abingdon Press, p. 15.

66. White, p. 15.

67. Cited in White, p. 40.

68. White, p. 75.

69. White, p. 76.

70. Julian Huxley, *What Dare I Think: The Challenge of Modern Science To Human Action and Belief*. (1931) London: Chatto and Windus, p. 8.

71. Grayling, *The Form of Things*, p. 21.

72. Jokinen, *Curtains: Adventures of an Undertaker in Training*, p. 85.

73. Grimes, *Deeply Into the Bone*, p. 4.

74. Grimes, p. 6.

75. Comte–Sponville, *The Little Book of Atheist Spirituality*, p. 9.

76. Ibid., p. 9.

77. Ibid., p. 9.

78. Yalom, *The Gift of Therapy*, p. 103.

79. Confucius, *The Analects*, III.4.

80. Cited in Bibby, *Beyond the Gods and Back*, p. 166.

81. Plato. Laws. 87. b-c.

82. Cited in Gary Wills, "The Dramaturgy of Death" in *The Best American Essays (2002 Edition)*. Edited by Stephen Jay Gould. (2002) Boston and New York: Houghton Mifflin Company, p. 334.

83. B. Joseph Pine and James H. Gilmore, *The Experience Economy: Work is Theatre and Every Business a Stage*. (1999) Boston: Harvard Business School Press, p. 110.

84. W.J. Rorabaugh, *Kennedy and the Promise of the Sixties*. (2002) Cambridge: Cambridge University Press, p. 226.

Phase One: Planning and Preparation

1. Cited in Pierre Berton's *Prisoners of the North*. (2004) Toronto: Doubleday Canada, p. 112.

2. Confucius, T*he Analects*, I.9.

3. W. Edwards Deming, *Out of the Crisis*. (2000 Edition) Cambridge: M.I.T. Press, p. 49.

4. Personal Conversation, October 7, 2009.

5. George A. Bonanno, *The Other Side of Sadness*. (2009) New York: Basic Books, p. 1.

6. Cited in David Hicks' *Ritual and Belief: Readings in the Anthropology of Religion (Second Edition)*. (2002) New York: McGraw–Hill, p. 305.

7. Stephen and Ondrea Levine, *Who Dies?* (1989 Edition) New York: Anchor Books, p. 223.

8. Peter Hessler, "Doctor Don" in *The Best American Essays 2012*. Introduced and edited by David Brooks. (2012) New York: Mariner Books, p. 156. In my opinion this entire essay should be required reading for any clergyperson moving into rural ministry.

9. Peter Urs Bender, *Secrets of Power Presentations*. (1991) Toronto: The Achievement Group, p. 54.

10. George Bowering and Jean Baird (Editors). *The Heart Does Break: Canadian Writers on Grief and Mourning*. (2009) Toronto: Random House Canada, p. 11.

11. Kenneth Doka, "A Primer on Loss and Grief" in *Living With Grief: At Work, At School, At Worship*. Edited by Joyce D. Davidson and Kenneth J. Doka. (1999) Washington, DC: Hospice Foundation of America, p. 9.

12. Doka, p. 10.

13. Edwin S. Shneidman, *The Suicidal Mind*. (1996) New York and Oxford: Oxford University Press, p. 4.

14. Shneidman, p. 7.

15. Joan Chittister, *For Everything A Season.* (1995, 2013 Editions) Maryknoll: Orbis Books, p. 154.

16. Ben Witherington III, *Jesus the Sage: The Pilgrimage of Wisdom.* (1994) Minneapolis: Fortress Press, p. 57.

17. Arlene Dickinson, *Persuasion: A New Approach to Changing Minds.* (2011) Toronto: Harper Collins, p. 141.

18. Elaine Ramshaw, *Ritual and Pastoral Care*, p. 18.

19. Ramshaw, p. 56.

20. Paul Johnson, *Psychology of Pastoral Care.* (1953) Nashville: Abingdon Press, p. 101

21. Johnson, p. 8.

22. Yalom, *The Gift of Therapy*, p. 17.

23. Barbara Killinger, *Integrity: Doing the Right Thing for the Right Reason.* (2007) Montreal and Kingston: McGill–Queen's University Press, p. 36.

24. Kent D. Richmond, *Preaching to Sufferers: God and the Problem of Pain.* (1988) Nashville: Abingdon Press, p. 83.

25. Cited in Philip Slayton's *Good Lawyers Gone Bad.* (2007) Toronto: Viking Canada, p. 136.

26. Arlene Dickinson, *Persuasion*, p. 9.

27. Walter Glannon, *Biomedical Ethics.* (2005) New York and Oxford: Oxford University Press, p. 36. Glannon includes an excellent introduction to the subject of confidentiality in this book.

28. I've included this resource in the bibliography.

29. Barbara Okun, Ph.D., and Nowinski, Ph.D., Joseph, *Saying Goodbye: How Families can Find Renewal Through Loss.* (2011) New York: Berkley Books, p. 264.

30. Carmine Gallo, *Talk Like TED: The 9 Public–Speaking Secrets of the World's Top Minds.* (2014) New York: St. Martin's Press, p. 185.

31. Monica McGoldrick and Froma Walsh (Eds.), *Living Beyond Loss: Death in the Family.* (1991) New York and London: W.W. Norton and Company, p. 24.

32. Paul Irion, "Ritual Responses to Death" in *Living With Grief: At Work, At School, At Worship.* Edited by Joyce D. Davidson and Kenneth J. Doka. (1999) Washington, DC: Hospice Foundation of America, p. 158.

33. Edward Myers, *When Parents Die: A Guide For Adults*. (1986) New York: Penguin Books, p. 110.

34. Edward Norbeck, "African Rituals of Conflict" in *Gods and Rituals: Readings in Religious Beliefs and Practices*. Edited by John Middleton. (1967) New York: The Natural History Press, p. 217.

35. Sam Berry, *Exit Laughing: How Humour Takes the Sting Out of Death*. Edited by Victoria Zackheim. (2012) Berkeley: North Atlantic Books, pp. 157-158.

36. Scott Weems, *Ha! The Science of When We Laugh and Why*. (2014) New York: Basic Books, p. 8

37. Carmine Gallo, *Talk Like TED*, p. 9.

38. Gallo, p. 160.

39. Victoria Zackheim, *Exit Laughing: How Humour Takes the Sting out of Death*, p. 196.

40. Cited in Sarah Murray's *Making An Exit*, (2011) New York: St. Martin's Press, p. 35.

41. Bonanno, *The Other Side of Sadness*, p. 163.

42. Herodotus, *Histories*, p. 390.

43. Carmine Gallo, *Talk Like TED*, p. 165.

44. Weems, p. 11.

45. Weems, p. 17.

46. David K. Switzer, *The Minister as Crisis Counselor*. (1980 Edition) Nashville: Abingdon Press, p. 78.

47. Cary L. Cooper, Rachel D. Cooper, and Lynn H. Eaker, *Living With Stress*. (1988) London: Penguin, p. 21.

48. Daniel B. Smith, *Muses, Madmen, and Prophets: Hearing Voices and the Borders of Sanity*. (2007) London: Penguin, p. 8.

49. Cited in John Gray's *The Immortalization Commission: Science and the Strange Quest to Cheat Death*. (2011) Toronto: Doubleday Canada, p. 91.

50. Oliver Sacks, *Hallucinations*. (2012) New York and Toronto: Alfred A. Knopf, p. 230.

51. Robert Graves, *Goodbye to All That*. (1928, 1998) New York: Anchor Books, p. 287.

52. Sacks, *Hallucinations*, p. 234.

53. Sacks, p. xiv.

54. Sacks, p. xiv.

55. Cited in John Lloyd and John Mitchinson's *The Book of the Dead*. (2009) London: Faber and Faber, p. 142.

56. Hooyman and Kramer, *Living Through Loss*, p. 17.

57. Johnson, p. 248.

58. Edward Norbeck, "African Rituals of Conflict", p. 213.

59. Garret Keizer, "Getting Schooled" in *The Best American Essays 2012*, p. 185.

60. Cited in Mark Harris' *Grave Matters*. (2007) New York: Scribner, p. 49.

61. Rollo May, *Freedom and Destiny*. (1999 Edition) New York: W.W. Norton and Company, p. 231.

62. Carmine Gallo, *Talk Like TED*, p. 240.

63. Bender, p. 52.

64. Carl R. Rogers, *On Becoming a Person*. (1961) Boston: Houghton Mifflin Company, p. 16.

65. Johnson, p. 73.

66. Cited in Bonanno, *The Other Side of Sadness*, p. 15.

67. Cited in A. C, Grayling's *The Meaning of Things: Applying Philosophy to Life*. (2001) London: Phoenix, p. 170.

68. Bender, p. 18.

69. Bender, p. 23.

70. Arlene Dickinson, *Persuasion: A New Approach to Changing Minds*. (2011) Toronto: Harper Collins, p. 6.

71. Bender, p. 105.

72. Rollo May, *Freedom and Destiny*, p. 100.

73. Gail Vaz–Oxlade, *Money Rules*. (2012) Toronto: Collins, p. 328.

74. Anthony de Mello, *The Song of the Bird*. (1984) Garden City: Image Books, p. 20.

75. We'll discuss this in the chapter on the inspirational phase of a funeral.

76. Steven Gerali, *What to Do When Teenagers Deal With Death?* (2009) Grand Rapids: Zondervan, p. 59.

77. Louis C. Faron suggests that one of the purposes of a funeral is to "intensify the kinship relations" of those of us touched by the death of an individual. "Death and Fertility Rites of the Mapuche Indians" in *Gods and Rituals: Readings and Religious Beliefs and Practices.* John Middleton (ed.). (1967) New York: The Natural History Press, p. 228.

78. Beverly Raphael, *The Anatomy of Bereavement.* (1983) New York: Basic Books, p. 3.

79. Quoted in Donald G. Krause, *The Art of War for Executives.* (2005) New York: Perigee Books, p. 18.

80. Jokinen, *Curtains: Adventures of an Undertaker in Training*, p. 116.

81. Bozarth–Campbell, p. 32.

82. Gladwell, *What the Dog Saw: And Other Adventures*, p. 268.

83. Bonanno, *The Other Side of Sadness*, p. 110.

84. Donald F. Klein, M.D. and Paul H. Wender, M.D., *Understanding Depression: A Complete Guide to Its Diagnosis and Treatment.* (1993) New York and Oxford: Oxford University Press, p. 15.

85. Klein and Wender, p. 42.

86. Cited in Northcott and Wilson, p. 159.

87. Northcott and Wilson, p. 159.

88. Doreen M. McFarlane, *Funerals With Today's Families in Mind.* (2008) Cleveland: The Pilgrim Press, p. 50.

89. McFarlane, p. 53.

90. Judith Herman, *Trauma and Recovery: The Aftermath of Violence from Domestic Abuse to Political Terror.* Basic Books (New York, NY), 1992, 1997 Edition, p. 133.

91. Herman, p. 188.

92. Herman, p. 174.

93. Bonnano, p. 198.

94. Comte–Sponville, *The Little Book of Atheist Spirituality*, p. 9.

95. Paula J. Caplan, Ph.D., *They Say You're Crazy.* (1995) Reading: Addison Wesley, p. 12.

96. Barbara Kellerman, *Reinventing Leadership.* (1999) Albany: State University Press of New York, p. 151.

97. Baird and Baird, p. 11.

98. Baird and Baird, p. 11.

99. Northcott and Wilson, p. 70.

Phase Two: Warm–Up

1. Bender, *Secrets of Power Presentations*, p. 18.

2. David Lodge, *The Art of Fiction*. (1992) London: Penguin Books, p. 4.

3. Cited in Pine and Gilmore's *The Experience Economy*, p. 104.

4. Keith Watkins, *The Great Thanksgiving*, p. 97.

5. Brian D. Spinks, "The Serious Business of Worship" in *The Serious Business of Worship: Essays in Honour of Brian D. Spinks*. Edited by Melanie Ross and Simon Jones. (2010) London and New York: T and T Clark, p. xi.

6. "Funeral Turns to Party After 'Corpse' Wakes Up" in *Calgary Herald* (May 13, 2012).

7. Therese A. Rando, *How to Go On Living When Someone You Love Dies*. (1991 Edition) New York: Bantam Books, p. 226.

8. Arnold Van Gennep, *The Rites of Passage*, p. 50.

9. Perry Berresford Ellis, *A Brief History of the Druids*, p. 171.

10. In reviewing religious ritual prior to the crusades Chris Tyerman writes, "nothing destroys the message of ritual more certainly than unease ... in its performance." Chris Tyerman. *God's War: A New History of the Crusades*. (2007) London: Penguin, p. 65.

11. Cited in D.W. Cleverley Ford's *The Ministry of the Word*. (1979) London and Sydney: Hodder and Stoughton, p. 224.

12. Dickinson, *Persuasion*, p. 130.

13. John Lloyd and John Mitchinson, *The Book of the Dead*. (2009) London: Faber and Faber, p. 41.

14. N.T. Wright, *Following Jesus: Biblical Reflections on Discipleship*. (1995) Grand Rapids: Wm. Eerdmans, p. 66.

15. Paul Irion, *The Funeral and the Mourners: Pastoral Care of the Bereaved*, p. 96.

16. Quoted in hooks, *Belonging: A Culture of Place*, p. 175.

17. William R. Baird, Sr. and John E. Baird, *Funeral Meditations*.(1966) Nashville: Abingdon Press, p. 10.

18. Hooyman and Kramer, *Living Through Loss*, p. 122.

19. Gavin Roynon, ed. *A Prayer for Gallipoli: The Great War Diaries of Chaplain Kenneth Best*. (2011) London and New York: Simon and Schuster, p. 15.

20. Steven E. Ozment, *The Reformation in the Cities: The Appeal of Protestantism in Sixteenth–Century Germany and Switzerland*. (1975) New Haven and London: Yale University Press, p. 96.

21. Claudia L. Jewett, *Helping Children Cope With Separation and Loss*. (1982) Boston: Harvard Common Press, p. 3.

22. Michelle Robinson, "Music in Worship: Supporting Orientation, Disorientation and Reorientation" in *Touchstone*. 33/1 (February 2015), p. 42.

Phase Three: Inspiration

1. Pat Schneider, *How the Light Gets In*, p. 9.

2. Schneider, p. 10.

3. Paul Radin, *Primitive Religion*. (1957 Edition) New York: Dover Publications, p. 184.

4. Radin, p. 185.

5. Radin, p. 11.

6. John Macquarrie, *The Faith of the People of God*. (1972) New York: Charles Scribner's Sons, p. 155.

7. Held at Roy Thomson Hall, August 27, 2011.

8. Cited in Rodney Stark's *Discovering God*, p. 258.

9. Elaine Ramshaw, *Ritual and Pastoral Care*, p. 58

10. *Ode to a Grecian Urn*.

11. Thomas Merton, *The Seven Storied Mountain*. (1976 Edition) New York and London: Harcourt Brace Jovanovich Publishers, p. 111.

12. Betty Jane Wylie, Beginnings, p. 132.

13. Kathleen E. Corley, *Maranatha: Women's Funerary Rituals and Christian Origins*. (2010) Minneapolis: Fortress Press, p. 126.

14. Bryan Massingale, *Racial Justice and the Catholic Church*. (2010) Maryknoll: Orbis Books, p. 107.

15. H. Ian Hogbin, "Pagan Religion in a New Guinea Village" in *Gods and Rituals: Readings in Religious Beliefs and Practices*. Edited by John Middleton. (1967) New York: The Natural History Press, p. 51.

16. Sarah Murray, *Making An Exit*. (2011) New York: St. Martin's Press, p. 20.

17. Diana Butler Bass, *Christianity After Religion: The End of Church and the Birth of a New Spiritual Awakening*. (2012) New York: HarperOne, p. 17.

18. Paul Irion, *The Funeral and the Mourners: Pastoral Care of the Bereaved*, p. 96.

19. Cited in Eric Friesen, "Music: The Language of the Artist" in *Queen's Quarterly* 119/1 (Spring 2012), p. 22.

20. Cited in Anthony Blond's *A Brief History of the Private Lives of the Roman Emperors*. (1994, 2008 Editions) London: Constable and Robinson, p. 156.

21. Phyllis Tickle uses this term when describing the work of John Wimber but these words can also apply to music's effectiveness in the context of the funeral ritual. Phyllis Tickle. *Emergence Christianity: What It Is, Where It Is Going, and Why It Matters*. (2012) Grand Rapids: Baker Books, p. 82.

22. Nicholas Wade, *The Faith Instinct: How Religion Evolved and Why It Endures*. (2010) New York and London: Penguin Books, p. 40.

23. Cited in Nora Foster Stovel's *Divining Margaret Laurence: A Study of Her Complete Writings*. (2008) Montreal and Kingston: McGill–Queen's University Press, p. 241.

24. *The Collected Essays, Journalism and Letters of George Orwell*, p. 166.

25. Cited in Oliver Sacks, *Musicophilia: Tales of Music and the Brain*. (2007) New York and Toronto: Knopf Canada, p. 252.

26. Oliver Sacks, *The Man Who Mistook His Wife for a Hat and Other Clinical Tales*. (1987 Edition) New York: Harper Perennial, p. 8ff.

27. Eric Friesen, "Oliver Sacks Interviewed" in *Queen's Quarterly* 115/3 (Fall, 2008), p. 445.

28. Friesen, p. 443.

29. Murray, p. 131.

30. Cited in David Hempton, *Evangelical Disenchantment: 9 Stories of Faith and Doubt*, p. 174.

31. Psalm 137.

32. Kathleen E. Corley, *Maranatha*, p. 50.

33. Corley, p. 60.

34. Cited in Tracey Rowland's *Ratzinger's Faith: The Theology of Pope Benedict XVI.* (2008) Oxford and New York: Oxford University Press, p. 133.

35. Cited in Scott Weems' *Ha!*, p. 64.

36. Weems, p. 179.

37. Elwin A. Wienandt, "Jazz at the Altar?" in *The Christian Century Reader*. Edited by Harold E. Fey and Margaret Frakes. (1962) New York: Associated Press, p. 388.

38. Wienandt, p. 389.

39. Sacks., p. 37.

40. Sacks, p. 244.

41. Sacks, pp. 244-245.

42. Sacks, p. 219.

43. Sacks, p. 344.

44. Temple Grandin, *Thinking In Pictures: And Other Reports From My Life With Autism.* (1995) New York: Doubleday, p. 191.

45. Sacks, pp. 250-251.

46. Cited in Sacks, p. 296.

47. Hooyman and Kramer, *Living Through Loss*, p. 79.

48. Sacks, p. 301.

49. Ludwig Feuerbach, *The Essence of Christianity.* Translated by George Eliot. (1957) New York: Harper Torchbooks, pp. 3-4.

50. Feuerbach, p. 9.

51. Colman, *Corpses, Coffins, and Crypts*, p. 151.

52. Colman, p. 149.

53. This suggestion is based on both personal experience and the recommendation of writers such as Dale Topp. Reference: Dale Topp, *Music in the Christian Community.* (1976) Grand Rapids: Wm. B. Eerdman's, p. 86.

54. "Aussie Funerals Rocking Affairs" in the *Calgary Herald,* July 5, 2008.

55. Richard John Neuhaus, *American Babylon: Notes of a Christian Exile.* (2010 Edition) New York: Basic Books, p. 161.

56. Robert J. Morgan, *Rise Again! The Story of Cape Breton Island,* Book One. (2008) Wreck Cove: Breton Books, p. 173.

57. Angela Sumegi, *Understanding Death*, p. 40.

58. Sumegi, p. 43.

59. Mark Chipperfield, "Football Songs Don't Belong at Catholic Funerals: Archbishop" in *The Calgary Herald,* September 11, 2010.

60. Irion, *The Funeral and the Mourners: Pastoral Care of the Bereaved*, p. 102.

61. William B. McCullough, "Grief: A Physician–Minister's Views" in *For the Bereaved: The Road to Recovery (3rd Edition)*. Edited by Austin H. Kutscher and all. (1990) Philadelphia: The St. Charles Press, 1990, p. 22.

62. Gardner Murphy, p. 322.

63. Charles Taylor, *The Malaise of Modernity*. (1991) Toronto: Anansi Press, p. 44.

64. A.E. Harvey, *Is Scripture Still Holy?* (2012) Grand Rapids: Eerdmans, p. 2.

65. Cited in Pat Schneider's *How the Light Gets In*, p. 67.

66. Cited in John Stubbs' *Reprobates*, p. 80.

67. Ronald Christ, "Jorge Luis Borges: The Art of Fiction" in *The Paris Review Interviews (Volume One)*. Edited by Philip Gourevitch. (2006) New York: Picador, p. 138.

68. Malcolm David Eckels, *Understanding Buddhism*. (2010) London: Watkins Publishing, p. 92.

69. Cited in Rollo May's *Freedom and Destiny*, p. 173.

70. Northrop Frye, "New Directions from Old" in *Myth and Mythmaking*. Edited by Henry A. Murray. (1968 Edition) Boston: Beacon Press, p. 123.

71. Wilfred Cantwell Smith, *What is Scripture?* (1993) Minneapolis: Fortress Press, p. 185.

72. W.H. Stevenson (Ed.). *William Blake: Selected Poetry*. (1988) London: Penguin, p. 52.

73. Douglas Bush, *Mythology and the Romantic Tradition in English Poetry*. (1969 Edition) New York: W.W. Norton and Company, p. 269.

74. McKeen, p. 362.

75. Cited in Douglas Bush, *Mythology and the Romantic Tradition in English Poetry*, p. 422.

Phase Four: Education — Eulogies and Tributes

1. Joyce Youings, *Sixteenth–Century England*, p. 20.

2. Peter S. Wells, *Barbarians to Angels: The Dark Ages Reconsidered.* (2008) New York and London: W.W. Norton and Company, p. 42.

3. William Shakespeare, *Richard II, III*, ii, 155 f.

4. William Shakespeare, *Henry VI*, Part I, Act I, Scene I, Line 15.

5. Oliver Sacks, *The Man Who Mistook His Wife For A Hat and Other Clinical Tales*, p. 110.

6. Sacks, p. 111.

7. Carmine Gallo, *Talk Like TED*, p. 51.

8. Smith, p. 64.

9. Smith, p. 66.

10. Cited in Claude Levi–Strauss' *Structural Anthropology*. Translated by Claire Jacobson and Brooke Grundfest Schoepf. (1963) New York: Basic Books, p. 23.

11. Cited in Edmund Wilson's *To the Finland Station: A Study in the Writing and Acting of History*. (1953 Edition) Garden City: Doubleday and Company, p. 448.

12. Smith, p. 66.

13. Kathleen Corley, *Maranatha: Women's Funerary Rituals and Christian Origins*, p. 30.

14. Anthony de Mello, *The Song of the Bird*. (1984) Garden City: Image Books, p. 49.

15. Malcolm Gladwell, *What the Dog Saw: And Other Adventures*. (2009) New York and Boston: Little, Brown, and Company, p. xiii.

16. Cited in Tim Bowling's "Ex Libris" in *Queen's Quarterly* 116/2 (Summer 2009). pp. 305-313.

17. William Shakespeare, *Henry IV*. 3.1.81.

18. Cited in Herodotus, *Histories*. (1996) Hertfordshire: Wordsworth Classics, p. xi.

19. Cited in Michael Posner, "The Year in Cinema" in *Queen's Quarterly* 119/1 (Spring 2012), p. 9.

20. James Van Praagh, *Unfinished Business: What the Dead Can Teach Us About Life*. (2009) New York: HarperOne.

21. Van Praagh, p. 2.

22. The person who came up with this idea had to be living with a hernia.

23. James Baldwin, "Notes of a Native Son" in *50 Essays: A Portable Anthology*. Edited by Samuel Cohen. (2004) Boston and New York: Bedford/St. Martin's, p 54.

24. Orson Scott Card, *Speaker for the Dead*. (1991 Edition) New York: Tom Doherty and Associates, p. 24.

25. Card, p. 51.

26. Cited in Hunter S. Thompson, *The Great Shark Hunt: Gonzo Papers, Volume 1*. (1979, 2003 Editions) New York and London: Simon and Schuster, p. 516.

27. Card, p. 131.

28. Card, *Speaker for the Dead*, p. 258.

29. Cited in Stephen Marche's "The Patroclization" in *Queen's Quarterly*. (Winter, 2010), p. 502.

30. Cited in Thomas Long, *Accompany them with Singing*, p. 185.

31. Sumegi, *Understanding Death*, p. 129.

32. Broadcast Live on Canadian Networks CBC, CTV, and CPAC. (April 16, 2014).

33. Thomas Long, p. 185.

34. Edward Searl, *In Memoriam: A Guide to Modern Funeral and Memorial Services (2nd Edition)*. (2000) Boston: Skinner House Books, p. vii.

35. Searl, p. 99.

36. Christian Riegel, *Writing Grief: Margaret Laurence and the Work of Mourning*. (2003) Winnipeg: University of Manitoba Press, p. 9.

37. Pritchett, *The Oxford Book of Short Stories*, p. xi.

38. Lukacs, *The End of an Age*, p. 52.

39. David Finch, "Old–fashioned Story telling Still Has Its Perks" in *The Calgary Herald*, September 21, 2008.

40. Cited in Dorothy Lander and John Graham–Pole. "Love Letters to the Dead: Immortal Gifts to the Lifelong Learner" in *Teaching Death and Dying*. Edited by Christopher M. Moreman. (2008) Oxford and New York: A.A.R./Oxford University Press, p. 228.

41. Effros, p. 62.

42. Cited in Malcolm Eckels' *Understanding Buddhism*, p. 104.

43. Robert Gerwarth, *Hitler's Hangman: The Life of Heydrich*. (2011) New Haven and London: Yale University Press, p. x.

44. hooks, p. 3.

45. David Riggs, *The World of Christopher Marlowe*. (2004) London: Faber and Faber, p. 51.

46. Kathleen E. Corley, *Maranatha*, p. 2.

47. Endre Farkas, "Waiting to Grieve" in *The Heart Does Break: Canadian Writers on Grief and Mourning*. Edited by George Bowering and Jean Baird. (2009) Toronto: Random House Canada, pp. 121-122.

48. Lander and Pole, p. 227.

49. Grimes, *Deeply Into the Bone*. p. 235.

50. Wylie, p. 146.

51. Cited in Nora Foster Stovel, *Divining Margaret Laurence*, p. 313.

52. Nicholas Wade, *The Faith Instinct*, p. 88.

53. Wade, p. 82.

54. Carmine Gallo, *Talk Like TED*, p. 213.

55. Murray, *Making An Exit*, p. 173.

56. Kevin Little, "A Final Resting Place for a Homeless Man" in *The Globe and Mail,* November 15, 2011.

57. Sandra Martin, "Deadication" in *The Globe and Mail*, December 27, 2008.

58. Please see http://video.nytimes.com/video/playlist/last-word/1194811622353/index.html (Accessed April 9, 2015) and the video at http://www.thelastlecture.com/ (Accessed April 9, 2015).

59. John W. De Gruchy, "Grappling With A Colonial Heritage: The English–speaking Churches Under Imperialism and Apartheid" in *Christianity in South Africa*. Edited by Richard Elphick and Rodney Davenport. (1997) Berkley and Los Angeles: University of California Press, p. 165.

60. Jokinen, *Curtains: Adventures of an Undertaker–in–Training*, p. 146.

61. Rando, *How to Go On Living When Someone you Love Dies*, p. 268.

62. Rando, p. 268.

Phase Five: Transition — The Message

1. Duff Crerar, *Padres in No Man's Land: Canadian Chaplains and the Great War (Second Edition)*. (2014) Montreal and Kingston: McGill–Queen's University Press, p. 183.

2. Cited in Robert Fulford's, "Ruined Landscapes of Memory" in *Queen's Quarterly*. 120/3 (Fall 2013), p. 375.

3. Cited in Radcliffe–Brown's *Structure and Function in Primitive Society*, p. 160.

4. Cited in Christine Kehl O'Hagan's "Tragedy Plus Time" in *Exit Laughing: How Humour Takes the Sting out of Death*. (2012) Berkeley: North Atlantic Books, p. 212.

5. Temple Grandin, *Thinking In Pictures*, p. 196.

6. James B. Twitchell, *Branded Nation: The Marketing of Megachurch, College Inc., and Museumworld*. (2004) New York: Simon and Schuster, p. 94.

7. Martin Amis, *The War Against Cliché: Essays and Reviews, 1971-2000*. (2001) Toronto and New York: Vintage Canada, p. 153.

8. Cited in Ross Bartlett, "Proclamation is Indispensible" in *Touchstone* (Volume 32, February 2014, Number One), p. 53.

9. Thompson, *The Great Shark Hunt*, p. 527.

10. Kent D. Richmond, *Preaching to Sufferers: God and the Problem of Pain*. (1988) Nashville: Abingdon Press, p. 20.

11. Richmond, p. 30.

12. Mike Heffernan, *Rig: An Oral History of the Ocean Ranger Disaster*. (2009) St. John's: Creative Publishers, p. 8.

13. Cited in Siddhartha Mukherjee's *The Emperor of All Maladies: A Biography of Cancer*. (2010) New York and London: Scribner's, p. 462.

14. Cited in D.W. Cleverley Ford's *The Ministry of the Word*. (1979) London and Sydney: Hodder and Stoughton, p. 110.

15. Lucy Mair, *An Introduction to Social Anthropology (Second Edition)*. (1972) New York and London: Oxford University Press, p. 195.

16. 1 Corinthians 9:24.

17. Paul Scott Wilson, *The Four Pages of the Sermon*. (1999) Nashville: Abingdon Press, p. 9.

18. Adam Gopnik, *Winter: Five Windows on the Season*. (2011) Toronto: Anansi Press, p. 178.

19. Cited in David Hempton, *Evangelical Disenchantment: 9 Portraits of Faith and Doubt*, p. 114.

20. Bender, p. 15.

21. Thomas Long, *Accompany Them With Singing*, p. 6.

22. Robert E. Kavanaugh, *Facing Death*. (1972) London and New York: Penguin Books, pp. 29-30.

23. Carmine Gallo, *Talk Like TED*, p. 130.

24. Cited in Rachel Berman's "Au Revoir" in *Queen's Quarterly* 121/3 (Fall 2014), p. 423.

25. Cited in Deming, *Out of the Crisis*, p. 388.

26. Bertrand Russell, "Philosophy For Laymen" in *Unpopular Essays*. (2009 Edition) London and New York: Routledge Classics, p. 26.

27. Irvin Yalom, *Staring at the Sun: Overcoming the Terror of Death*. (2009) San Francisco: Jossey–Bass, p. 83.

28. Rob Bell, *Love Wins: A Book About Heaven, Hell, and the Fate of Every Person Who Ever Lived*. (2011) New York: HarperOne, p. 110.

29. Richmond, Kent D. *Preaching to Sufferers*, p. 108.

30. Ecclesiastes 3:2a.

31. Richmond, p. 121.

32. Mukherjee, *The Emperor of All Maladies*, p. 462.

33. Leslie Marmon Silko, "Language and Literature from a Pueblo Indian Perspective" in *50 Essays: A Portable Anthology*. Edited by Samuel Cohen. (2004) Boston and New York: Bedford/St. Martin's, p. 346.

34. Peter Beresford Ellis, *A Brief History of the Druids*. (2002 Edition) London: Constable and Robinson, p. 55.

35. Quoted in William McKeen's *Outlaw Journalist: The Life and Times of Hunter S. Thompson*. (2008) New York and London: W.W. Norton and Company, p. 16.

36. Elizabeth Spires, "Elizabeth Bishop: The Art of Poetry" in *The Paris Review Interviews (Volume One)*. (2006) New York: Picador, p. 285.

37. Elaine Ramshaw, *Ritual and Pastoral Care*, p. 78.

38. Jan G. Linn, *22 Keys to Being a Minister: Without Quitting or Wishing for Early Retirement*. (2003) St. Louis: Chalice Press, pp. 26-27.

39. Baird, Sr. and Baird, *Funeral Meditations*, p. 99.

40. Cited in Douglas Bush, *Mythology and the Romantic Tradition in English Poetry*. (1969 Edition) New York: W.W. Norton and Company, p. 261.

Phase Six: Closing Moves

1. Radin, *Primitive Religion*, p. 27.

2. Radin, p. 28.

3. Charlie Campbell, *Scapegoat: A History of Blaming Other People*. (2011) New York and London: Overlook Duckworth, p. 43.

4. William Loader, *The Dead Sea Scrolls on Sexuality: Attitudes Towards Sexuality in Sectarian and Related Literature at Qumran*. (2009) Grand Rapids: William B. Eerdmans, p. 244.

5. John Cooper, T*he Queen's Agent: Francis Walsingham at the Court of Elizabeth I*. (2011) London: Faber and Faber, p. 17.

6. Cooper, p. 325.

7. Based on the experience of a colleague whom shall remain nameless, I cannot stress enough that it has to be a METAL bowl.

8. Broadcast August 27, 2011.

9. John Stubbs, *Reprobates*, p. 267.

10. Mircea Eliade, *Rites and Symbols of Initiation*, p. 70.

11. Paul Irion, *The Funeral and the Mourners*, p. 110.

12. Catherine Bell, *Ritual*, p. 36.

13. "Niching" is a term coined by Kimberly Stevenson who is currently working in the funeral industry here in Calgary. Niching simply refers to the placement of an urn in a niche or some other storage location.

14. Das, *Awakening the Buddha Within*, p. 320.

15. Nigel Cawthorne, *Stalin: The Murderous Career of the Red Tsar*. (2012) London: Arcturus, p. 120.

16. Irvin D. Yalom, *Staring at the Sun: Overcoming the Terror of Death*, p. 44.

17. Helmut Thielicke, *Being A Christian When the Chips Are Down.* Translated by H. George Anderson. (1977) Philadelphia: Fortress Press, p. 24.

18. Thielicke, p. 27.

19. Christon Archer and all, *World History of Warfare.* (2002) Lincoln: University of Nebraska Press, p. 72.

20. Wade Davis, *The Wayfinders: Why Ancient Wisdom Matters in the Modern World.* (2009) Toronto: Anansi Press, p. 27.

21. N.J. Berrill, *Man's Emerging Mind.* (2010 Edition) Oxford and New York: Oxford University Press, p. 126.

22. Anders Winroth, for example, uses this term in his recent book *The Age of the Vikings.* (2014) Princeton: Princeton University Press, p. 24. Peter Brown also uses this term in *The Ransom of the Soul: Afterlife and Wealth in Early Western Christianity.* (2015) Cambridge and London: Harvard University Press, p. 193.

23. Catherine Cottreau–Robins, "Searching for the Enslaved in Nova Scotia's Loyalist Landscape," *Acadiensis* XLIII, no. 1 (Winter/Spring 2014), p. 130.

24. Annemarie de Waal Malefijt, *Religion and Culture: An Introduction to Anthropology of Religion.* (1968) New York: MacMillan, p. 52.

25. Berrill, p. 127.

26. John Casey, *After Lives*, p. 17.

27. Winroth, pp. 223-224.

28. Riane Eisler, *The Chalice and the Blade: Our History, Our Future.* (1988) New York: Harper and Row, p. 2.

29. Winroth, p. 90.

30. Jacques Soustelle, *Daily Life of the Aztecs.* (2002 Edition) London: Phoenix Press, p. 200.

31. Many of us may think that the Egyptians were the only ones who practiced mummification but that wasn't the case. But regardless of who did what a helpful introduction to this process is found in Angela Sumegi's *Understanding Death* (p. 54).

32. Northcott and Wilson, p. 23.

33. Cited in Peter Haining's *Cannibal Killers.* (2005 Edition) London: Magpie Books, p. 147.

34. Angela Sumegi, *Understanding Death*, p. 13.

35. Wade Davis, *The Wayfinders*, p. 105.

36. Effros, p. 62.

37. Cited in A.C. Grayling, *The Meaning of Things*, p. 180.

38. Herodotus, *Histories*, p. 89.

39. Herodotus, p. 65.

40. Peter S. Wells, *Barbarians To Angels: The Dark Ages Reconsidered*. (2008) New York and London: W.W. Norton and Company, p. 36.

41. Wells, p. 139.

42. Allan Kellehear, *A Social History of Dying*. (2007) Melbourne: Cambridge University Press, p. 23.

43. Stevenson, p. 46.

44. Murray, *Making An Exit*, p. 55.

45. Murray, p. 73.

46. Hoffman, *The Seven Storied Tower*, p. 181.

47. N.J. Berrill, p. 22.

48. Lloyd and Mitchinson, *The Book of the Dead*, p. 397.

49. Lloyd and Mitchinson, p. 391.

50. Bonanno, *The Other Side of Sadness*, p. 172.

51. Soustelle, *Daily Life of the Aztecs*, p. 200.

52. Wells, *Barbarians to Angels*, p. 34-35.

53. Wells, p. 42.

54. Wells, p. 36.

55. Wells, p. 42.

56. Thomas P. Keenan, *Technocreep: The Surrender of Privacy and the Capitalization of Intimacy*. (2014) Vancouver and Berkeley: Greystone Books, p. 131.

57. Eire, *A Very Brief History of Eternity*, p. 180.

58. Penny Colman, *Corpses, Coffins, and Crypts: A History of Burial*. (1997) New York: Henry Holt and Company, p. 73. This is an extremely engaging book that provides an accessible introduction into the subject of burials and graveside rituals.

59. Ellis, *A Brief History of the Druids*, p. 137.

60. Myers, *When Parents Die*, p. 107.

61. Bowering and Baird, *The Heart Does Break*, p. 12.

62. Morrison, p. 79.

63. Herman J. Selderhuis, *John Calvin: A Pilgrim's Life*. (2009) Downers Grove: Inner–Varsity Press, p. 234.

64. Susan White, *Christian Worship and Technological Change*, p. 75.

65. Baird, Sr. and Baird, *Funeral Meditations*, p. 12.

66. Jokinen, *Curtains: Adventures of an Undertaker in Training*, p. 32.

67. Duff Crerar describes the dangers and challenges of wartime funerals in his book entitled *Padres in No Man's Land: Canadian Chaplains and the Great War (Second Edition)*, p. 103.

Evaluation

1. Chris Hadfield, *An Astronaut's Guide to Life on Earth*. (2013) New York and Toronto: Random House Canada, p. 37.

2. Joan Chittister, *For Everything a Season*, p. 117.

3. Herodotus, *Histories*, p. 534.

4. W. Edwards Deming, *Out of the Crisis*, p. 256.

5. Cited in Lama Surya Das' *Awakening the Buddha Within: Tibetan Wisdom for the Western World*. (1997) New York: Broadway Books, p. 215.

6. Douglas Stone and Sheila Heen, *Thanks for the Feedback: The Science and Art of Receiving Feedback Well*. (2014) New York: Viking, p. 3. In my opinion this entire book is an excellent introduction to the practice of feedback and evaluation. It's a resource many will find helpful.

7. Stone and Heen, p. 6.

8. Stone and Heen, p. 18.

9. Irvin Yalom, *The Gift of Therapy*, p. 37.

10. Rollo May, *Freedom and Destiny*, p. 186.

11. Ron MacLean, *Cornered*. (2011) Toronto: HarperCollins, p. 30.

12. Buffet, Jimmy, *A Pirate Looks at Fifty*. (1998) New York: Random House, p. 140.

13. Quoted in Noel M. Tichy and Stratford Sherman, *Control Your Destiny or Someone Else Will*. (2005 Edition) New York: Harper Business Essentials, p. 28.

14. Ibid., p. 28.

15. Rear Admiral (Retired) Paul T. Gilchrist, *Feet Wet: Reflections of a Carrier Pilot*. (1990) Novato: Presidio, p. 270.

16. Rogers, p. 22.

17. Morton Hunt, *The Story of Psychology*. (2007 Edition) New York: Anchor Books, p. 637.

18. R. Kevin Seasoltz, *A Virtuous Church: Catholic Theology, Ethics, and Liturgy for the 21st Century*. (2012) Maryknoll: Orbis Books, p. 186.

19. Ben Witherington III. *Jesus the Sage: The Pilgrimage of Wisdom*. (1994) Minneapolis: Fortress Press, p. 32.

20. Bender, p. 27.

21. Hooyman and Kramer, *Living Through Loss*, p. 354.

22. Dickinson, *Persuasion*, p. 226.

23. Bender, p. 34.

24. Paul Irion, *The Funeral and the Mourners*, p. 137.

25. Irion, p. 76.

26. Quoted in Tichy and Sherman, p. 131.

27. John Stubbs, *Reprobates*, p. 206.

28. James A. Pike, *The Next Day*. (1957) Garden City: Doubleday and Company, p. 22.

29. Gail Vaz–Oxlade, *Money Rules*, p. 122.

30. Barbara Ehrenreich, *Living With A Wild God: A Nonbeliever's Search for the Truth About Everything*. (2014) New York: Twelve, p. 22.

31. Pat Schneider, *How the Light Gets In: Writing as a Spiritual Practice*. (2013) New York and Oxford: Oxford University Press, p. 6.

32. It's extremely important to confront our weaknesses as we journal as that is one way we achieve humility as I've previously defined it. Schneider suggests that changing our inner world has a direct effect on our external world.

33. Joan Didion, "On Keeping A Notebook" in *50 Essays: A Portable Anthology*. Edited by Samuel Cohen. (2004) Boston and New York: Bedford/St. Martin's, p. 85.

34. Michael Kirby, "Grief in the Law Enforcement Workplace: The

Police Experience" in *Living With Grief,* p. 31.

35. Bobby Orr, *Orr: My Story.* (2013) Toronto: Viking, p. 5.

36. Jan G. Linn, *22 Keys to Being a Minister: Without Quitting or Wishing for Early Retirement.* (2003) St. Louis: Chalice Press, p. 43.

37. Yalom, *The Gift of Therapy,* p. 32.

38. Ecclesiastes 3:2b.

39. 'Adam Smith', *The Money Game.* (1968) New York: Random House, p. 120.

40. Peter Constantine (Ed.) *The Essential Writings of Machiavelli.* (2007) New York: The Modern Library, p. 295.

41. Bender, p. 27.

42. Douglas Stone and Sheila Heen, *Thanks for the Feedback*, p. 94.

43. Carmine Gallo, *Talk Like TED*, p. 102.

44. Stone and Heen, p. 95.

45. Linn, p. 56.

46. John Gray, *The Immortalization Commission*, p. 225.

47. Cited in Eric Maisel, *The Atheist's Way*, p. 16.

48. Cited in Jeffrey Kahn's *Angst: Origins of Anxiety and Depression.* (2013) Oxford and New York: Oxford University Press, p. 64.

Conclusion

1. Cited in Bryan Tennyson's "School Days, School Days ... Cocagne Academy in the 1840s". *Acadiensis* Volume 5, Number 2 (Spring 1976), p. 137.

2. Paul Tillich, *The Shaking of the Foundations.* (1948) New York: Charles Scribner's Sons, p. 115.

3. E.E. Evans–Pritchard, *Theories of Primitive Religion.* (1965) New York and Glasgow: Oxford University Press, p. 39.

4. Phyllis Kosminsky, *Getting Back to Life When Grief Won't Heal.* (2007) New York: McGraw–Hill, p. 136.

5. Kosminsky, p. 151.

6. Murray, *Making An Exit*, p. 139.

Selected Bibliography

Baird, Sr. William R., and John E. Baird. 1996. *Funeral Meditations.* Nashville: Abingdon Press.

Bell, Catherine. 1997, *Ritual: Perspectives and Dimensions.* Oxford and New York: Oxford University Press.

Bell, Rob. 2011. *Love Wins: A Book About Heaven, Hell, and the Fate of Every Person Who Ever Lived.* New York: HarperOne.

Bender, Peter Urs. 1991. *Secrets of Power Presentations.* Toronto: The Achievement Group.

Bonanno, George A. 2009. *The Other Side of Sadness.* New York: Basic Books.

Bornstein, Daniel E. 2009. *Medieval Christianity.* Minneapolis: Fortress Press.

Bowering, George, and Jean Baird, eds. 2009. *The Heart Does Break: Canadian Writers on Grief and Mourning.* Toronto: Random House Canada.

Bozarth–Campbell, Alla. 1986 Edition. *Life is Goodbye, Life is Hello: Grieving Well Through All Kinds of Loss.* Minneapolis: CompCare Publishers.

Brooks, David, ed. 2012. *The Best American Essays 2012.* Boston and New York: Mariner Books.

Bush, Douglas. 1969 Edition. *Mythology and the Romantic Tradition in English Poetry.* New York: W.W. Norton and Company.

Card, Orson Scott. 1991 Edition. *Speaker for the Dead.* New York: A Tor Book.

Casey, John. 2009. *After Lives: A Guide to Heaven, Hell, and Purgatory.* Oxford and New York: Oxford University Press.

Chittister, Joan. 1995, 2013 Editions. *For Everything A Season.* Maryknoll: Orbis Books.

Cloud, Henry. 2010. *Necessary Endings.* New York: HarperBusiness.

Colman, Penny. 1997. *Corpses, Coffins, and Crypts: A History of Burial.* New York: Henry Holt.

Comte–Sponville, Andre. 2007. *The Little Book of Atheist Spirituality.* Translated by Nancy Huston. New York: Viking.

Confucius. 1979. *The Analects.* Introduced and Translated by D.C. Lau. London: Penguin.

Cooper, Cary L., Rachel D. Cooper, and Lynn H. Eaker. 1988. *Living With Stress.* London: Penguin.

Corley, Kathleen E. 2010. *Maranatha: Women's Funerary Rituals and Christian Origins.* Minneapolis: Fortress Press.

Cowan, Douglas E. and Gary G. Bromley. 2008. *Cults and New Religions: A Brief History.* Malden: Blackwell Publishing.

Crerar, Duff. 2014. *Padres in No Man's Land: Canadian Chaplains and the Great War (Second Edition).* Montreal and Kingston: McGill–Queen's University Press.

Danticat, Edwidge, ed. 2011. *The Best American Essays 2011.* Boston and New York: Mariner Books.

Davidson, Joyce D., and Kenneth J. Doka. 1999. *Living With Grief: At Work, At School, At Worship.* Washington, DC: Hospice Foundation of America.

Davis, Kingsley. 1948. *Human Society.* New York: MacMillan.

Davis, Wade. 2009. *The Wayfinders: Why Ancient Wisdom Matters in the Modern World.* Toronto: Anansi Press.

de Mello, Anthony. 1984. *The Song of the Bird.* Garden City: Image Books.

Dickinson, Arlene. 2011. *Persuasion: A New Approach to Changing Minds.* Toronto: Harper Collins.

Dolan, Jay P. 1992. *The American Catholic Experience: A History from Colonial Times to the Present.* Notre Dame: The University of Notre Dame Press.

Dunne, John S. 1974. *The City of the Gods: A Study in Myth and Mortality.* London: Sheldon Press.

Driver, Tom F. 1991. *The Magic of Ritual: Our Need for Liberating Rites that Transform Our Lives and Our Communities.* New York: Harper Collins.

Dunbar, Robin. 2004. *The Human Story: A New History of Mankind's Evolution.* London: Faber and Faber.

Eckels, Malcolm David. 2010. *Understanding Buddhism.* London: Watkins Publishing.

Eire, Carlos. 2010. *A Very Brief History of Eternity.* Princeton and Oxford: Princeton University Press.

Eliade, Mircea. 1958. *Rites and Symbols of Initiation: The Mysteries of Birth and Rebirth.* Translated by Willard R. Trask. New York: Harper Torchbooks.

Ellis, Perry Berresford. 1994, 2002. *A Brief History of the Druids.* London: Constable and Robinson.

Feuerbach, Ludwig. 1957 Edition. *The Essence of Christianity.* Translated by George Eliot. New York: Harper Torchbooks.

Fey, Harold E., and Margaret Frakes, eds. 1962. *The Christian Century Reader.* New York: Associated Press.

Ford, D.W. Cleverley. 1979. *The Ministry of the Word.* London and Sydney: Hodder and Stoughton.

Fraser, Kathleen. 2009. *When I'm Gone: Practical Notes for Those You Leave Behind.* Erie: The Boston Mills Press.

Gallo, Carmine. 2014. *Talk Like TED: The 9 Public–Speaking Secrets of the World's Top Minds.* New York: St. Martin's Press.

Geertz, Clifford. 1973. *The Interpretation of Cultures.* New York: Basic Books.

Gladwell, Malcolm. 2009. *What the Dog Saw: And Other Adventures.* New York and Boston: Little, Brown, and Company.

Gollner, Adam Leith. 2013. *The Book of Immortality: The Science, Belief, and Magic Behind Living Forever.* Toronto: Doubleday Canada.

Gray, John. 2011. *The Immortalization Commission: Science and the Strange Quest to Cheat Death.* Toronto: Doubleday Canada.

Grayling, A.C. 2001. *The Meaning of Things: Applying Philosophy to Life.* London: Phoenix.

Grayling, A.C. 2007 Edition. "Funerals" in *The Form of Things: Essays on Life, Ideas, and Liberty in the 21st Century.* London: Phoenix.

Grimes, Ronald L. 2000, 2002. *Deeply Into the Bone: Re–Inventing Rites of Passage.* Berkeley: University of California Press.

Harris, Mark. 2007. *Grave Matters.* New York: Scribner.

Hempton, David. 2008. *Evangelical Disenchantment: 9 Portraits of Faith and Doubt.* New Haven and London: Yale University Press.

Herman, Judith. 1997 Edition. *Trauma and Recovery.* New York: Basic Books.

Herodotus. 1996. *Histories.* Translated by George Rawlinson. Hertfordshire: Wordsworth Classics.

Hodge, Gerald. 2008. *The Geography of Aging: Preparing Communities for the Surge in Seniors.* Montreal and Kingston: McGill–Queen's University Press.

Hoffman, Curtiss. 1999. *The Seven Storied Mountain: A Mythic Journey Through Space and Time.* Cambridge: Perseus Publishing.

hooks, bell. 2009. *Belonging: A Culture of Place.* New York and London: Routledge.

Hooyman, Nancy R., and Betty J. Kramer. 2006. *Living Through Loss: Interventions Across the Life Span.* New York: Columbia University Press.

Hunt, Morton. 2007 Edition. *The Story of Psychology.* New York: Anchor Books.

Irion, Paul E. 1954. *The Funeral and the Mourners: Pastoral Care of the Bereaved.* Nashville: Abingdon Press.

Jenkins, Philip. 2002. *The Next Christendom: The Coming of Global Christianity.* New York: Oxford University Press.

Johnson, Paul E. 1953. *Psychology of Pastoral Care.* Nashville: Abingdon Press.

Joiner, Thomas. 2005. *Why People Die by Suicide.* Cambridge: Harvard University Press.

Jokinen, Tom. 2010. *Curtains: Adventures of an Undertaker in Training.* Toronto: Random House Canada.

Kellehear, Allan. 2007. *A Social History of Dying.* Melbourne: Cambridge University Press.

Kenner, Hugh. 1998. *The Elsewhere Community.* Concord: Anansi.

Killinger, Barbara. 2007. *Integrity: Doing the Right Thing for the Right Reason.* Montreal and Kingston: McGill–Queen's University Press.

Klein, Donald F., and Paul H. Wender. 1993. *Understanding Depression: A Complete Guide to Its Diagnosis and Treatment.* New York and Oxford: Oxford University Press.

Kosminsky, Phyllis, Ph.D. 2007. *Getting Back to Life When Grief Won't Heal.* New York: McGraw–Hill.

Kutscher, Austin H., ed. 1990. *For the Bereaved: The Road to Recovery (3rd Edition).* Philadelphia: The St. Charles Press.

Levine, Stephen and Ondrea. 1989 Edition. *Who Dies?* New York: Anchor Books.

Levi–Strauss, Claude. *1963. Structural Anthropology.* Translated by Claire Jacobson and Brooke Grundfest Schoepf. New York: Basic Books.

Long, Thomas G. 2009. *Accompany them with Singing: The Christian Funeral.* Louisville: Westminster John Knox Press.

Lukacs, John. 2002. *The End of an Age.* New Haven and London: Yale University Press.

Linn, Jan G. 2003. *22 Keys to Being a Minister: Without Quitting or Wishing for Early Retirement.* St. Louis: Chalice Press.

Mair, Lucy. 1972. *An Introduction to Social Anthropology (Second Edition).* New York and London: Oxford University Press.

Maisel, Eric. 2009. *The Atheist's Way: Living Well Without Gods.* Novato: New World Library.

Malinowski, Bronislaw. 1954 Edition. *Magic, Science, and Religion and Other Essays.* Garden City: Anchor Books.

May, Rollo. 1981, 1999 Editions. *Freedom and Destiny.* New York: W.W. Norton and Company.

McFarlane, Doreen M. 2008. *Funerals With Today's Families in Mind.* Cleveland: The Pilgrim Press.

McGoldrick, Monica and Froma Walsh, eds. 1991. *Living Beyond Loss: Death in the Family.* New York and London: W. W. Norton and Company.

McKeen, William. 2008. *Outlaw Journalist: The Life and Times of Hunter S. Thompson.* London and New York: W.W. Norton and Company.

McKeon, Richard, ed. 1941. *Aristotle, Basic Works.* New York: Random House.

Meslier, Jean. 2009. *Testament: Memoir of the Thoughts and Sentiments of Jean Meslier.* Translated by Michael Shreve. Amherst: Prometheus Books.

Middleton, John, ed. 1967. *Gods and Rituals: Readings in Religious Beliefs and Practices.* New York: Natural History Press.

Morrison, James K. 1991. "The Clinical Use of Imagery to Induce Psychotherapeutic Grieving" in *Death Imagery: Confronting Death Brings us to the Threshold of Life.* Edited by A.A. Shiekh and K.S. Sheikh. Milwaukee: American Imagery Institute.

Mukherjee, Siddhartha. 2010. *The Emperor of All Maladies: A Biography of Cancer.* New York and London: Scribner's.

Murray, Sarah. 2011. *Making An Exit.* New York: St. Martin's Press.

Myers, Edward. 1986. *When Parents Die: A Guide For Adults.* New York: Penguin Books.

Neuhaus, Richard John. 2010. *American Babylon.* New York: Basic Books.

Northcott, Herbert C. and Donna M. Wilson. 2008. *Dying and Death in Canada (Second Edition).* Buffalo: Broadview Press.

Ober, William B. 1998 Edition. *Bottoms Up! A Pathologists Essays on Medicine and the Humanities.* New York: Harper and Row.

Okun, Ph.D., Barbara and Joseph Nowinski, Ph.D. 2011. *Saying Goodbye: How Families can Find Renewal Through Loss.* New York: Berkley Books.

Ozment, Steven E. 1975. *The Reformation in the Cities: The Appeal of Protestantism to Sixteenth–Century Germany and Switzerland.* New Haven and London: Yale University Press.

Pike, James A. 1957. *The Next Day.* Garden City: Doubleday and Company.

Pine, Joseph B. and James H. Gilmore. 1999. *The Experience Economy: Work is Theatre and Every Business a Stage.* Boston: Harvard Business School Press.

Pritchett, V.S., ed. 1981. *The Oxford Book of Short Stories.* New York: Oxford University Press.

Radcliffe–Brown, A.R. 1952, 1965 Editions. *Structure and Function in Primitive Society: Essays and Addresses.* New York: Free Press.

Radin, Paul. 1957 Edition. *Primitive Religion.* New York: Dover Publications.

Ramshaw, Elaine. 1987. *Ritual and Pastoral Care.* Minneapolis: Fortress Press.

Rando, Therese A. 1991 Edition. *How To Go On Living When Someone You Love Dies.* New York: Bantam Books.

Raphael, Beverley. 1983. *The Anatomy of Bereavement.* New York: Basic Books.

Reed, Elizabeth L. 1970. *Helping Children With the Mystery of Death.* Nashville: Abingdon Press.

Richmond, Kent D. 1988. *Preaching to Sufferers: God and the Problem of Pain.* Nashville: Abingdon Press.

Riegel, Christian. 2003. *Writing Grief: Margaret Laurence and the Work of Mourning.* Winnipeg: University of Manitoba Press.

Rogers, Carl R. 1961. *On Becoming A Person.* Boston: Houghton Mifflin.

Rorabaugh, W. J. 2002. *Kennedy and the Promise of the Sixties.* Cambridge: Cambridge University Press.

Ross, Melanie, and Simon Jones, eds. 2010. *The Serious Business of Worship: Essays in Honour of Brian D. Spinks.* London and New York: T and T Clark.

Sacks, Oliver. 1987 Edition. *The Man Who Mistook His Wife for a Hat and Other Clinical Tales.* New York: Harper and Row.

Sacks, Oliver. 2007. *Musicophilia: Tales of Music and the Brain.* New York and Toronto: Alfred A. Knopf.

Sacks, Oliver. 2012. *Hallucinations.* New York and Toronto: Alfred A. Knopf.

Schneider, Pat. 2013. *How the Light Gets In: Writing as a Spiritual Practice.* New York and Oxford: Oxford University Press.

Searl, Edward. 2000. *In Memoriam: A Guide to Modern Funerals and Memorial Services (2nd Edition).* Boston: Skinner House Books.

Shakespeare, William. 1936. *Cymbeline. The Complete Works.* Edited by G. L. Kittredge. Boston: Ginn and Company.

Shneidman, Edwin S. 1996. *The Suicidal Mind.* New York and London: Oxford University Press.

Smith, Christian. 2003. *Moral, Believing Animals: Human Personhood and Culture.* Oxford: Oxford University Press.

Soustelle, Jacques. 2002 Edition. *Daily Life of the Aztecs.* London: Phoenix Press.

Spong, John Shelby. 2009. *Eternal Life: A New Vision.* New York: HarperOne.

Stark, Rodney. 2007. *Discovering God: The Origins of the Great Religions and the Evolution of Belief.* New York: Harper Collins.

Stenger, Victor J. 2007. *God: The Failed Hypothesis.* Amherst: Prometheus Books.

Stevenson, Leslie. 1974, 1987. *Seven Theories of Human Nature (Second Edition).* New York and London: Oxford University Press.

Stone, Douglas and Sheila Heen. 2014. *Thanks for the Feedback: The Science and Art of Receiving Feedback Well.* New York: Viking.

Stovel, Nora Foster. 2008. *Divining Margaret Laurence: A Study of Her Complete Writings.* Montreal and Kingston: McGill–Queen's University Press.

Stubbs, John. 2011. *Reprobates: The Cavaliers of the English Civil War.* New York: W.W. Norton and Company.

Sumegi, Angela. 2014. *Understanding Death: An Introduction to the Ideas of Self and the Afterlife in World Religions.* Chichester: Wiley Blackwell.

Switzer, David K. 1980 Edition. *The Minister as Crisis Counselor.* Nashville: Abingdon Press.

Tichy, Noel M. and Sherman Stratford. 2005 Edition. *Control Your Destiny: Or Someone Else Will.* New York: Harper Business Essentials.

Thielicke, Helmut. 1997. *Being A Christian When the Chips Are Down.* Translated by H. George Anderson. Philadelphia: Fortress Press.

Turner, James. 1987 Edition. *Without God, Without Creed: The Origins of Unbelief in America.* Baltimore and London: Johns Hopkins University Press.

Van Gennep, Arnold. 1960. *The Rites of Passage.* Chicago: The University of Chicago Press.

Vaz–Oxlade, Gail. 2012. *Money Rules.* Toronto: Collins.

Wade, Nicholas. 2010. *The Faith Instinct: How Religion Evolved and Why It Endures.* New York and London: Penguin Books.

Watkins, Keith. 1995. *The Great Thanksgiving.* St. Louis: Chalice Press.

Weems, Scott. 2014. *Ha! The Science of When We Laugh and Why.* New York: Basic Books.

Wells, Peter S. 2008. *Barbarians to Angels: The Dark Ages Reconsidered.* New York and London: W.W. Norton and Company.

White, Susan J. 1994. *Christian Worship and Technological Change.* Nashville: Abingdon Press.

Wills, Garry. 2002. "The Dramaturgy of Death" in *The Best American Essays (2002 Edition).* Edited by Stephen Jay Gould, 331-343. Boston and New York: Houghton Mifflin Company.

Wilson, Paul Scott. 1999. *The Four Pages of the Sermon.* Nashville: Abingdon Press.

Winroth, Anders. 2014. *The Age of the Vikings.* Princeton: Princeton University Press.

Wylie, Betty Jane. 1997. *Beginnings: A Book For Widows (Fourth Revised Edition).* Toronto: McClelland and Stewart.

Yalom, Irvin D. 2009. *Staring at the Sun: Overcoming the Terror of Death.* San Francisco: Jossey–Bass.

Yalom, Irvin D. 2009 Edition. *The Gift of Therapy: An Open Letter to a New Generation of Therapists and Their Patients.* New York: Harper Perennial.

Youings, Joyce. 1984, 1986. *Sixteenth–Century England.* Middlesex and New York: Penguin Books.

Zackheim, Victoria, ed. 2012. *Exit Laughing: How Humour Takes the Sting out of Death.* Berkeley: North Atlantic Books.

About the Author

Michael K. Jones is a former United Church of Canada Minister born and raised in Atlantic Canada. He is a graduate of St. Thomas University (BA) in Fredericton, New Brunswick, and the Atlantic School of Theology (MDiv) in Halifax, Nova Scotia. Following his ordination in 1993 he began his ministry in Northern Alberta where he served the communities of Valleyview and DeBolt. From there he moved with his spouse Trish to Calgary, Alberta where he continues to live and work. His previous publication is entitled *Empty Houses: A Pastoral Approach to Congregational Closures*.

www.ingramcontent.com/pod-product-compliance
Lightning Source LLC
Chambersburg PA
CBHW030917090426
42737CB00007B/222